TWELVE DESPERATE MILES

TWELVE
DESPERATE MILES

THE EPIC WWII
VOYAGE OF THE SS CONTESSA

TIM BRADY

Crown Publishers | New York

Published in the United States by Crown Publishers, an imprint of the Crown Publishing Group,
a division of Random House, Inc., New York.

www.crownpublishing.com

CROWN and the Crown colophon are registered trademarks of Random House, Inc.

Library of Congress Cataloging-in-Publication Data

Brady, Tim, 1955–

Twelve desperate miles : the epic WWII voyage of the SS Contessa / Tim Brady.—1st ed.

p. cm.

1. World War, 1939–1945—Riverine operations—Morocco. 2. World War, 1939–1945—
Riverine operations, American. 3. World War, 1939–1945—Campaigns—Africa, North.
4. Operation Torch, 1942. 5. Contessa (Steamer) I. Title.

D766.99.M6B73 2012

940.54'234—dc23   2011026090

ISBN 978-0-307-59037-4

eISBN 978-0-307-59039-8

Printed in the United States of America

Book design by Lenny Henderson

Maps by David Lindroth Inc.

Jacket design by Whitney Cookman

Jacket photography: Hulton-Deutsch Collection/CORBIS (top); Bettman/CORBIS (bottom)

10 9 8 7 6 5 4 3 2 1

First Edition

CONTENTS

DRAMATIS PERSONAE

(in order of appearance)

René Malevergne (aka "The Shark," "Monsieur Prechak")—River pilot of the French Moroccan Port Lyautey. When France fell to Hitler's army in the summer of 1940, he joined the French "underground" forces in Morocco, subverting the Vichy regime in Africa. He was ultimately tapped by Allied forces for a special mission. Husband to Germaine; father to Claude and René.

Paolantonacci, Brunin, Ravel, Brabancon, and Rocca—Colleagues of Malevergne in Port Lyautey.

Captain William Henry John—Welsh-born master of the SS *Contessa,* veteran of the British Royal Navy in World War I, for more than twenty years a resident of New Orleans, and longtime employee of the Standard Fruit Company. He and his ship were called to duty by the U.S. War Shipping Administration in the spring of 1942 and began transporting U.S. troops and supplies from New York to North Ireland that summer. Husband to Bessie; father to Peggy and Betts.

Rear Admiral Karl Doenitz—Leader of Germany's U-boat campaign. He would also briefly succeed Adolf Hitler as the last führer of the Third Reich in the waning days of the war.

General George Patton—Appointed commander of the I Armored Corps in July 1942, Major General George Patton received another command come August, when he was tapped by Eisenhower to head the Western Task Force of Operation Torch, the invasion of North Africa.

General George Marshall—Appointed Army Chief of Staff by President Franklin Delano Roosevelt in September 1939. He would remain in that post, based in Washington, throughout the war. In 1944, Marshall became the first five-star general in the U.S. Army in World War II.

General Dwight David Eisenhower—In late May 1942, General Dwight David Eisenhower flew to London, where he assumed command of the European Theater of Operations (ETOUSA). From offices there, he would oversee the pending invasion of North Africa.

General Lucian Truscott—Newly promoted Brigadier General Lucian Truscott was in England, charged with the development of an Army Ranger unit patterned after British commando forces, as the invasion of North Africa evolved.

Captain Harry Butcher—Naval aide to General Eisenhower in London. Butcher was ordered by his commander to keep a diary of the activities of Eisenhower's office. Butcher published *My Three Years with Eisenhower* after the war.

General Alan Brooke—Chief of the Imperial General Staff; essentially, head of the British army; Marshall's counterpart in initial discussions on where to attack the Axis. Brooke argued strenuously against Operation Roundup, the American plan to invade France in 1942.

Vice Admiral Wion de Malpas Egerton and **Commodore Lennon Goldsmith**—Royal Navy commanders of the first and second convoys in which the *Contessa* sailed.

Admiral Henry Kent Hewitt—A thirty-five-year veteran of the U.S. Navy. Admiral Hewitt commanded the Atlantic Fleet amphibious forces in the summer of 1942. He would soon butt heads with General George Patton as they planned together (and separately) the combined navy and army operations of the Western Task Force of Operation Torch.

The Apostles—Nickname given to the OSS operatives who arrived in North Africa in the wake of the February 1941 Murphy-Weygand Agreement, which allowed for trade between the United States and Vichy North Africa. These spies slipped into North Africa in the guise of U.S. customs agents charged with making sure American goods were not shipped to Germany.

Colonel William "Bill" Eddy—World War I vet, scholar, and expert on Middle Eastern affairs, Eddy was sent to Tangier in 1941 to serve, nominally, as a naval attaché. His actual duties were to gather intelligence for the OSS and serve as the overseer of the Apostles in northwest Africa.

Robert Murphy—American consul in Paris in the 1930s. Murphy became FDR's man in North Africa—liaison to the Vichy government and collector of information at the onset of the war.

David King—Having served in the French Foreign Legion and the U.S. Army during World War I, King came to Casablanca as an OSS operative in 1941.

Gordon Browne—An archaeologist by trade, Browne was a relatively new OSS recruit stationed in Tangier. He and Franklin Holcomb happened to be in Casablanca at a propitious moment for René Malevergne and the future of Operation Torch in September 1942.

Franklin Holcomb—Son of Marine Corps Commandant Thomas Holcomb. Franklin worked out of Tangier as assistant naval attaché to William Eddy. He was on assignment with Browne on a tour of the interior of Morocco when the pair came to Casablanca.

Hal Wallis—Chief of production at Warner Brothers Studios in Hollywood, Wallis was overseeing the editing and promotional campaign of a new film called *Casablanca* in the late summer of 1942. He was completely unaware of any Allied plans involving North Africa.

General Alfred Gruenther—Called over to London in August 1942 from a station in San Antonio, Texas, to assume the post of chief of staff for Eisenhower, Mark Clark, and the North African campaign, Gruenther had a steep learning curve in order to catch up to fast-developing plans.

Major General Mark Clark—Appointed by Eisenhower as overall deputy commander in chief of Allied forces in North Africa.

Carl Clopet—Casablanca hydrographer exfiltrated from Morocco to London in order to aid Allied planning for the invasion of Africa.

Goalpost planning team—Included British members of Louis Lord Mountbatten's staff and American officers serving under General Lucian Truscott. Both were brought together in Washington in mid-September 1942 to help coordinate the Port Lyautey attack force in the invasion of Morocco. British members were Commanders Dick Costabadie and John Homer and Major Robert Henriques. American members of Truscott's planning team included Majors Ted Conway and Pierpont Morgan Hamilton. Hamilton was the grandson of the famed financier J. P. Morgan and the great-great-grandson of Alexander Hamilton.

Western Task Force Transportation group—Army Services of Supplies was headed by Lieutenant General Brehon Somervell, who would hold the position for the duration of the war. Somervell's chief duties in the fall of 1942 were to supply the needs of the first major operation of the Allied command, Operation Torch, the invasion of North Africa. Serving as chief of transportation in the Army Service Forces, directly beneath Somervell, was General Charles P. Gross, whose principal task that fall was to fulfill the shipping needs for the army's invasion. Gross commanded Brigadier General John R. Kilpatrick, who headed the Hampton Roads Port of Embarkation in Virginia. Colonel Cyrus J. Wilder was the executive officer of the Port of Hampton Roads.

Lieutenant Colonel Frederick de Rohan—Commander of the 60th Infantry Regimental Combat Team of the 9th Infantry Division, Truscott's principal infantry fighting in the Goalpost operation.

Lieutenant Colonel Jack Toffey—Commander of the Third Battalion of the 60th Infantry Regimental Combat team. His troops landed north of the River Sebou on D-day with the goal of aiding in the assault of the Port Lyautey airfield and taking the bridge north of the port.

Colonel Demas "Nick" Craw—Army Air Force liaison to General Lucian Truscott's command. He was slated to command the Port Lyautey airfield once it was in Allied hands.

Colonel Harry Semmes—Semmes served with distinction as a captain in Colonel George Patton's newly created tank corps during the First World War. After establishing himself as a patent attorney between the wars, Semmes reenlisted at the start of World War II and soon found himself serving once again in an armored division under Patton.

Lieutenant Commander Robert Brodie Jr.—Brodie was captain of the U.S. destroyer *Dallas,* which was picked to open the River Sebou for the SS *Contessa.*

Walter Cronkite—United Press reporter assigned to the battleship *Texas.* He had just finished an assignment in which he'd reported on the experience of traveling in a convoy between New York and England.

U.S. Navy armed guard—In June 1942 a fourteen-man naval armed guard unit was assigned to the SS *Contessa* prior to its first voyage to England. Among the members of the guard who would sail with the *Contessa* to North Africa were Lieutenant William Cato, who commanded the unit for its first two voyages on the *Contessa*; the New Jersey contingent of Patsy Lambusta of Newark, Paul "Slick" Manganaro of Glassboro, and Adolph Krol of Camden; Bill Pottiger from Michigan; Hazelton Gilchrest "Hakie" McLaughlin from Bar Harbor, Maine, who was one of the few members of the guard who had experience on the sea; Wally Mason of Quincy, Massachusetts; and Ambrose "Kid" Schaffer of Ohio, a former professional prizefighter.

Lieutenant Albert Leslie—Leslie assumed command of the armed guard unit on the voyage of the *Contessa* to Morocco. He was also appointed a cocaptain of the vessel by the U.S. Navy through the duration of the trip. Leslie was a World War I navy vet who had stayed in the service for a number of years afterward and had also worked for the U.S. Coast Guard. He was living in Pittsburgh at the start of World War II.

The *Contessa* crew—The crew included the chief engineer, Englishman John Henry Langdon, a longtime employee of Standard Fruit; the second engineer, Arthur Baumgart, a native of Poland who, like Langdon, was a naturalized citizen of the United States and long an employee of Standard Fruit; the chief mate, Alexander Vallerino, and chief steward, Mario Violini (nicknamed "The Unsinkable"), natives of Italy but now citizens of the United States; Harry Haylock, the ship's carpenter, who had sailed many times under Captain John and was originally from Honduras; second officer Jan Norberg, from Norway; and quartermaster Ture Jansen, a Swede. The chief radio officer, Alfred Turner, was one of the few native-born Americans on the *Contessa* crew.

Bill Sigsworth—Captain William John's brother-in-law, a last-minute addition to the *Contessa*'s crew. He was drafted aboard in Hampton Roads and was to make his first voyage as a seaman to North Africa.

Norfolk County Jail—Among the eighteen crew members taken aboard the *Contessa* from the Norfolk County Jail were Ahmed Ali, Ali Salik, Ahmed Mohammed, Said Mohammed—all British nationals from Gulf of Aden ports—Henry Drummond, a young Australian, an American sailor named John Riccio, and a Finn named John Sutinen.

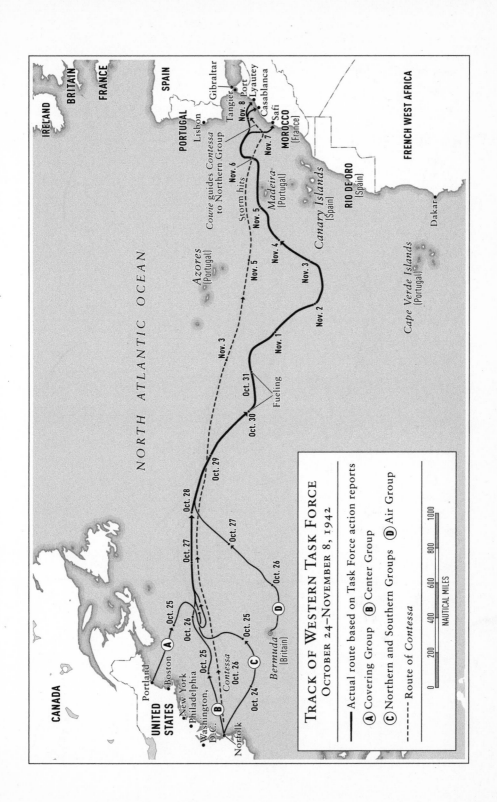

TRACK OF WESTERN TASK FORCE
OCTOBER 24–NOVEMBER 8, 1942

——— Actual route based on Task Force action reports

Ⓐ Covering Group Ⓑ Center Group

Ⓒ Northern and Southern Groups Ⓓ Air Group

- - - - - Route of Contessa

NAUTICAL MILES

0   200   400   600   800   1000

CANADA

UNITED
STATES

Portland
Boston
New York
Philadelphia
Washington,
D.C.
Norfolk

NORTH ATLANTIC OCEAN

Bermuda
(Britain)

Azores
(Portugal)

Madeira
(Portugal)

Canary Islands
(Spain)

Cape Verde Islands
(Portugal)

RIO DE ORO
(Spain)

FRENCH WEST AFRICA

Dakar

IRELAND
BRITAIN
FRANCE
SPAIN
PORTUGAL
Lisbon
Gibraltar
Tangier
MOROCCO
(France)

Nov. 8 Port
Lyautey
Casablanca
Safi

Nov. 7

Nov. 6

Cowie guides Contessa
to Northern Group

Storm hits

Nov. 5

Nov. 5

Nov. 4

Nov. 3

Nov. 3

Nov. 2

Nov. 1

Nov. 1

Oct. 31

Fueling

Oct. 30

Oct. 29

Oct. 28

Oct. 27

Oct. 27

Oct. 26

Oct. 26

Oct. 25

Oct. 25

Oct. 25

Oct. 26

Contessa
Oct. 26

Oct. 24

Oct. 25

Oct. 25

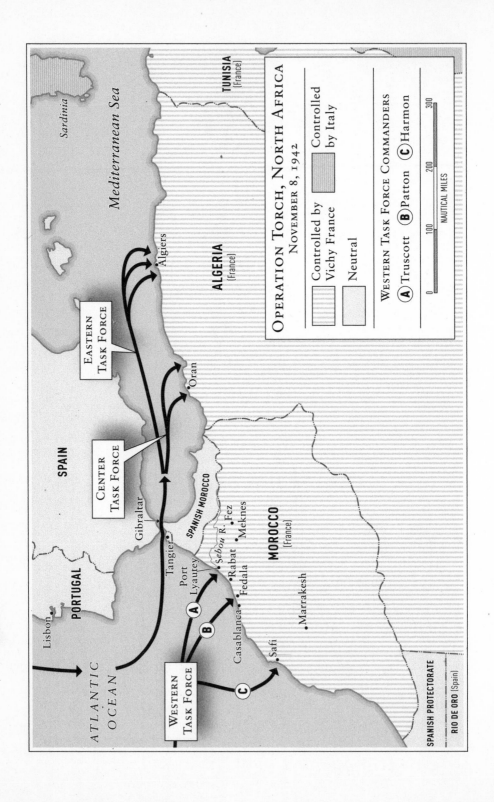

OPERATION TORCH, NORTH AFRICA
November 8, 1942

Controlled by Vichy France

Controlled by Italy

Neutral

WESTERN TASK FORCE COMMANDERS
(A) Truscott (B) Patton (C) Harmon

0   100   200   300
NAUTICAL MILES

Sardinia

Mediterranean Sea

TUNISIA
[France]

ALGERIA
[France]

Algiers

Oran

SPAIN

EASTERN TASK FORCE

CENTER TASK FORCE

Gibraltar

Tangier

SPANISH MOROCCO

Sebou R.   Fez

Port Lyautey

Rabat   Meknes

Fedala

Casablanca

MOROCCO
[France]

Marrakesh

Safi

PORTUGAL

Lisbon

ATLANTIC OCEAN

WESTERN TASK FORCE

(A)

(B)

(C)

SPANISH PROTECTORATE

RIO DE ORO [Spain]

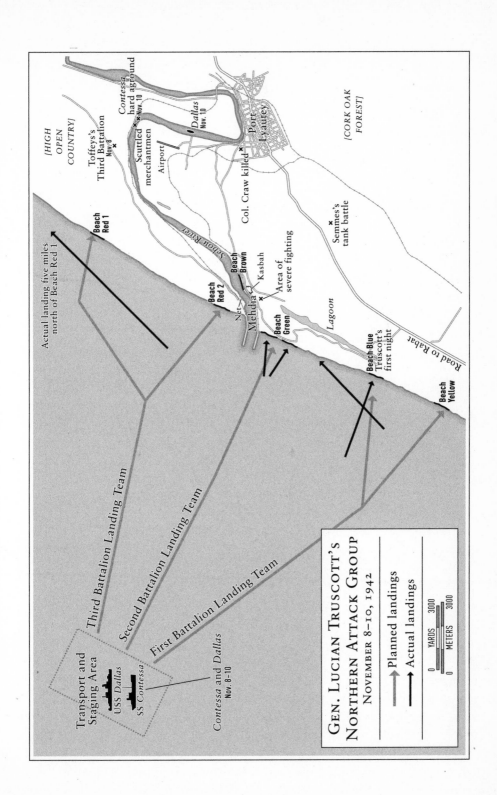

GEN. LUCIAN TRUSCOTT'S
NORTHERN ATTACK GROUP
NOVEMBER 8–10, 1942

Planned landings
Actual landings

0   YARDS   3000
0   METERS   3000

Transport and Staging Area

USS *Dallas*   SS *Contessa*

Contessa and *Dallas*
Nov. 8–10

First Battalion Landing Team

Second Battalion Landing Team

Third Battalion Landing Team

Actual landing five miles
north of Beach Red 1

Beach Red 1

Beach Red 2

Beach Brown

Net
Mehdia

Beach Green

Beach Blue
Truscott's
first night

Beach Yellow

[HIGH OPEN COUNTRY]

Toffey's
Third Battalion
Nov 8

Contessa
hard aground

Scuttled
merchantmen
Nov. 10

Dallas
Nov. 10

Airport

Col. Craw killed

Port
Lyautey

Sebou River

Kasbah

Area of
severe fighting

Semmes's
tank battle

Lagoon

[CORK OAK
FOREST]

Road to Rabat

PROLOGUE

A Good Citizen of Mehdia

MOROCCO, 1940

When war came to France and the nation was lost to Hitler and the collaborationists, people in French Morocco acknowledged their feelings in sad and quiet gestures. A shrug here. A meaningful squeeze of hands there. Those who had a hard time accepting the Axis-aligned Pétain government—and they were many—went about their business in a haze of unease, uncertainty, and largely unspoken opinions. The authorities in Port Lyautey, where retired merchant marine sailor René Malevergne worked, were initially indulgent of the distrust they felt around them, but soon the forgiving manner of the police was replaced by sidelong glances and open suspicion. At the same time, the feelings of the resisters grew more defiant as the weeks and months of Vichy governance stretched from summer into fall. There were soon opportunities for people like Malevergne to secretly defy the regime.

By October 1940, repercussions of the war's fearful and disastrous effects on the populations of Europe came to inhabit North Africa. Refugees from France, Poland, Czechoslovakia, and elsewhere in Europe were thick in Morocco, crowding Casablanca and Rabat but also evident in smaller cities like Port Lyautey. There were food shortages, not so much caused by the increase in population in the region, but because local farmers were withholding their produce, disturbed that it was being shipped to France to be consumed by les Boches—the German occupiers. Tensions between those who aligned themselves with the Vichy regime and those who entered the nascent and secretive world of the Free French Resistance began to escalate.

For the most part, Germany stayed out of French Morocco, but its

1

gaze and interest in the country was sensed by everyone from refugees to French colonials to Moroccan natives. The realization that the Nazis were a power that could overwhelm a nation with remarkable speed was, by this time, ingrained in the populace. In Casablanca, something called the German Armistice Commission set up shop on the Boulevard de la Gare in the heart of the city; its members—as arrogant as a goose step—strutted presumptuously around town with a keen eye on the ways and means of Vichy.

It was in this atmosphere, several months into the new regime, that an old friend of Malevergne's named Ravel found him strolling through the Port Lyautey market one day and pulled him aside, asking a simple yet dangerous question: "Are you a Gaullist or Pétainist?"

For a patriot like Malevergne, who not only had fought against the Germans in World War I but had a brother who had been critically wounded and left handicapped at Verdun, it was absurd to think of any sort of alliance with the Nazis. "Even if de Gaulle did not exist," Malevergne told his friend, "I think I would be a Gaullist."

Born in Limoges in 1892, René Malevergne served in the French navy during the war and came to Morocco soon after the conflict's end. He used his naval experience to earn a job in the French civil service, working in a maritime post at the port, about seventy miles north of Casablanca. Within a few years, he was promoted to its chief pilot. His job was to offer his navigational skills and guidance to ocean ships entering the waters of the River Sebou through the hidden shoals and pounding surf of the Atlantic that marked the river's entrance. It was a highly skilled post. The Sebou was the second-longest river in Morocco, running all the way down from the Atlas Mountains in the interior out to sea, but at its deepest it allowed for a draft of just seventeen feet for all the oceangoing vessels that sailed up its dozen winding miles from the Atlantic to the Port of Lyautey. To navigate both the fearsome entrance to the Sebou and its shallow, bending path to the port was the work of an expert.

Malevergne's position was highly regarded in the region. He was also a handsome man, with an easy smile, a dimpled chin, and dark hair that swept back from his brow in rippled waves. Malevergne stood just five feet four inches tall and carried himself with his shoulders thrown back—facts that tended to accentuate the small paunch that had come to him in middle age, making him appear slightly heavier than he was. He was a solid citizen of Mehdia, and he added to this sense of establishment in 1930, when he married a local girl, Germaine Martin. In a few years' time, she gave birth to two young sons, René and Claude, and the family built a white cottage in Mehdia in the shadow of an old sixteenth-century Portuguese fort known locally as the Kasbah. René, Germaine, and the boys were happily ensconced in this world when the troubles of 1940 arrived.

A man who knew an Atlantic port like Lyautey as well as Malevergne did could be a very valuable commodity to the secret causes of the Free French—a fact that was understood not only by Ravel and his cohorts but also by Vichy authorities and Malevergne himself. In times like these, the fact that he was middle-aged, was married, and had two young boys did not constrain those who might want his help. He was, after all, the harbor pilot. Malevergne was not terribly surprised, then, to hear Ravel, in a quiet voice over cigarettes, tell him in somewhat vague terms of the group to which he belonged in Rabat, the capital of Morocco, about 21 miles southwest of Mehdia.

Malevergne decided not to tell his friend that he'd had an invitation just three days earlier from the other side. A captain in the French navy had asked Malevergne to stop by his offices in Port Lyautey. There, he had given the river pilot his telephone number and asked that Malevergne call if he was contacted by anyone from any of the "clandestine organizations [that] are even now preparing all sorts of escapes."

Despite this oblique warning that he was being observed by the authorities, Malevergne was receptive to Ravel and the Resistance, and when yet another old friend, Jean Claude Paolantonacci, the chief customs inspector in Lyautey, paid him a visit in Mehdia a few weeks later, Malevergne listened intently. This time the message was more concrete:

We are meeting in Rabat next month, Pao said. *There is a plan to facilitate a passage in England. You are needed.*

In late November, Malevergne bade his wife, Germaine, and his two young boys good-bye and made the journey to the capital to learn more about the plans. He rode his bicycle through the cork oak forest between Mehdia and Rabat, watchful for both the local police and the unsavory nomads who still occasionally camped in the woods. In Rabat, he met with the Gaullists, who included Paolantonacci and Ravel; a Belgian proconsul from Port Lyautey named Allegre; Brabancon, the Belgian general consul; and a businessman named Brunin, who was the leader of the group.

As it turned out, the conspirators had already been plotting with British undercover agents to foster the escape to England of forty Belgian aviators currently trapped in Morocco. A vessel would be coming from Lisbon to Casablanca and then Port Lyautey sometime toward mid-December. Could Malevergne pilot the ship to and from the port and then arrange for the embarkation of the Belgian fliers at a predetermined inlet on the Atlantic shore, one that would be feasible for getting the Belgians to the ship in the rough seas?

To Malevergne, it all seemed slightly hypothetical and unreal. He was a river pilot, not a secret agent. And yet to all of the questions, all of the *if*s, *and*s, and *but*s that came out of that meeting, his answer was always the same: if the ship arrived safely at Mehdia, yes, he could pilot it to and from Port Lyautey; if all went well in the port, yes, he could steer the ship back out to the ocean; and once the ship was out of the river, yes, he could guide it toward a safe rendezvous with the pilots on the Atlantic coastline.

As a parting aid, the group gave him an assistant to help with his tasks, a man named Rocca who was said to have been a French war hero, a winner of the Légion d'Honneur in the First World War, and to have "a grim hatred of the Nazis." Rocca's cover was that he would be Paolantonacci's newly hired customs agent working with Malevergne in Mehdia.

Malevergne went home to await the arrival of the Portuguese ship, but almost immediately he became suspicious of Rocca. Something indefinable in his manner was just wrong. It was a feeling Malevergne could not shake.

When the ship, the *São José,* arrived on December 12, Malevergne went aboard and discovered that her captain was also nervous about the operation. It felt like a bad omen to Malevergne, but nonetheless, he piloted the *São José* up the Sebou to Port Lyautey. Once there, Malevergne determined to check with his contacts in the underground just to make sure. Should they continue?

Once more he pedaled and rode his motorized bicycle down the two-lane macadam road to Rabat and sat down with a pair of his coconspirators, who tried to reassure him. Brunin even told him dryly that "deep down the French authorities would not be angry at the departure of forty Belgians from Morocco."

Malevergne's misgivings were not assuaged. He went back to Port Lyautey and was further discomfited by the relaxed Rocca, who told him that everything was fine. There was nothing to worry about. But Malevergne could see the French navy bustling about the port as if something were afoot, and his sense of paranoia was acute.

He went to Paolantonacci with his concerns about Rocca. In Lyautey, the only three people who knew of what was about to happen with the *São José* were Paolantonacci, Rocca, and Malevergne. Malevergne knew Pao would never betray him, and he himself had told no one. Why did the French navy seem to sense something was up too? Why was he feeling their glances?

By this time, Pao, too, was nervous. Decisions had to be made. The hour for commitment to the escape was near. The friends made a plan to smoke out Rocca. They decided to tell him that the embarkation place had changed to the village of Sidi Bouknadel, between Mehdia and Rabat. It was not a practical place for *barcassiers* to transport the pilots to the waiting *São José,* a fact that any Moroccan sailor, which Rocca was not, would know.

The next day, the security precautions of the French navy in the port became even more obvious. The authorities were thick as sardines on the docks of the harbor. There was one other bad sign for Malevergne, the most ominous: Rocca had disappeared. Once again Malevergne contacted Pao, who contacted Brunin. Finally the man who had tried to be so reassuring to Malevergne just a few days earlier gave in to anxiety. Brunin called off the escape and dispersed the Belgian pilots among the various safe houses in Rabat.

Malevergne went home to Mehdia on the evening of the December 15 with a deep sense of foreboding. For a moment, he thought of using the phone number that had been given to him by the French naval lieutenant a few weeks earlier. One call and he could be saved. *But what about Brunin, Paolantonacci and the others?* he thought. What would happen to them? Malevergne knew that he could not make the call, that he could not betray his friends, and he told Germaine to expect the worst.

Their son Claude had a fever that evening, and Malevergne and Germaine passed a sleepless night. Rain came in the morning, and as Malevergne stirred the fire in the cottage beneath the Kasbah, he wondered if he should call the doctor about the boy. It turned out he didn't have time. A car pulled up to the front of the house. It was 7:00 a.m. when the local police inspector, accompanied by two other officers, knocked on the door.

"What is it, gentlemen?" Malevergne asked.

The inspector was a man Malevergne had known for a number of years. "We need you," he said with embarrassed eyes. "You must come with us."

"Are you arresting me?" Malevergne asked. "You said 'must.'"

The inspector did not answer. What was there to say? Yes, he must go with the police.

Malevergne kissed his wife and boys good-bye. He gave a last backward glance at his home in Mehdia. Looking at the men who were taking him away, taking him to an uncertain future that at that moment promised nothing but ill, the river pilot actually felt sorry for them "and pitied them for the work they had to do."

They drove him first to the police station in Port Lyautey and then quickly on to Rabat, where, for the first time in his life, René Malevergne heard a prison door clang shut behind him.

PART I

CHAPTER 1

New York, June 1942

As much as any place in the country in late June 1942, World War II was being waged in New York Harbor. Fanned out on shorelines that stretched from Perth Amboy and Elizabeth in New Jersey to the Bronx and South Brooklyn in New York and thick along the southern end of Manhattan rested "docks, piers, and wharves of every conceivable size, condition, and state of repair," all preparing ships for the duties of a nation at war. The bay was thick with vessels too. Scores lay anchored and waiting for their turn at the docks. Warships and merchant vessels, transports and tugs (up to 575 employed by the Port of New York) plied the waters of the upper bay while the Statue of Liberty looked silently on and the sounds of heavy machinery mixed with the deep blast of ships' horns to echo around the basin.

More than three dozen shipyards, including the giant Navy Yard in Brooklyn, also rimmed the harbor. Destroyers, cruisers, and battleships from the U.S. Navy sat suspended in dry docks being feverishly overhauled, outfitted, repaired, and scrubbed. The flashing arcs of welding torches could be seen day and night, while the pounding echoes of hammers smashing against steel hulls reverberated around the bay. Scores of merchant vessels were in the process of conversion to defense-capable ships by order of the War Shipping Administration (WSA). Other boats, commercial to pleasure craft, trawlers to yachts, were being turned into sub chasers mounted with three-inch guns and loads of depth charges. Brand-new PT boats, the speedy little darlings of naval action in the Pacific, zipped around the harbor in test runs conducted from Bayonne, New Jersey, where they were being manufactured by the score.

The yards and docks were punctuated by skeletal derricks and cranes, radio antennae, conning towers, and ships' masts of every size and description, all standing outlined against the skylines of Manhattan,

Newark, and Brooklyn. Upward of a thousand warehouses, set just back from the shorelines and capable, within the whole sweep of the harbor, of storing a combined forty million square feet of goods and matériel, thrummed with the comings and goings of railroad cars and trucks. Here is where the tools of war, the machinery, the weaponry, the dry goods and hardware, the canvas, cotton, and wool, the matches, batteries, boots, and cigarettes, arrived from the factories in the interior of the nation. Here they were stored, and here they were loaded onto those waiting ships, along with the young men who would use them.

Thousands of members of the army's II Corps, the first large contingent of the long-promised American invasion force, which was scheduled to sail to England at the end of the month, had arrived in New York in preparation for the trip and waited in Brooklyn to be shipped from Bush Terminal. They were far from the only military in the city: "90 day wonders," the nickname given to college boys drawn from mostly dry lands all over the country, who were given three months to learn the ropes of a midshipman's life in the U.S. Navy, were housed up at Columbia; army brass and navy officers in dress whites, overseeing the comings and goings in the city for the U.S. Department of War, took the best tables at the Copa; but thousands of sailors—merchant marines, coast guard, and U.S. Navy—had their own good times, wandering the streets of Manhattan, wondering what war would bring them even as they gawked skyward at the Empire State and Chrysler buildings and soaked in the neon lights of Broadway. Caps pushed back on their heads to reveal a hint of hairline, they took big, galumphing strides through the city, eyeing the young women of New York and being eyed in return, like the happy-go-lucky crooners in wartime movies yet to be made.

For all the excitement and anticipation in New York, however, few in the city slept peacefully. While it was apparent that the nation's involvement in the war in Europe was about to begin in earnest, no one knew for sure where or when that action would start. For those millions here and across the country who were uneasy about what the war in Europe would bring (and who wasn't?), the fact that New York was full of soldiers, sailors, ships, and the supplies of battle, standing on the brink of war but not yet in it, deepened the sense of anxiety, even as it gave them something akin to relief that the United States was about to engage the enemy.

Ever since the Japanese had bombed Pearl Harbor, now more than seven months ago, there had been such a constant stream of bad news that many in New York and the rest of the country were demoralized. Just the day before—on Father's Day—the guest pastor at Riverside Church had sermonized against the "spiritual defeatism" that seemed to be consuming the intellectual set on the Upper West Side. The fury and destructiveness of war in Europe and in the Pacific was so bad that a malaise had settled over many in the country. Would there ever be beauty and grace in the world again?

Dean Charles Gilkey of the University of Chicago Chapel tried to buck up the Riverside congregation by reminding them that Beethoven created some of his greatest music and Keats his greatest poetry during the darkest days of the Napoleonic Wars. The American Civil War produced Abraham Lincoln, he told them, adding: "The best things are so constantly in conflict with the worst things around us, that it is all the more important in bad times for every one of us to 'hold his own end up.'"

Despite these bolstering words, it would have been hard to criticize congregants who left the pews and returned to the city streets with their spirits less than soaring. Not only was New York in the midst of hot, sticky weather—eighty-five degrees and humid—but gas shortages inhibited exits out of the steaming metropolis to upstate or Long Island resorts.

There was some tentative-sounding good news on the war in the Pacific. At a place called Midway, the Japanese fleet seemed to have been dealt a hard blow by the U.S. Navy and its aircraft; but in Europe, it was difficult to find anything to cheer about. The Germans were readying a new offensive against the Soviet Union that threatened to topple the Russians, leaving only the United States and Great Britain to maintain the fight against the Nazis. In France, Jews had just been ordered by the

Vichy government to wear yellow stars. In North Africa, the latest news had it that Tobruk had fallen to General Erwin Rommel, the "Desert Fox," leaving all of Egypt wide open to his Panzer divisions. Elsewhere, there were rumors, so awful that they were hard to credit, of Nazis using gas to exterminate Jews sent to camps on the eastern front.

For all this, perhaps the most debilitating aspect of war to the citizens of the New York and the rest of the East Coast was how near it seemed to the very harbor that sheltered this mass collection of ships and humanity. For months now, German submarines had been terrorizing the coastal waters of the eastern United States, sinking merchant ships with a vengeance just beyond the Narrows.

Under the command of Admiral Karl Doenitz, Germany had, at the start of the war in Europe, sent out forty-six U-boats to prey on British shipping. Initially, they were dispatched into the Atlantic as individual vessels, but in September 1940, Doenitz began sending out these submarines in groups that came to be known as "wolf packs." Their numbers were increased into the hundreds, and their successes in sinking ships led German commanders to dub the early phase of the operation the "Happy Time."

An increase in British protection of Allied convoys began to curtail the numbers of ships going to the bottom, but as soon as the United States entered the war in December 1941, Doenitz initiated an operation called Paukenschlag—Drumbeat—which sent U-boats to the very shores of the United States to begin a brutal mauling of American shipping. The German command had been genuinely surprised by the Japanese attack on Pearl Harbor and was only prepared to send half a dozen of its subs to American coastal waters in December 1941. But the fact that shipping traffic was so thick along the Eastern Seaboard, and that the United States was so ill prepared to deal with attacks, allowed this handful of U-boats to destroy ship after ship in the region.

From the Gulf of Mexico to the Caribbean Sea, and tight to the coast all the way from Florida to Nova Scotia, the German subs wreaked havoc on defenseless ships. They lurked so close to American shores that one of their principal means of locating targets was to use the backdrop of city lights to outline and illuminate their prey. So successful was the enterprise that the Germans resurrected the nickname of their first successful operation and labeled this one, with a decided lack of creativity, the "Second Happy Time."

A Norwegian tanker was sunk off the coast of Nantucket in early January 1942, two days later a British ship was sunk off of Long Island, and four days after that a Standard Oil tanker went down off the coast of North Carolina. In late February, near Barnegat Light in New Jersey, a torpedo plowed into the port side of the tanker *R. P. Resor* so close to the Jersey shore that an able seaman on watch could see the outline of the retreating U-boat against the individual lights of homes and docks along the coast. Earlier in the month, the SS *Lemuel Burrows* was torpedoed and sunk just off Atlantic City, with twenty crewmen killed in the process. The second engineer on the ship wrote that it was the resort itself that doomed the ship. "We might as well run with our lights on. The lights [of Atlantic City] were like Coney Island. It was lit up like daylight all along the beach."

As the weeks passed, Doenitz began to send more subs to American waters. In early April, a German U-boat commander was so close to Jacksonville Beach in Florida as he watched the burning of a tanker he'd just hit (the *Gulfamerica* on her maiden voyage) that he could see tourists running to the shore from restaurants and hotels to gawk at the sight. He had originally intended to finish the tanker off with his deck guns, but when he saw the gawkers, he was afraid his shells would scream into the innocent bystanders. The commander decided to position his submarine to the landward side of the tanker and fire out toward the open sea. Later, he wrote a congratulatory note in his ship's log, as if he'd been providing just another tourist sight for the Floridians gathered on the shore: "All the vacationers had seen an impressive special performance at Roosevelt's expense. A burning tanker, artillery fire, the silhouette of a U-boat—how often had all of that been seen in America?"

Through the early months of 1942, few measures were taken by the

U.S. military to prevent this carnage. Merchant shippers and marines pleaded with the navy to supply them with arms. More patrol boats and air patrols were needed to scour the East Coast for German subs. Shipping convoys surrounded by military vessels had been used to good effect by the British for almost two years: why weren't they being employed here? Likewise, shoreline blackouts along British coasts had prevented the sort of stage-light backdrops that made the killings easy for U-boat commanders. Couldn't we at least dim the lights?

Despite the pleas for action from the shipping industry and the public, it took the sinking of more than three hundred ships along the East Coast and in the Gulf and Caribbean before Admiral Ernest King, the chief of naval operations, finally took measures to protect the sea-lanes. Air and boat patrols were gradually increased and the navy agreed to provide armed guards to merchant shipping.

Coastal lighting restrictions were a thornier issue. It turned out that despite the hazard to ships, shoreline businesses—resorts, amusement areas, restaurants, and others—were less than thrilled at the prospect of going completely black for the duration of the crisis, and the navy acceded to their requests for something less than a pitch-dark coast line. A "dim out" was ordered instead, and the shielding of lights, rather than the extinguishing of them, became standard operating procedure.

The hardest nut to crack, for those trying to persuade King to specific action, was the implementation of the convoy system. For a man who was predisposed to dislike anything British, the positive effect of the system on wartime England's shipping industry was not persuasive in its favor. King and a number of World War I veterans of the U.S. Navy argued that because convoys had to sail at the speed of their slowest members, they prevented faster vessels from performing to their utmost capabilities. King and others also felt the convoy system taxed already overcrowded ports upon arrival, resulting in delays and backups that slowed the process even further. And there was a confirmed belief in the U.S. Navy that there simply weren't enough warships available in the fleet to provide protection for groups of merchant ships, to wage war against the Axis, and to meet the needs of the naval war in the Pacific.

The staggering number of vessels lost to U-boats, however, was putting such a severe strain on American shipping capabilities that an alarmed George Marshall became involved in the discussion. He sent a note to King, writing, among other dire warnings, that "the losses by submarines on our Atlantic Seaboard and in the Caribbean now threaten our entire war effort." Marshall acknowledged that escort ships were at a premium but wondered if King was searching in every nook and cranny for vessels. "Has every conceivable . . . means been brought to bear on this situation?" Marshall asked.

The man who was recently named by Marshall to head American forces in the European theater and who was a day away from flying to England to take that command, Dwight Eisenhower, was far more blunt in his assessment of the admiral, at least to his diary. "One thing that might help this war," Eisenhower wrote, "is to get someone to shoot King."

By the end of spring, the U.S. Navy had acquiesced, if grudgingly, to the convoy system. Transatlantic merchant and transport shipping would be protected by escorts in full beginning in July. This was the principal reason why New York Harbor was so brimming with ships being readied for the war on June 22, 1942, when the SS *Contessa* rounded Sandy Hook, sailed through the Narrows and into the upper bay, pointed toward pier 1, Bush Terminal, on the south end of Brooklyn.

Painted a bright white with a "V" on its single smokestack, the *Contessa* cut a weary but still handsome figure as she sailed through the waters of the harbor. Requisitioned by the War Shipping Administration in April and directed in May to New York, where "defense work" was to be undertaken to convert her into a transport ship for service on behalf of the army, the *Contessa* was arriving from La Ceiba in Honduras, a standard stop on her usual Caribbean cruises.

Owned by the Standard Fruit Company New Orleans but registered out of Honduras, she was what was commonly called a "banana boat," a steamer that made her trade by hauling loads of fruit and sightseers between the United States and various ports in the Caribbean. She had been plying the waters of the Gulf and Atlantic seaboards for a dozen years, ever since she was built and christened in Glasgow, Scotland, in 1930.

Named after the Italian village from which the founders of the Standard Fruit Company (the Vaccaro family, whose name also supplied the "V" on her smokestack) had emigrated, the *Contessa* was an oil-burning vessel, 397 feet long and 5,500 tons, with a triple-reciprocating engine, similar to the Liberty ships that had just begun to be churned out for merchant service in the war. Above the water she was roomy enough for up to sixty first-class passengers, who could dine in spacious comfort as well as enjoy the wicker-chaired lounge, a music room, a smoking room with game tables, deluxe cabins, and even an outdoor swimming pool. But it was her shallow draft and good size that allowed her to gather large loads of fruit from riverside plantations without getting trapped in stream muck. She'd grown accustomed to negotiating river ports in her many years of Caribbean service.

The *Contessa* was no *Queen Mary*, but as Standard Fruit declared in company brochures advertising her charms, she was "large enough for every element of comfort, and not too large to permit delightful social relationships with fellow vacationists." For a hundred and ten bucks and up, passengers found hot and cold running water in every stateroom; "Punkah Louvres [to] ensure warm and cool air as desired"; recreation that included shuffleboard and quoits; and even musicians to entertain the passengers at sea and on the shore.

Beyond the defense work for which she was coming to Brooklyn, the *Contessa* was here to pick up a load of troops to take to England, to learn what her convoy assignment would be for the voyage across the Atlantic, and to be boarded by one of the U.S. Navy armed guard units that were now being assigned to each of the merchant ships in the WSA fleet.

Not the *Contessa*, her crew, her master, Captain William Henry John, nor the Standard Fruit Company were innocents as far as wartime

dangers were concerned. Not only had they been sailing in the dangerous waters of the Caribbean and the American seaboard for the past
several months, including this trip up the East Coast to New York, but
many within the company had intimate knowledge of war's perils. In
fact, three of Standard Fruit's own ships, including two that John knew
intimately, had already been sunk in the spring of 1942 by German
U-boats.

The *Amapala,* built in 1924, was a 4,148-ton steamer that worked,
like the *Contessa,* between New York, Havana, and Honduras, hauling passengers and bananas between ports. The *Ceiba* was an older and
smaller ship, built in 1911 and hauling 1,698 tons. In March 1942, the
Ceiba was sunk by a U-boat off the coast of North Carolina on its way
to New York. Almost home on its way from Honduras to New Orleans,
the *Amapala* was attacked a month later—a couple of weeks before the
Contessa sailed for New York.

The third Standard Fruit vessel lost in the first months of the war, the
one that John had not sailed on, the *Miraflores,* had been sunk in February 1942. She disappeared with all thirty-four hands and no trace, on her
way from Haiti to New York, sometime after the middle of the month.

John was a forty-nine-year-old Welshman who had come to New
Orleans in 1919, immediately after serving in the British Royal Navy
during World War I. He spent four years working as port captain for a
sugar company in New Orleans before signing up with Standard Fruit
Company in New Orleans in 1923. His first ship was the *Ceiba,* upon
which he served as second and then first mate, before becoming master
of his first ship for Standard Fruit, the *Morozan.* In quick succession he
moved up the company ladder, serving as master on a series of ships of
ascending value to Standard Fruit: the *Gatun,* the *Granada,* the *Teguci-
galpa,* the *Cefalu,* the *Amapala,* and finally the *Contessa.*

A straight-backed and trim sailor, John stood five feet ten and
weighed 175 pounds. He had thick eyebrows and kept a crisp part to his
wavy salt-and-pepper hair, which he combed back in Clark Gable style.
Any movie-star appeal was sabotaged, to some extent, by his mustache.

Salt and pepper like the top of his head, it sat abbreviated beneath his nostrils, giving him less the look of Gable than that of a clerk prone to crisp pronunciation and a clipped manner of speech.

Neither image quite suited him. There was nothing supercilious about him, but he was no dashing hero either. John was a soft-spoken man with a gentlemanly polish that made him excellent company for his ships' captain's dinners. He was comfortable in his position and seemingly so natural to it that even members of his own family referred to him as "Captain John."

Born in 1893 in Pembroke, Wales, not far from Cardiff, Captain John joined the British merchant marine as a cadet in an officers' training program at the age of fifteen. He spent four years learning the ropes on steam-powered, coal-burning freighters before matriculating to the Nautical Academy in Portsmouth to study for his second mate's papers. After a couple more years in the merchant navy, he had his master's rating as well, then wound up in the Royal British Naval Reserve, with which he served through the First World War.

Postwar Britain offered limited opportunities for relatively inexperienced officers in the merchant marine, so John decided to try his luck elsewhere. With his new wife, an attractive Welsh girl named Bessie Sigsworth, and the first of two daughters, Peggy (a second daughter, Betts, would be born in the United States in 1925), John moved to New Orleans in 1919. As it turned out, John had something of a flair for the American South. Though he kept his Welsh accent, he liked the exotic flavor of New Orleans. He donned panama hats and drank scotch and ginger ale when he was off the bridge and resting at his new home in New Orleans. The family was so comfortably ensconced in Louisiana culture that by the time the war had begun, daughter Peggy was a sorority sister and beauty queen at LSU, with the daughter of Huey Long as a housemate. Wife Bessie had brought her mother, father, and brother over from Wales to join the family in New Orleans.

None of this, of course, made the onset of war and the move of the *Contessa* to New York in 1942 any easier. It was safe to say that Bessie, if not Captain John himself, wondered if it wasn't time for this old sailor to call it a career. Though John was still a man who stood tall and straight on the bridge, still a man whose orders were issued and taken with confidence and alacrity, his salad days were long gone.

New York Harbor was a familiar sight to Captain John. Standard Fruit had delivered fruit to, and booked cruises out of, Manhattan for years and kept an office on Broadway. As captain of both the *Contessa* and the *Amapala*, John had sailed to and from the port with regularity in the 1930s. Steering toward Bush Terminal in Brooklyn was, however, a new experience.

Stretching into the harbor beneath Sunset Park and the sprawling Brooklyn army base, the terminal was a busy warren of warehouses, designed by Cass Gilbert, with multipaned windows and arched bridge skyways connecting one building to the next. The terminal was the largest point of embarkation for army personnel and equipment in the city, and it was hopping on that June day. Outside, dockworkers and cranes loaded one ship after another, as a long line of trains and trucks were backed up waiting to deliver supplies to the docks, including munitions so dangerous that a twenty-five-dollar fine for smoking at the piers was judged not steep enough by the mayor of the city. Within the buildings, a sea of clacking typewriters were manned by straight-backed clerks and junior officers, holding checklists and clipboards, monitoring the comings and goings of newly minted infantrymen waiting to ship off to England.

The *Contessa* was to berth at pier 1 for a full month as it was prepared for its first convoy voyage at the end of July. Here it would be painted battleship gray and receive "splinter protection"—steel plates—on the bridge and at newly installed gun mounts to prevent the wooden deck from splintering under fire. It would be outfitted with a fire-control communication system, a magazine for ammunition storage, and nine guns fore, aft, and bridge: eight 20-millimeters and one 4-incher. Fourteen members of a navy armed guard would join the crew, which would number sixty-nine, counting Captain John. In addition, one hundred troops bound for Ireland would board the *Contessa* before she sailed.

John and the crew could be forgiven for any sense of melancholy as they steered toward Bush Terminal. Gone now were the swimming pool and passengers playing quoits on deck. Gone were the parties, the musicians, and the elaborate captain's dinners on the last night of the cruise. Gone were the warm-water ports of La Ceiba, Caracas, Havana, and Veracruz and the smell of bananas wafting from the refrigerated holds. Hard to believe, but the *Contessa* was soon going to be a ship of war, sailing purposefully, just beyond the harbor, into the teeth of those menacing German wolf packs lying in wait in the chilly North Atlantic waters.

John, who had already experienced his share of conflict, didn't have to be warned that global war was a horrific thing. To enter it twice in a lifetime, as were so many others, was certainly a surreal thing. Adding to that sense for John was a personal connection to what was happening in the ocean between New York and the ports of Great Britain.

As a twenty-five-year-old navigation officer on HMS *Snapdragon,* a convoy destroyer sailing in the Mediterranean between Malta and Port Said in October 1918, John was on duty when a German U-boat sank a cargo ship within the *Snapdragon*'s group. As the rest of the convoy sailed on, the *Snapdragon* was ordered to stay behind to search for and punish the German sub. After four hours of fruitless sniffing in the ocean, the destroyer was just about to give up the hunt when the U-boat suddenly broke the surface of the water, at point-blank range right in front of her. The *Snapdragon* swung its guns toward her and sent five 4-inch shells pounding into her hull. Like a dead fish, the U-boat slowly turned belly up in the water before beginning its descent to the bottom. As the sub disappeared, the German crew soon emerged in life rafts, bobbing on the surface of the ocean, and the *Snapdragon* sailed near to haul the sailors aboard.

Among the survivors was the ship's commander, a cocksure German lieutenant, as John remembered him, far more insulted at the fact that he'd lost a ship and had been captured than grateful that his life had been saved. When John asked how things were in Berlin—this was just a month before the long and horrible war would come to a close—he was told, again with arrogant self-assurance, that the only difference between the Germany of October 1918 and the Germany of July 1914 was that the public houses now closed at midnight.

The lieutenant's name was Karl Doenitz, the man who was now Rear Admiral Karl Doenitz, the *Befehlshaber der Unterseeboote,* commander of the submarines in the German navy. The cocky lieutenant had become leader of Project Drumbeat on the shores of North America; he was the dark knight who'd sunk hundreds of Allied and merchant ships, including two Standard Fruit vessels that William John had known like the back of his hand.

Quite frankly, Captain John wished that Karl Doenitz had gone down with his U-boat twenty-four years earlier. Instead, John was faced with a private sense of irony: what if one of this man's submarines drew a bead on the *Contessa*?

CHAPTER 2

Airborne to London

I f Captain William John was a hesitant enlistee in the cause, the man dozing in the four-engine Stratoliner flying high above the Atlantic on its way from Washington to Nova Scotia, and then to London, was his exact opposite: a man born, bred, and absolutely ready for this war. For General George S. Patton Jr. the prospect of battle ahead couldn't have been more exhilarating. He shared the cabin with a group of staffers and recently promoted Brigadier General James Doolittle, whose air raid of Tokyo in April had made him the first genuine hero of World War II. All were seated comfortably in the cushioned seats of this novel airliner and cruising at twenty thousand feet above the ocean on a flight that would take most of August 6 and into the morning of August 7, 1942, before it landed in London.

A little more than a week earlier, Patton had been stuck in the deserts of California southeast of Palm Springs, training a newly created American armored command designed to offer an answer to the German's Panzer divisions currently wreaking havoc in the North African terrain. Away from the center of U.S. military command in Washington, Patton worried that despite his longtime friendship with Eisenhower, the new commander of the European Theater of Operations United States Army (ETOUSA), and despite the respect that Chief of Staff George Marshall had for his ability, he was too far from the heart of what was happening to be assured that he would be an integral part of the first battle in the European theater.

In fact, Marshall had recently sent him hustling back to California after an initial summons to Washington in June. The rebuke had come after Patton had essentially questioned a decision Marshall had made about the deployment of American armored forces to aid the British, just defeated at Tobruk. Patton had asked not once but twice for another division to help with the fight, after being pointedly told that there simply were not the resources for such a demand. In response, the chief of staff had sent his commander back to the desert, posthaste, fully intent on making sure Patton understood who was in charge of U.S. military efforts in this war.

Marshall had let Patton stew in California for a full month, uncertain whether his future role in the army would offer him the sort of field command that he knew he deserved and craved. Patton was not a man skilled in headquarters politics, to say the least. He was also—as would soon be exhibited—a general who would pursue with a bullish stubbornness what he felt was needed for his command. These traits, along with his blunt and profane style, had won him at least as many enemies as friends during his long army career. And Patton knew that those who disliked him tended to do so with a vengeance.

Then a second call came from Marshall's office; then had come the order for him to fly to Washington; then had come news that he was to be an integral part of the first American attack on Axis forces in the war; and now all was right with the world. Once he'd arrived in Washington, he had gotten the order to fly to London to discuss the assault with Eisenhower and the European command. And here was the flight itself.

The first fully pressurized aircraft ever built and one of only ten in the air at the time, the Stratoliner had been requisitioned by the federal government for use by VIP travelers when the war began. It could fly five to ten thousand feet higher than the standard nonpressurized airplanes in the arsenals of both Allied and Axis forces and actually had curtained sleeping compartments with spring mattresses. The flight gave Patton such a sense of comfort, as he and the others cruised in darkness over the Atlantic, that after some brief chitchat with his companions—"all talk was of fishing and shooting," Patton later told his diary—he was actually able to adjourn to one of those bunks and take a lengthy nap on the plane. Good to be able to relax in the clouds.

For those who knew Patton well, snoozing was an unfamiliar posture in which to find him. This was a man of action, a man of combat, a man accustomed to barking commands in language so blue and in a tenor so surprisingly high-pitched that everyone commented on both. "I sometimes wondered if [Patton's] macho profanity was unconscious compensation for his most serious personal flaw," wrote General Omar Bradley, "a voice that was almost comically squeaky and high-pitched, altogether lacking in command authority."

Patton had a well-known predisposition for not suffering fools or mistakes gladly. Those close to him usually forgave his temper, knowing most of his outbursts—at least in the field—were the soundings of an overly passionate man whose central intention was to improve his soldiers. Those who didn't like him thought he was intemperate, unwise, and impulsive to a fault.

His colorful style had already drawn the attention of the media. He'd been featured on the cover of *Life* magazine in the summer of 1941, after he'd made a splash in war games held that spring in Louisiana. One of the anecdotes reported told of Patton, a licensed pilot, grabbing a plane in the midst of the games to get a better sense of how his tanks were performing in the field. He was worried in particular that they guard against bunching, which would make a thick and plentiful target for the enemy. When he spied a logjam of armored vehicles halted at a crossroads, he buzzed his own troops, as close as safety would allow, screaming down at the transgressors, "Get those goddamn tanks off the roads and into the bushes." Good stuff for the reporters.

At age fifty-six, if he wasn't quite as fit as he'd been thirty years earlier when he was an Olympic teammate of Jim Thorpe in Stockholm, Patton was nonetheless in trim shape. Just that past spring, while training armored forces for desert fighting in California, he'd insisted that his officers prove their fitness by running ten miles a day in the oppressive heat. Patton led them on their jogs.

In contrast to his crusty exterior, Patton was imbued with a deep sense of style and was a romantic at heart. He was a writer of poetry, dressed with gallant flair, and was prone to dramatic words and gestures.

When he bid adieu to his beloved Second Armored Division before heading off to California to train the desert armored forces in the spring of 1942, Patton raised his glass to his colleagues and their spouses at his going-away party. "Here's to the wives," he said. "My, what pretty widows you're going to make!"

George Patton was the sort of character who collected nicknames easily. His soldiers called him "The Green Hornet" or "Flash Gordon" for his heroic mannerisms and splashy style of dress. He had essentially given himself his most famous moniker while delivering yet another impassioned speech to officers in the Second Armored Division in the very early days of the conflict. The war, he told them, "will be won by blood and guts alone." So "Blood and Guts" he became, though Patton himself despised the name. To friends and family, who saw more of his charm than others, he was simply "Georgie."

Patton was raised in a home of comfort and privilege in Los Angeles. His father served for a time as district attorney for the county, was a successful businessman, and ran unsuccessfully for Congress and the U.S. Senate as a Democrat. His mother came from a wealthy family whose patriarch had arrived in California as a fur trapper in the days of Spanish rule and hacienda living. Benjamin Davis Wilson subsequently became one of the earliest mayors of Los Angeles and was the owner of a vast ranch bordering the city. It was here, romping through the hills and valleys that would one day be modern Pasadena, that Georgie grew up.

Patton's father came from Virginia, and his ancestry included a whole passel of soldiers of the South. George's grandfather, a colonel in the Confederate Army and a graduate of the Virginia Military Institute, was killed at Cedar Creek. A great-uncle died in Pickett's charge at Gettysburg. Two other great-uncles served Virginia in the Civil War, and Patton's father, like his father before him, graduated from VMI and steeped his own son in military history and the legacy of the Lost Cause.

Georgie wanted to be called, and fully intended to be, "Lieutenant General George S. Patton Jr." from his earliest days forward.

His education was unique and curious. Patton's father believed that the learning process should consist almost entirely of a child "soaking in" the classics by having them read aloud. From his toddlerhood all the way to adolescence, young Georgie's ears and mind were given a steady diet of legends and epics, poetry and Scripture. It was said that he could recite whole passages of *The Iliad* as a seven-year-old boy and liked to play with his sister as Hector and Achilles outside the gates of Troy on the grounds of the Patton estate in the San Gabriel Valley, east of Los Angeles. He didn't go off to school until he was twelve. Perhaps not surprisingly, he was a notoriously bad speller for his whole life.

Like his forebears, George Jr. went to VMI, but he left after only a year to take an appointment at West Point. There, Patton excelled in all subjects but math, won points for deportment and discipline, was a star hurdler on the track team, and won the high honor of being appointed corps adjutant in his last year of school.

He married Beatrice Ayer, the daughter of a wealthy Massachusetts manufacturer, a year after graduating, and together they began an army life in the cavalry. Stationed first in Illinois and then in Fort Myer, Virginia, where Patton served as aide-de-camp to General Leonard Wood, chief of staff of the army, George Jr. was spotted as a rising star from his earliest days. He combined the physical traits and style of a nineteenth-century cavalry officer, with a blunt aggressiveness that would serve him well in twentieth-century warfare. While in Illinois, Patton took up polo at a Lake Forest club and became an accomplished player and excellent horseman. Later, while in Europe, he studied fencing and became a master swordsman and would wind up instructing the skill at Fort Riley, Kansas.

That trip to Europe came in about 1912, when Patton was chosen to represent the United States Olympic team as a member of the pentathlon squad, a sport that combined five of the primary skills of a cavalry officer, including fencing, swimming, equestrian steeplechase riding, cross-country running, and pistol shooting. Patton finished in fifth place overall in the competition, which was marked by some controversy. Patton scored an unexpectedly poor twenty-seventh in pistol shooting, though it was later claimed by some witnesses that a miss of Patton's was actually caused by the fact that he'd hit the target in the precise same spot twice, one bullet burying the next.

Patton's flair and take-no-prisoners reputation was enhanced during service in Mexico, where he chased Pancho Villa under the command of Brigadier General John J. "Blackjack" Pershing. In one incident, which became legendary, Patton, along with half a dozen infantrymen, drove to the hideout of a General Cardenas from Villa's staff. A shootout ensued, during which Patton shot and killed two of the Mexicans, including Cardenas, with his ivory-handled pistol. He drove back to Pershing's headquarters with the bodies strapped to the hood of his steaming army car. The story was widely covered in the national press, making Patton a minor celebrity of the incursion into Mexico.

Pershing took a shine to "Georgie," seeing in him many of the same instincts for combat he saw in himself. When Pershing was appointed commander of the American Expeditionary Force (AEF) in Europe after the U.S. entry into World War I, he asked that Patton accompany him to France and serve in his headquarters. Then based with the AEF in Paris and recently promoted to captain, Patton became headquarters commandant. Among many new acquaintances, he met Captain George Marshall soon after his arrival.

Patton, however, chafed at headquarters duties and was soon lobbying to move to some position that would offer a chance for more action. When Pershing decided to establish an American corps of tanks, a weapon that was new to the war and just coming into its own, Patton was asked if he'd like to serve under its commander, Colonel Samuel Rockenbach. George asked his father for advice on the matter and was told to "select the weapon with which you can inflict the most punishment while suffering the least casualties." Sound counsel, in Patton's estimation, and off he went to study this new armed vehicle at both French and British training centers.

Patton established himself as the American army's leading expert and proponent of the machinery. He learned how to operate the tanks, trained others in the newly formed tank brigade, and ultimately, in September 1918, led his corps into battle at Saint-Mihiel and then Meuse-Argonne, where he was wounded on the first day of action. Patton won a battlefield promotion to colonel and earned a Distinguished Service Cross and the Purple Heart for his service and wounds.

Patton became one of the most visible and highly regarded young officers in the war. He developed a style of personal leadership that would carry over into the next war and would soon be apparent in North Africa. He was no remote, commanding figure to his troops; whether in training or combat, he was there among them on a daily basis, cursing, exhorting, letting them know in no uncertain terms that his role was to make them better and braver soldiers. He was hardly beloved by his soldiers, but he was respected; and Patton gained a reputation as a fighter and a strict disciplinarian who was capable of leading and inspiring his troops. He also liked to see a salute snapped off with a smart style that came to be known in the ranks as a "George Patton."

His eccentricities were also becoming legend within the army. Patton liked to write poetry on what he called "the manly virtues [that war] engenders." It was also in France that he became relatively open about his belief in his own reincarnations. One of the young lieutenants under his command in the tank corps in France, Harry Semmes (who would subsequently serve with Patton in North Africa and write a biography of the general after World War II), recorded an instance when Patton was driving through the French countryside in an area he'd never seen before to visit an American station. He had an odd feeling that he'd been in this same locale as a soldier in another life. "As the car approached the top of a hill," Semmes wrote, "Captain Patton, to whom the vicinity was entirely unfamiliar, reached forward and asked the soldier driver if the camp wasn't out of sight and just over the hill to the right. The driver replied, 'No sir . . . but there is an old Roman camp where we are going over there to the right. I have seen it myself.' " According to Semmes, Patton proceeded to the camp but, once there, had another intuition. Wasn't their theater of action straight ahead? He asked at the station headquarters. It was nighttime, and Patton had no way of knowing where the fighting was. " 'We have no theater [there],' " Patton was told, " 'but I do know that there is an old Roman theater only about three hundred yards away.' "

After the war, Patton was stationed near Washington, at Camp Meade, Maryland, and spent much of his time, with limited success, petitioning Congress for funds to build the army's armored forces. It was during these years that he first met and became friends with "Ike" Eisenhower, another West Point grad and rising star in the U.S. Army who, like Patton, had settled into an underfunded and often undervalued peacetime army. The two would spend a year together at Fort Riley in the mid-1920s, as well as study at the Command and General Staff College at Fort Leavenworth. Patton also graduated from the Army War College at Carlisle, Pennsylvania, which was required education at the time for any officer hoping for advancement in the army.

From Fort Riley, Patton took Beatrice and his family to the first of two interwar postings in Hawaii, where, among other duties, he wrote a plan for the defense of the island should she be attacked by air. He also honed his polo-playing skills. Back near Washington, at Fort Myer in Virginia in the early 1930s, Patton was reunited with his friend Eisenhower under the command of General Douglas MacArthur. Here he met for the first time Captain Lucian K. Truscott, another officer who would become a crucial figure in the career of George Patton and one with whom he was about to become reacquainted in London. All four were involved in the notorious squashing of the 1932 Bonus March.

In July of that year, thousands of World War I vets, financially devastated by the Great Depression, marched on Washington, demanding payment on bonuses that had been promised them as veterans of the

Great War. The problem was that the soldiers had been given bonds that weren't due to be redeemed for another dozen years, and the federal government had neither the means nor the inclination to hurry the payments.

The order to clear the marchers from Washington was passed from the administration to the army, and MacArthur personally oversaw the routing of the vets and their families. Eisenhower, MacArthur's aide, was at his side, embarrassed by what followed. Patton, who commanded the cavalry, including Lucian Truscott, was in charge of much of the dirty work. Two vets were killed in the mayhem, and the camp erected by the marchers was burned to the ground. It was a moment of which no officer involved was overly proud.

As the Second World War approached, the U.S. Army began the process of sorting out just what kind of military it needed to be and who might be its most accomplished commanders. One of the chief bones of contention was the use of armored divisions. Despite the obvious success of German blitzkrieg tactics in Europe, there were many in the United States who felt that one of the principal weapons of those attacks, the tank, was still a work in progress, that its most important function, at which it had shown only partial effectiveness in World War I, was in support of infantry. Tanks, which in the First World War had been subject to frequent breakdowns and terrain-induced stalls, were still not ready to lead troops into combat went this line of thinking. Some even assumed the horse would be a continued and important component of the war. In fact, it wasn't until 1940 that the U.S. Army created its First and Second Armored Divisions.

In the spring of 1941, newly promoted Major General George Patton was named commanding general of one of those divisions, the Second, and he led this force through a pair of successful war games in Louisiana and South Carolina that year. Again, however, his successes did not come without detractors. While Patton viewed his aggressive use of armored vehicles as an effective display of their capabilities, others in the exercises felt he was skirting the spirit of the games and disrupting important tests of the army's infantry for showboating purposes. The importance of these exercises was heightened for the commanders involved because, as Patton himself well knew, they were an opportunity to shine and impress. Making the cover of *Life* magazine didn't guarantee success in the prewar army, but in the fierce jockeying for consequential command in the coming war, a little national publicity didn't hurt either.

While there was no consensus on the character of George Patton within the army, there didn't need to be for him to have a seat on that August 1942 flight to London. In Eisenhower and Marshall he had the two most powerful supporters he could have within the European Command. And if his impulsiveness, his lack of patience, his inability to step lightly around the abilities and egos of other men in the U.S. Army had created a whole slew of rivals—well, as he would have suggested, war had begun, and the time for the political niceties and privileges of the interwar high command had passed. This battle would be won by blood and guts alone.

Of course, to the British high command, General George Patton, like all American commanders, was essentially an untested commodity in the sort of war that was being waged in Europe. He and Doolittle, along with Eisenhower, who'd flown to England in June, and George Marshall, who had hitched a ride on this same Stratoliner three weeks earlier, were all novices and had a steep climb up the learning curve to reach the point where they would know as much about the intricacies of World War II as their hosts. And the British were more than a little put off by the fact that the Americans were not inclined to be tutored.

From a strategic point of view, Marshall's journey, beginning on July 18, was one of the most momentous of the war. He had flown with Chief of Naval Operations Ernest King; FDR's eyes and ears, Harry Hopkins; and an accompanying crew of military brass from each branch of the service. The heavy hitters had come to meet with their Allied counterparts, the chiefs of staff of the British services, as well as Marshall's man in England, Eisenhower. This was the colloquy that would outline the direction the Allies in Europe were to travel through the coming months of 1942 and, by extension, the whole war. The entry of the United States into the fighting—the engagement that everyone from New York Harbor to the Golden Gate Bridge had been expecting for months now—was about to begin, the particulars to be hashed out by Marshall and company in England.

For months, the two governments had been trying to settle a basic dispute about how to fight the war against Nazi Germany. The simple facts were that Joseph Stalin and the Soviet Union were in desperate need of some relief from the onslaught that they faced from Germany. They had been imploring the United States and Great Britain to open a second front from the moment the United States had entered the war. No one, East or West, was certain how long the Soviets could last against Hitler's attack, but the dire straits and desperate conditions of the Russian people after a year of massive assault were well known. Already hundreds of thousands were dead on the eastern front, and earlier that summer Germany had begun to mount another offensive aimed at the heart of the Soviet nation.

The question was what strategy the Allies should pursue to wage war and alleviate the situation in the east. Marshall, Eisenhower, and most of the U.S. Army command favored a cross-channel assault against Germany in France. With typical American brio and a strategy that had been prevalent in the American army since the days of U. S. Grant and the American Civil War, their central idea was simply to pursue the enemy directly and with as much force as possible. If an attack against Germany in France in 1942 was now unlikely, given the quickly advancing calendar, then it should be made the following spring. Eisenhower himself had outlined the strategy, labeled Operation Roundup, while working under Marshall in the spring of 1942, still in Washington.

The British were dead set against the idea. It was premature, they said. The Americans were naive to think that they could mount a successful battle on the beaches of France against an already entrenched and powerful Nazi force. It would be slaughter, and since the initial invasion would have to be carried out largely by British forces, due to American army inexperience and the need for the United States to become further mobilized, Her Majesty's high command was not enthusiastic, to say the least. To his daily log, Marshall's counterpart, General Alan Brooke, called Marshall's notion of a cross-channel attack "just fantastic." The British proposed instead to attack the Wehrmacht through Norway, through North Africa, or by means of relentless bombings of Germany spiced by strategic commando raids against Nazi defenses in France that would force the Third Reich to stretch its defenses to razor-thin peril across two thousand miles of European coastline.

Gathered at the trapezium-shaped War Office building in Whitehall, London, home of the British department of war, Brooke and Marshall were the chief protagonists in the debate, and they quickly fulfilled a long tradition in American and British relationships. That is to say, Marshall felt that Brooke was patronizing, and Brooke felt that Marshall was too inexperienced, someone who had never served as an officer in the field and was therefore a political general with no real sense of what war was about.

The Norway attack was rather quickly dismissed as strategically pointless to the western Allies and ineffective in terms of alleviating pressure on the eastern front. The British pushed hard for an attack against North Africa, but the problems of an assault there were many in American minds. First among these was the question of what would be the response of the neutral nations in the area: Spain and Vichy France. French North Africa had not been occupied by the Axis powers, as was France itself. But since German trust in the capabilities and loyalty of the Vichy government was limited, the question was, how long would the Nazis stay removed from the French protectorates in North Africa?

Spain's role in the matter was likewise crucial. As Eisenhower would later put it, "there was a lively danger" that the Germans would attack through Axis-friendly Spain, threatening the strategically crucial

British-held Gibraltar and the invasion itself. With Gibraltar in the hands of Germany the Allied forces would be sealed off within the Mediterranean, a devastating situation for the invaders.

Finally, there was the matter of what the French themselves would do. Would French colonists consider an invasion force in North Africa liberators or an enemy violating the neutrality of the region? Would the French in North Africa fight or not?

And once engaged in North Africa, the Allies would, by virtue of commitment of resources to the action, be fully engaged. Even if the French met them on the beaches of the Mediterranean and Atlantic waving banners and cheering, the Allied forces would still have to battle German Panzer divisions, which would soon be racing across the desert to halt them. The fear in American quarters was that an attack in North Africa would ultimately run from the Red Sea to the Atlantic and take the rest of 1942 and well into 1943 to carry out. It would inevitably force a delay in the assault against the strength of Germany's European forces in France.

For American doubters of the strategy, the question was why American forces should waste manpower and treasure in an invasion against French and German forces in Africa that would be logistically difficult to pull off—given the fact that the invasion would take place on a continent distant from the United States and America's growing base in England—and strategically questionable for a couple of reasons. First, the Germans would not have to divert as many of their resources from the war against the Soviet Union to cover North Africa as they would if the Allied attack were a cross-channel invasion of France. Second, assuming a successful invasion (a big question mark in many people's minds), how could the capture of North Africa help in the ultimate goal of striking directly and fatally at the heart of Nazi Germany? Between a victorious Allied army in North Africa and Adolf Hitler stood the Mediterranean Sea, Italy, and the Alps—hardly a smooth path to Berlin.

Essentially, American military leaders—Marshall and Eisenhower chief among them—felt that chasing Germans "a thousand miles south of London . . . when there were plenty of Wehrmacht troops stationed less than twenty-five miles from Dover" was an absurdity. And there was more than a little grousing that the British preference for a North African invasion was grounded as much in that nation's desire to maintain its control over Egypt, the Suez Canal, and its Middle Eastern interests as in its desire to quicken the pace of the war and ultimately achieve Allied victory.

But there were considerations beyond the strategic. This was the first great joint venture in the war for the Allies, and while by means of its wealth and production capabilities, the United States had supplanted Great Britain as the most important member of the coalition, it still had to be respectful of the political considerations involved. The truth of the matter was that at this moment, the two needed to cooperate, and the Soviet Union desperately needed some relief from the intensity of German attack. There was also a domestic political consideration for the man who would ultimately decide on the pursuit of Operation Torch, as it came to be known. Franklin Delano Roosevelt knew that the American people were anxious to join the fray in Europe, knew that to wait until 1943 to attack the enemy was politically risky.

A few days after arriving in London, Marshall sent a cable back to Roosevelt telling the president that the Joint Command was at an impasse. The British could not be convinced to participate in Sledgehammer, the plan to invade France directly across the channel, and the Americans remained skeptical about an invasion of North Africa.

It was Roosevelt who made the decision to accept the British plan of invading North Africa. Much to the delight of Winston Churchill and the British high command, he responded to Marshall's cable with one of his own, announcing his decision. Operation Sledgehammer, the direct assault against France, was not to be—at least in 1942. The Allies would acquiesce to the British and attack North Africa.

Stephen Ambrose describes Eisenhower as "darkly depressed by the decision." In fact, his feelings ran so strong that this usually temperate general, a man who had gone so far as to ban all pessimistic talk at his command headquarters in London, told his second in command, General Mark Clark, "July 22, 1942,"—the day the decision to invade North Africa had been agreed upon—"will go down as the blackest day in history!"

Eisenhower was not the sort of soldier to stew a long time over a decision that belonged to the commander in chief, however. Plus, he was simply too busy and too burdened with the responsibilities of his command to continue to fight a political battle that he could not win. He immediately sat down with the British and began to outline an invasion of North Africa.

What was initially envisioned was a double-pronged assault on the French Vichy territories in North Africa. The French North African empire swept nearly eight hundred miles from Tunisia, on the Mediterranean just to the west of Libya, around the northwest corner of the continent and down the Atlantic coast, encompassing the nation of French Morocco. Spanish Morocco, a tiny wedge of land directly across from Gibraltar on the northern tip of Africa and encasing the city of Tangier, remained a protectorate of Spain.

The plan called for one arm of the assault to swing toward Algiers on the Mediterranean. This would be composed largely of British forces. The second punch of the invasion was to be a roundhouse directed at French Morocco on the Atlantic side of the continent.

To Marshall and Eisenhower, the western assault was crucial in preventing a possible German invasion of Gibraltar through Spain. By taking Morocco, the Allies would be able to maintain communication from the Mediterranean if Franco allowed Hitler to overrun Gibraltar.

It was this force, wholly American, that the man sleeping in the back of the Stratoliner had been tapped to lead. What they needed, Eisenhower and Marshall agreed, was a soldier who would take Morocco quickly and efficiently. They needed a fighting general like George Patton.

CHAPTER 3

Incorrigible

Housed in a seven-by-nine-foot cell and fed black bread and "a doubtful liquid with a few scraps of meat in a dirty wooden bowl," René Malevergne passed his first couple of days in solitude at the Rabat prison, except for the periodic presence of guards opening and shutting his cell door to hand him these foul meals. On the third day, he was taken to the regional director of security and interrogated about his associations, at which time he learned that his coconspirators had been rounded up as well. He was told that if he gave the authorities the truth about the plans, he would soon see his wife and children. Malevergne was shown correspondence that had been found in the hands of the captain of the *São José*, but Malevergne knew that the letter had nothing incriminating in it and said so to his questioner.

But the ship's captain was plotting to take Belgian pilots out of Morocco to England, he was told.

So what? said Malevergne. *It was my duty as port pilot to board any ship coming into the harbor.*

Malevergne was left with a handful of blank sheets of paper and told to write out his confession. The pages remained blank when the inspector returned, and as a consequence, Malevergne was subjected to four more hours of questioning.

He was asked about the secret embarkation point at Sidi Bouknadel beach, the one he and Pao had concocted to fool Rocca. "Such an operation would be idiotic," Malevergne told his interrogators truthfully. "It would be inconceivable at that time [of day] because it could not go unnoticed in that part of the coast."

He was told that Germaine had burned some English pounds in the fireplace after Malevergne had been arrested, trying to hide incriminating evidence. Where had he come by English pounds?

"If she burned the money, our savings are gone," he told them. *They came from the Bank of England in Casablanca. I purchased them several years ago.*

It was one o'clock the next morning when he began to wilt, admitting that he might have talked with his companions about contriving a plot to aid the Belgian pilots out of Morocco, like "probably ten million Frenchmen at this moment who speculate about such a crime, if it is a crime." Forced to sign a statement to that effect, Malevergne was taken back to his cell with the promise that he would be able to see his wife and children the next day and allowed to accompany the authorities as they searched his home.

In the morning, he was driven to his home in Mehdia, but unfortunately Germaine and the boys were not there. They'd left for Rabat to stay with friends. Malevergne watched with a sickened and violated feeling as an officer went through his papers, as well as family photos and letters. He was then taken to his workplace in Port Lyautey, where once again the authorities searched his papers. As he left, his colleagues bade him tearful good-byes. It felt like it would be a very long time before he saw them again.

On the day before Christmas Eve, 1940, Malevergne was transferred, along with his accused coconspirators, Allegre, Brunin, Brabancon, and Paolantonacci, and eight of the Belgian pilots, to the military prison in Casablanca. Circumstances here were more lenient than they'd been in Rabat. Along with the others with whom he was allowed to visit, Malevergne began to craft a strategy against the charges and to coordinate stories. His defense consisted primarily of convincing the authorities that his chief accuser, Rocca, the man he'd hired and suspected of duplicity almost from the beginning, was an unreliable witness: a well-known drunk and liar.

Malevergne's stay in Casablanca was brief. Just after the New Year, he was taken with a dozen other inmates to a prison in Meknes, a city in the foothills of the Atlas Mountains in northern Morocco, to await trial in front of a military tribunal. His surroundings were once again harsh: a small cell with a cement slab to sleep upon; twenty-minute walks in the morning and afternoon "in a sort of cage, a little larger than the cell"; no communication with other prisoners; chickpeas or bean soup for dinner. He was, however, given paper and writing implements, and here, toward the end of January, Malevergne began to keep a diary.

In his second week in Meknes, Malevergne met with an attorney and learned that a hearing of his case had been set for the following week. On the appointed day, he was taken with his attorney to the judge's chambers, where to his surprise he found the traitor Rocca. He let his rage speak through his glance until the judge was out of the room. "Do you think that the Légion d'Honneur which you wear is well placed?" Malevergne hissed at him.

Rocca squirmed. "I was arrested before you were," he told Malevergne sheepishly. "At the interrogation, I was not able to take it."

A worm, Malevergne thought. Before the judge reentered the chambers, he asked Rocca to tell the court that he'd been drinking the day he'd made his accusations against the conspirators. That they were full of exaggerations and lies. Somehow he hoped that this plea would affect Rocca, but a few minutes later, after a clerk had read aloud Rocca's damning deposition, the court asked the witness if he affirmed the statement. Rocca simply nodded.

As he had initially, Malevergne argued that whatever was discussed between him and his fellow conspirators, it had been just that: discussions. No actions had ultimately been taken to get the Belgian pilots out of Morocco. He was guilty only of talk. Unfortunately, that was enough to send Malevergne's case to trial.

The river pilot was whisked by rail back to Casablanca. As he passed through Port Lyautey on the ride to Casablanca, the train made a ten-minute stop. Malevergne's heart ached at the thought that he was just a few miles from his wife and that it might be a very long time before he saw Germaine and his boys again. It might be never again. He saw a railroad employee in the city, an old friend, and left a message for his family: *Please tell my wife that I was in the station this morning and taking a plane from Casablanca in a short while.*

In Casablanca, Malevergne was taken by car from the train station to the airport, where he and half a dozen of his conspirators, including, again, Paolantonacci, Brunin, Brabancon, and Allegre, as well as the Portuguese captain of the *São José,* boarded an Air France plane bound first for Oran and then for Algiers, all on the way back to Vichy, France.

In Algiers they were kept overnight in a prison whose warden was a former resident of Port Lyautey and gave the group a decent reception. Unfortunately, the Portuguese captain misunderstood these kindnesses. He thought they constituted the sort of soothing gesture that a priest offers to a condemned man before a coming execution. The captain became slightly unhinged and could not be convinced by Malevergne and the others that there was no illusion here; the warden was simply being nice. The morning could not come quickly enough, and they were escorted to another plane for the last leg of the journey to France.

After landing in the city of Vichy, the prisoners were transported to the nearby city of Clermont-Ferrand, home of the Michelin Tire Company. They found themselves jailed in a crowded prison of 260 inmates, crammed into a facility meant for fewer than 200. The prisoners had come from all over the colonies, from French Equatorial Africa to French West Africa to Morocco and Algiers. All of them had been, in Malevergne's words, "compromised in the affairs of the Resistance," but they came from all types of backgrounds: some were thieves, spies, or deserters. "A lady of light morals" named Betty was also incarcerated. Some, like René Malevergne, were simply categorized as "incorrigibles."

New prisoners arrived from Morocco on a regular basis, including the Port Lyautey orchestra conductor and two women who were acquaintances of Malevergne: a Madame Mikaeaf and a nurse named Miss Krener. There was a daily flow of inmates into and out of the prison. Those who went to trial and were convicted were immediately replaced by newcomers, so that the overall total of inmates remained pretty steadily around 260. To keep up their spirits, prisoners would invent songs of honor for each prisoner as he or she was taken off to the court for trial.

The "dean" of the group was Pierre Mendès-France, a former under secretary of state for finance (and future prime minister of France), who offered counsel to prisoners awaiting trial, including Malevergne. Mendès-France, who would soon become Malevergne's cellmate, was not optimistic about the river pilot's fate, nor was he sanguine about his own. Regarding Mendès-France's own situation, at least, Malevergne agreed. The charges against the former minister were trumped up and had no basis, but as Malevergne recorded in his diary, because Mendès-France was a politician and a Jew, "they want to condemn."

February turned to March, March to April, and April to May. Prisoners came and went. The poor Portuguese ship captain had been taken to a hospital after another breakdown in the prison. There he languished. The Port Lyautey orchestra conductor received nine months in prison. A group of Belgian pilots—not those whom Malevergne and his cohorts had planned to help escape—were given harsh sentences for trying to escape to England. Malevergne learned that one of them, a Lieutenant Fernandez, upon hearing his sentence tore off the insignia of rank on his uniform and flung it to the ground. "I won it for shedding my blood for France," he told the court. And when his own lawyer tried to pick it up, Fernandez told him, "Leave it alone. I don't want it anymore."

Mendès-France was tried and indeed convicted. He got six years in prison and had little hope for an appeal. Malevergne reported that almost immediately upon returning to their cell to await final dispensation of his sentence, Mendès-France began plotting his escape (which was ultimately successful).

Meanwhile, Brunin and Paolantonacci learned that they were to be tried in the nearby city of Gannat, while Brabancon and another Belgian consulate employee, a man named Capart, were to be tried with Malevergne at Clermont-Ferrand. Malevergne and the others were assigned a lawyer, who prepared an extensive brief on their behalf.

A visit from his brother cheered Malevergne. It had been ten years since they'd last embraced. His brother's wounds, suffered while serving under Pétain at Verdun, had not improved with the passage of time. Pétain had changed much in the years since the war, his brother told René. It must have seemed like a serious understatement to Malevergne. "I was unstrung" by the visit, he told his diary.

On June 21, Malevergne was brought to court with Brabancon and Capart and heard the charges against him: "That, being a French citizen, he did, during the course of the year 1940, at various unspecified times, in time of war, give information of a military nature to a foreign power, to wit, Great Britain or its agents, with the intent of helping that power against France, and furnished to said agents information on the possibilities of embarking English forces on the Moroccan Coasts."

Due to the nature of the charges, Malevergne's trial was held in a military court and at the bench before him sat seven officers, along with a government commissioner and the clerk who had read the charges.

Brabancon's and Capart's cases were heard first, and each took about twenty minutes to defend himself. Then Malevergne was called forward. Once again, his defense was centered on the unreliability of Rocca, the chief witness against him. In his testimony, Malevergne challenged specific details in the deposition and was questioned closely on the same by the commissioner.

There was a recess after Malevergne presented his story, and when the court reconvened, it was time for the lawyers to take the floor. Malevergne worried that his counsel was a little long-winded and wearying the judges with his summation. But the lawyer finished with a flurry, demanding that Malevergne be freed.

Malevergne himself was given an opportunity to say a final word in his own defense. All of the confused allegiances of French patriots in the years of Vichy were delineated in his sincere plea: "I ask you to stop insulting me by supposing that for a single instant I could pretend to serve any other flag but our own," said the man who had agreed to aid the escape to Great Britain of men pledged to fight against the Axis powers, including Vichy France.

When Malevergne finished speaking, he and his two companions, Brabancon and Capart, stood before the court to hear the judgment. It came quickly: Brabancon, six months in prison; Capart, three.

It was now Malevergne's turn to be sentenced. He faced the seven officers arrayed before him and stood as the clerk snapped open a sheet of paper to announce the decision. As the clerk read the verdict, it took Malevergne a moment to fully comprehend what had just happened. In fact, he thought he'd heard wrong and asked the clerk to repeat what had just been read.

Who knew why he should be spared while the others stood convicted, but there it was. Before the court-martial in Clermont-Ferrand, René Malevergne stood acquitted.

CHAPTER 4

Claridge's

The flight to London took twenty-one hours, and Patton, despite the rest he'd gotten on the Stratoliner, was cranky upon arrival. He and his companions—Doolittle, Colonels Kent Lambert, who was part of Patton's staff, and Hoyt Vandenberg, who was with Doolittle, along with several other staff officers from the United States Army Air Force (both the army and navy had air commands before the air force formed its own separate branch of the United States military)— were driven to the famed Claridge's Hotel, where accommodations awaited them. The city looked bleak to Patton. He noted in his diary later that it appeared "half alive with very few people, even soldiers, about." For good measure, he commented acidly that "all the women are very homely and wear their clothes badly."

One of the first persons Patton met the next morning at Norfolk House in London, headquarters for the Joint Allied Command, was an old friend, Major General Lucian Truscott, who was there to brief him and Doolittle on the existing outline for the invasion. First, second, and third drafts of the plans had been gone through by members of the British chiefs of staff's offices and Eisenhower's command, and the British were becoming more and more insistent that the Mediterranean side of the invasion predominate, Truscott told him. Naval resources were simply insufficient to attack both the Atlantic coast in Morocco and the coast of Algiers, they said. The more important part of the battle, because it was nearer to German forces in Tunisia, was on the Mediterranean side.

Not surprisingly, Patton's mood was unimproved by this outline for invasion. The emphasis on the Mediterranean assault meant that he'd have to fight for resources for his western attack. Perhaps not surprisingly, Patton felt that his western command would be crucial to the overall success of the campaign. He asked Truscott and his staff to help him draw up initial estimates and plans for his needs to help bolster his argument for shifting resources to that area. Then he suggested that Truscott join him in the actual invasion. According to Truscott, Patton was insistent: "Dammit, Lucian," he said, "you don't want to stay on any staff job in London when there's a war going on. Why don't you come with me? I'll give you a command."

A soldier acknowledged for his abilities at training men, Truscott had been sent to London earlier that year to observe the methods of Great Britain's amphibious and commando forces under the command of Lord Admiral Louis Mountbatten. In the process, Truscott had become the U.S. Army's chief expert on these relatively novel and ultimately crucial components of modern warfare. Early in the summer he had helped organize and staff the first American version of the British commando forces, which would become the U.S. Army Ranger group, headed by Colonel William O. Darby and trained, that summer, in Northern Ireland and Scotland.

Like Patton, Truscott had originally been a cavalry officer. The two had first met ten years earlier when both served under General Douglas MacArthur at Fort Myer, near Washington. Both had participated in the infamous rout of the Bonus Marchers from the Capitol Mall in July 1932. They'd subsequently become friends and met periodically over the years, including in 1941 in Louisiana, serving with opposing forces during that summer's army war games. Though Lucian Truscott Jr.'s background was a far cry from Patton's, the two shared a number of interests and had similar straightforward styles. They were combat soldiers, good at leading and inspiring their troops and getting the most out of them in war.

Born to hardscrabble circumstances in 1895 in Texas, Truscott was raised primarily in Oklahoma, the son of an itinerant country doctor who frequently moved his family around from one fresh-timber town to the next in the newly formed Sooner State. The most notable moment in Lucian's youth was an accident that wound up scarring Truscott for the rest of his life. As a child wandering around in his father's office, Lucian

Jr. got his hands on a bottle of carbolic acid and decided to take a sip. His father probably pumped his stomach to emit the poison, but the acid wound up shredding the lining of his throat, leaving Truscott with a distinctive voice, described by one writer, as similar to "a rock-crusher."

To help the family make ends meet, Truscott went to a normal school and got his teaching certificate at the ripe old age of sixteen. He took his first job at a country school near his family's home in Stella, Oklahoma, but teaching turned out not to be the life for him. When the United States entered World War I, Truscott enlisted in an officers' training program designed to quickly turn young recruits with potential into military leaders. A first generation "90-day wonder," Truscott was sent off to Arizona for three months to learn how to command troops.

Truscott never made it to Europe for the war, remaining instead in the Southwest; but soon after the armistice, he had decided that he was suited for the military and would stay in the army. In the succeeding years, his career took him to many of the peacetime army stops that George Patton had made, including Hawaii and Texas, where Truscott, like Patton, indulged in a newfound passion for polo. Truscott was also stationed at Fort Riley and wound up teaching at the Command and General Staff School at Fort Leavenworth. The gravelly voice, skilled horsemanship, and leathery demeanor of an Oklahoma cowboy gave him instant presence, and Truscott developed a reputation as a fine and tough trainer of men.

It was at that Fort Myer posting in 1932 where he met Patton that Truscott first crossed paths with Eisenhower, too. Ike was serving as an aide to Army Chief of Staff Douglas MacArthur.

Truscott spent the remainder of the 1930s slowly moving up in the ranks of the peacetime army. He was reunited with Eisenhower just before the war, serving on "Ike's" staff in Fort Lewis in the state of Washington, prior to the war games in Louisiana and his departure for the combined staffs assignment in London.

In contrast to Patton's bluff and drama, Truscott could appear to be a laconic and distant figure. Robert Henriques, an Englishman who was part of Mountbatten's combined staff in London and ultimately a close and important aide to Truscott in the Operation Torch planning in both England and the United States, was less than impressed when he first met Truscott. In fact, he thought that the American was a little "dim." In meetings, Henriques reported, Truscott was "withdrawn almost to extinction and almost inarticulate. Like a student, conscientious but not very bright, he attended every conference as an observer and exclusively fulfilled this function, sitting at the table for hours with a perfectly blank face. When invited to comment by Mountbatten . . . he usually shook his head."

Henriques would soon realize that his initial assessment was far from accurate. He'd mistaken Truscott's thoughtfulness and consideration for dullness. He was somehow more "comprehensible" in the United States than in England, Henriques felt. "That soft Texan drawl, inaudible in London, now seemed infinitely friendly, purposeful, easy on the ear. . . . That Texan handshake and slow, very wide smile was instantly reassuring." Later, he would write of Truscott: "He inspired intense affection. . . ."

While there were moments in the months ahead when Patton questioned whether he'd made the right decision in his spontaneous request that Truscott join his North African adventure, they were fleeting. Unassuming Lucian Truscott would prove to be one of the great generals of the war.

After briefing Patton on the Torch plans as they existed, Truscott left the general in the hands of Eisenhower, who invited "Georgie" to a drink and a dinner of dehydrated chicken soup at Eisenhower's apartment. With the two generals was Eisenhower's aide, Captain Harry Butcher, attached to the general from the U.S. Navy, who made a record of the meeting.

Despite the possibility of acrimony between them—Patton, the more combat-experienced and older officer, had been passed over as chief of staff in the European Theater in favor of Eisenhower, while Eisenhower like everyone else, had to forgive Patton's brusque nature and impulsivity—the two genuinely liked each other and recognized that each had probably been appropriately cast for his respective role in this operation. Eisenhower was the perfect headquarters man and Patton the perfect field general. From the outset of their get-together, they spoke like old, forthright friends, discussing a few personnel decisions, including the switch of Truscott to Patton's command. Patton worried aloud to Eisenhower about intelligence estimates of French strength on the Moroccan coast, as well as the difficulties of finding suitable landing places in ocean swells that ran upward of fifty feet at times.

The two generals talked of army personalities and their likes and dislikes in officers. Eisenhower had trouble with "officers who feel they have fulfilled their responsibility when they simply report a problem to a superior and do not bring the proposed solution with them." In contrast, Patton said he didn't necessarily want a smart staff but a loyal one. Butcher, who had never met Georgie Patton, liked him and felt the get-together went well. "Patton is a good fellow," he wrote, "curses like a trooper, and boasts that while he is stupid in many particulars there is one quality he knows he has—the ability to exercise mass hypnotism. 'In a week's time,' [Patton] said, 'I can spur any outfit to a high state of morale.'"

To his diary, Patton was more cryptic about the meeting. "Had supper with Ike and talked until 1:00 a.m. We both feel that the operation [i.e., Torch] is mostly political. However, we are told to do it and intend to succeed or die in the attempt. If the worst we can see occurs, it is an impossible show, but, with a little luck, it can be done at a high price and it might be a cinch."

Patton wound up walking back to Claridge's from Eisenhower's apartment because he couldn't find a taxi at that late hour in blackout London, almost getting lost in the process. He mentioned the fact to his wife, Bea, in a letter two days later: "There were no taxies [sic] so I walked and would have been walking yet had I not run into a policeman who, by scent apparently, took me [to Claridge's]."

Patton's humor was not improved two days later when the U.S. Navy was brought into discussions on Operation Torch. Captain Frank Thomas, representing the commander in chief of the Atlantic Fleet, Admiral Royal Ingersoll, had much to say about the difficulties of the attack, particularly on the western front. He claimed that to get the necessary forces to Morocco would require the greatest armada in history, a fleet of between two hundred and four hundred transports and two hundred accompanying warships. The resources of the navy were already stretched beyond thin by the needs of waging a war in the Pacific and opening supply lines in the North Atlantic to Great Britain. Now it would have to send an immense armada to North Africa, land troops on its shores, maintain another cross-Atlantic supply line, and provide protection for all of the forces coming and going from this theater. There were simply not enough transports, not enough landing craft, not enough warships on the ocean to provide for all of the needs of an invasion force.

Steam was pouring from Patton's ears by the time the captain had finished offering the navy's reservations about the plans. Whether the animosity he would exhibit for the next couple of months toward this branch of the service was born in this meeting hardly matters; Patton was a soldier who, once committed to an assignment, found ways of doing it, and he could not abide those who hemmed and hawed about the matter. He was getting ready to fight in North Africa come hell or high water, and it seemed to him that the navy "was certainly not on their toes." In the meeting Patton challenged some of Thomas's assertions, and voices were raised.

Eisenhower steered them all toward a bottom line when he reminded everyone present that Torch was an order from the president of the United States and, whether it was liked or not, would be carried out. And pointedly, Eisenhower told the assembled naval officers that whether or not there was a single warship to guard the invasion, he was going to be a part of it "if I have to go alone in a rowboat."

Aside from his pique at the navy, Patton left the gathering with a distinct sense that too deep a bow was being made to British sensibility and guidance. He noted in his diary that evening, "It is very noticeable that most of the American officers here are pro-British, even Ike. . . . I am not, repeat not, pro-British."

Perhaps to open Patton's mind to his host country's charms, Truscott arranged for a dinner at Claridge's to which Truscott invited the man whose work he'd been studying since arriving in England, Lord Mountbatten. Several other British officers were present, and Patton was indeed impressed with them, telling Truscott the next day that they were "damn fine fighting men." He even accepted an invitation from one of them to another dinner the next evening, at which he was guaranteed to meet a "typical member of the English aristocracy." Patton had expressed skepticism that such a cliché still existed in Britain.

Patton arrived at the appointed hour the next evening decked out in his finest, a pose that he could pull off like few others in the U.S. Army. "With gleaming boots and spurs, riding breeches, shining buttons, rows of ribbons on his well cut blouse," he was, in Truscott's estimation, "a magnificent figure of a soldier."

Soon he was met by his counterpart. "A dowager of sixty-five or thereabouts with several chins seeking rest upon a more than ample bosom." She entered the room with her hair stacked in a "towering coiffure [that] quivered with her every movement." She wore furs, trailing skirts, and "strings and strings of pearls," and her hands sparkled with rings. "A picture from a page in history," said Truscott.

Seated next to her at the table, Patton charmed the guests with tales of army life, including his escapades with Pershing in Mexico and the notches on his gun from his days chasing Pancho Villa and his minions. His hostess registered just the right degree of "horror, astonishment, and doubt" at Patton's stories, and Truscott felt the evening had been a genuine success. A colorful mixing of two disparate worlds.

Less successful for Patton were efforts to boost resources for his western assault. In fact, by the middle of August, U.S. Navy and British arguments in favor of an emphasis on the Mediterranean invasion had swayed planners to the extent that Patton's assault on the Moroccan coast had been canceled. The combined U.S. and British navies continued to claim that they didn't have the resources to invade in three separate forces (two in the Mediterranean and one in Morocco); besides, the Moroccan surf was too pounding, too unpredictable to plan for an amphibious assault; and finally, by focusing on two points in the Mediterranean rather than the northwest coast of Africa, the Allies would be that much closer to the Germans in Tunisia. Patton would now lead forces against the city of Oran in northwestern Algeria as part of the Mediterranean attack. His force's move into Morocco would come from the north rather than from the Atlantic in the west.

By this time, Patton was simply committed to whatever plan was decided upon. To Bea, he wrote of the changes, "I think this is fortunate for me, so far as a longer life goes, but it is bad for the country—very dangerous in fact. Ike is not as rugged mentally as I thought; he vacillates and is not a realist."

A grave sense of the risks and dangers of what the Allies were undertaking began to color sensibilities in both Washington and London. The fact that untried, untested, and barely trained U.S. Army forces would be thrust into the war on the beaches of North Africa was one thing; the fact that they were to be carried and escorted by inadequate naval forces after journeys of thousands of miles for those traveling from American shores and hundreds of miles for those brought by the Royal Navy from England was another. No one knew how French forces would react; no one knew if Hitler would induce Franco to send the Spanish army to Gibraltar or perhaps take it himself, cutting off Allied forces in the region. And finally, by agreement and order of FDR and Winston Churchill, along with the desperate wishes of Soviet Russia and the sentiments of the free world, all of this needed to be done in the fast-dwindling months of 1942.

To Eisenhower, the French response represented the key to success or failure. There were fourteen French divisions in North Africa. Five hundred French planes. If Vichy forces in North Africa were to offer united opposition to the invasion, Axis forces could have the time to rush reinforcements to the region before major coastal objectives were taken. They might also have time to force an assault on Gibraltar.

In a gathering of the principal American military leaders of the assault—Eisenhower, Clark, Doolittle, and Patton—on the eve of Patton's return to the United States, all but Patton agreed that the odds were against a successful invasion. Patton put them at fifty-two to forty-eight in favor. To his diary that night he wrote, "I feel that we should fight, but for success we must have luck. . . . We must do something now. I feel that I am the only true gambler in the whole outfit."

Patton left for the States on August 19 to begin the process of organizing his invasion force. Truscott remained behind in England as Patton's surrogate in the ongoing planning for Torch. Before he left, "Georgie" paid one final visit to Eisenhower. While there, he pulled from his pocket a document that he'd drafted that morning. It turned out to be a proposed demand of the French for the surrender of Casablanca, intended for that day when he arrived in the city. As much as it hurt him for two former Allies to be engaged in such fighting, the note read in part, unless Casablanca surrendered within the next ten minutes, Patton would order the navy to shoot the hell out of the city.

"No wonder Ike's so pleased to have him," Butcher noted in his diary.

CHAPTER 5

Halifax to Belfast

The Standard Fruit Company helped to popularize Caribbean cruise vacations in the 1920s and '30s. Well-heeled passengers sailing from New York and New Orleans often made their first visits to Havana, Kingston, Veracruz, and Tampico, as well as Haiti, Honduras, and Nicaragua, on banana boats.

From time to time ships' captains like William John had an opportunity to rub elbows with the famous and near-famous on these cruises. Standard Fruit Company newsletters show photos of John greeting a Chicago opera star on board the *Contessa*, a pair of Hollywood producers, and the year's Miss New Orleans. Actor William Bendix, who would soon play famed New York Yankee Babe Ruth in *The Babe Ruth Story* and star as Chester Riley in television's *The Life of Riley*, met and became a close friend of Captain John on the *Contessa*. So, too, did the British actor Leo G. Carroll, who appeared in a whole slew of movies, among them *North by Northwest*, *The Desert Fox*, and *Strangers on a Train*. Like Bendix, he starred in his own 1950s television series, *Topper*.

Along with a touch of glamour, Standard Fruit liked to promote the possibility of using its steamers for honeymoon cruises and was happy to publicize the fact that Captain John's own daughter, Peggy, the LSU belle, and her new husband, Louis Koerner, enjoyed the comforts of the *Contessa* immediately after their May 1940 marriage. An article in the *New Orleans Times-Picayune* tells of their twelve-day voyage to Havana, Cristobal, Puerto Cabezas, and La Ceiba. According to the story, "surprise shore parties arranged by Captain John" awaited the couple at each stop, and for the bride "the whole idea was perfect. She could think of no better way to start a happy marriage than under a tropical moon with her father steering the course." The groom was said to be happy with the circumstances too (in fact, John's grandson, Louis Koerner, was probably conceived on the cruise).

The *Contessa* had a sister ship in the Standard Fruit fleet, the *Cefalu,* which John had captained in 1931 during the Nicaraguan crisis. It was about the same size, was christened the same year (1930), and cost the same amount: $999,250. They became the pride of the Standard Fleet when they arrived in New Orleans that year and were nicknamed the "Million Dollar Twins" in company promotional materials. Each had two decks above, two decks below, and three storage decks for carrying bananas.

On the *Contessa*, there were ten staterooms on the promenade deck, along with a lounge on the foredeck and a smoking room and bar to the aft. The saloon deck, directly beneath, held an additional twenty cabins, along with the dining room. Passenger fares in the early thirties ranged from a minimum of $190 for a nine-day cruise to $580 for the two largest staterooms on the promenade.

Two masts, front and rear, rose from the deck, along with a forty-one-foot-long forecastle, 135-foot-long bridge decks, and thirty-six-foot-long poop decks. Bananas were loaded by the stem into four refrigerated holds. Upwards of fifty thousand stems could be contained in these insulated areas, refrigerated to forty-eight to fifty-two degrees by a carbon dioxide gas system, with blowers working constantly to circulate the air. The holds were partitioned by portable walls that allowed the bananas to be loaded and hung.

The smell of fruit would waft up to passengers lounging in mahogany furniture on a highly polished wooden deck made of fir or splashing in the swimming pool, which, truth be told, was only about the size of a modern-day hotel whirlpool—about twelve by twelve and filled with seawater rather than fresh. But still very popular with vacationers. The *Contessa* usually carried a trio or quartet of musicians as well.

Meals were prepared and served by the steward's department and could be elaborate affairs. The Sunday dinner after Captain John's daughter's wedding included hors d'oeuvres like pickled walnuts and crabmeat cocktails, turtle soup, fillets of trout and sliced cucumber, sautéed kidney, chicken liver and shrimp à la Newburg, and, for entrees, stuffed Vermont turkey and prime rib. These were followed by salad, cheeses, fruits, nuts, raisins, and a plum pudding in brandy sauce.

All of this was history by the time the *Contessa* sailed from Brooklyn's Bush Terminal a little more than a month after its arrival. Stripped of its swimming pool and its mahogany; the rattan furniture and built-in berths gone; the cabins partitioned into jam-packed sleeping quarters with pipe-framed beds for the troops crammed aboard; and the gleaming white paint and the distinctive "V" on its smokestack, the banana boat was now just another gray military ship hauling troops overseas. The *Contessa* had been turned from a pleasant cruise ship into a functional military transport.

She sailed singly from pier 1 to Halifax, Nova Scotia, to join convoy HX 201. From Halifax she would sail in this, her first convoy, across the Atlantic to Belfast, where she would deposit her load of troops. Then it was on to Swansea in Wales, not far from Captain William John's hometown, Cardiff, where the remainder of her cargo would be unloaded.

There was a one-day stop in Boston for a convoy conference en route to Halifax, where orders were given by the commodore on how the voyage would proceed, including orders detailing signal instructions, setting a convoy speed, and creating an order and stations for the ships. HX 201 was composed of thirty-three vessels, primarily of American and British registry but with a handful of Dutch and Norwegian ships in the mix. The *Contessa* was the only ship of Honduran registry. The convoy sailed in a rectangular pattern, four ships north to south and nine ships east to west. Four destroyers were to escort the convoy at all times during the crossing. They cruised, roughly speaking, on the four corners of the ships' formation.

On August 2, the commodore's vessel, the *Manchester Port*, left the Halifax harbor and was followed in a succession spaced a few minutes apart by each ship in the convoy. The *Contessa* was the eighth vessel out and, as the convoy formed, took her place in the third column (north to south) and second row of ships. She was distinguished in the group by the "V" on her stack and a horizontal awning visible behind the stack. To her port side was a British ship, the *Torr Head*. Off her stern was the *Holyhead,* also out of Great Britain. Off her bow was an American ship, the *Santa Isabel,* which flew a flag with the letter "B," signaling that she was carrying explosives.

The American experience with the convoy system was new in August, but the learning curve would be quickly climbed in those last months of 1942. One of the earliest realizations was that not only did individual ships not want to be carrying ammunition; they didn't want to be in the vicinity of ships loaded with explosives. The SS *Mary Luckenbach,* a cargo ship sailing just a month later than the *Contessa* in a convoy on its way to Murmansk (what would become the most dreaded merchant sea route in the war) and carrying a load of TNT, virtually vaporized when she was hit by a torpedo in the North Sea. Not only was she gone in an instant, but reports detailed damage to eleven ships around her caused by the explosion.

There were other, more immediate, hazards for the ships in the convoy to consider, beyond being blown to smithereens. Perhaps chief among these was collision with the other ships in the convoy. The likelihood of such a crash was enhanced considerably when ships were sailing at night or were ordered to zigzag, change course, or maneuver to avoid torpedoes. For seamen accustomed to plying the oceans on their own, being thrust into packs of dozens of ships could make for adventurous sailing, especially when they were asked to maneuver like a squad of Zor Shriners. Collisions would turn out to be one of the leading causes of damage to and sinking of merchant ships during the war.

Straggling was also hazardous. Living up to their wolf-pack nickname, German U-boats would mimic the behavior of their lupine models and linger at the heels of convoys, waiting for weak members of the herd to fall behind, unable to keep up with their fellows, at which time the subs would attack, and pity the merchant crew that was left lagging.

U-boat strategies changed as the American convoy system developed, and the numbers of German submarines deployed to North Atlantic and Atlantic Seaboard routes by Admiral Doenitz increased through 1942. The Germans used spies and intercepted radio messages to suss out ship movements. Then the U-boats would form a line, spaced at approximately fifteen-mile intervals, perpendicular to suspected convoy routes. The first to spot a group of Allied ships would let them pass and fall in behind, signaling the location to its compatriots. The pack would form and trail, waiting for limping prey to fall behind. Another means of attack was to stage simultaneous assaults on a convoy from multiple directions. There was also a sharklike approach in which a U-boat would stay submerged as a convoy's escorts sailed by, only to rise to periscope depth right in the middle of the clustered ships behind, ready to fire its deadly torpedoes.

To the *Contessa* and many of the American ships of HX 201, all of this convoy/U-boat lore was new and being collected as they left the Halifax harbor and assembled out in the ocean. There was a light fog off the coast of Nova Scotia, and the commodore, a British vice admiral with the singular name Wion de Malpas Egerton, ordered that the ships in the group trail railroad ties on cables behind them, in order to better hold position within the group. These ties sent up a phosphorescent spray of water as they skimmed over the ocean, which helped illuminate the path of the leading ship even in fog and nighttime travel.

As Admiral King well knew, convoys sailed at the pace of their slowest vessel, which in the case of HX 201 meant a rate of just under nine knots on the first day. For the *Contessa*, which steamed at sixteen knots full speed, this was achingly slow, and like others in the group, she had to be aware of her station to avoid crowding the stern of the *Santa*

Isabel ahead. Even at this pace, however, one of the convoy members was unable to maintain speed and had to head back to Halifax unescorted.

The third day out, one of the escort destroyers, a British ship, spent a morning dropping depth charges, which rocked and alarmed convoy vessels in her vicinity, including the *Contessa*. The destroyer also blasted "Hail Britannia" through her loudspeakers at the end of the exercise, prompting some in the group to assume that she'd sunk a U-boat with the charges. Instead, she was just churning waves.

The morning of August 5 broke in a thick fog that would last all day. To compound difficulties for ships trying to maintain their stations, the commodore received an order to divert the convoy route at noon. Adding tension to the maneuvers was the fact that explosions were heard at 1250 and again at 1400 hours. By the time the exercise was over, the explosions had stopped, and the fog had cleared at 1700, the commodore's log noted the absence of five ships from the convoy, including the *Contessa*.

A straggler now in the vast Atlantic with German U-boats out there somewhere, trying to hunt them down, Captain William John and the 260 men on board, including the crew, the armed guard, and the 190 troops on their way to Ireland, were probably of various opinions about their status. For John and many in the crew, there was no doubt some relief that the close quarters and constricting pace of the convoy were temporarily relieved. As night passed, however, and the morning came with yet another fog and still no sight of the convoy, the green troops on board—mostly newly enlisted men, some in, some barely out of their teens—must have felt very lonely traveling without the strains of "Hail Britannia" being piped from a crackling loudspeaker system nearby.

As experienced and independent as the *Contessa* crew was, they, too, would have felt jangled nerves as the day progressed and the vessel continued to travel singly across the ocean. It would have been natural for William John to think of Doenitz and company, lurking in the waters before them. It would have been easy to think, too, of the *Amapala*, which he'd captained in the mid-1930s and which now lay at the bottom of the Gulf of Mexico.

Her April sinking had occurred just outside the mouth of the Mississippi River, soon after her captain, Master Harold Christiansen, had spotted a submarine after entering the gulf. The *Amapala* had begun zigzagging at full speed but couldn't shake the sub. Christiansen radioed an SOS to the U.S. Coast Guard and waited for the U-boat to close. The German ship stayed on the surface and started blasting the fruit boat with its two deck cannons and a machine gun. For twenty minutes the defenseless *Amapala* was lambasted. A fireman, José Rodriguez, was wounded, along with a radio operator named Ira Rubin. Christiansen had to finally order the Standard Fruit vessel abandoned. When its four lifeboats were lowered, however, the Germans continued to fire, sinking one of the safety vessels. Thankfully, all hands were picked up by the remaining boats.

Two hours after the SOS, a U.S. plane emerged out of the sky and scared the Germans off. Still, there were no ships to gather the crew of the *Amapala,* and the men had to spend a night in the lifeboats before a coast guard vessel came to save them. Poor Rodriquez died of his wounds and was buried at sea. The *Amapala* was still floating, but a wreck, after the action. The Coast Guard wound up sinking her where she'd been attacked.

Within the Standard Fruit Company, the fate of the *Amapala* was linked to an incident that had happened when John had been captain of the ship six years earlier. At that time, the vessel was sixty miles from New Orleans, carrying a couple dozen passengers, who were celebrating the ship's last night at sea. A pair of honeymooners at the party won a black umbrella as a door prize, and the bride committed a cardinal sin of sea travel: she opened the umbrella in the dining room. The steward quickly insisted that she shut it, but superstition held that the ship would sink by dawn.

In fact, that night the *Amapala* was rammed by a tanker on its way from New Orleans to New Jersey. The lifeboats were lowered and a gaping hole was made in her bow, but the *Amapala* stayed afloat. No passengers were injured and, as it turned out, the lifeboats were hauled back aboard unused. The ship wound up beached, however, and there were some at Standard Fruit who linked her ultimate fate, the sinking at the hands of the U-boat, to what had happened that night in the dining room.

Captain John was respectful of sea lore but not the sort of man to be cowed by its superstitions. Forty-nine years old as the *Contessa* sailed to Ireland, and with a career at sea that stretched back to his boyhood in Wales, he'd already experienced enough of a sailor's life to be able to sort out its real dangers from those that were engendered by active imaginations.

At 9:00 p.m. on the night of August 6—about the same time that George Patton and the Stratoliner were touching down in London—the *Contessa* spotted the rest of convoy HX 201 and rejoined the group to continue the voyage to Belfast and beyond.

The remainder of her maiden convoy trip would be made without incident. She found her way to Northern Ireland within the safe confines of HX 201, deposited her troops at the army camp in Bangor, the port just outside Belfast, and proceeded on to Swansea, Wales, where she disposed of an unspecified cargo that she'd hauled from Brooklyn in her holds.

Great Britain had the unmistakable appearance of a war zone. The docks at Swansea were thick with barrage balloons and antiaircraft guns. These had apparently impeded the Luftwaffe from pounding the harbor, but, as if to make up for this omission, German planes had pulverized the city of Swansea and its surrounding communities instead. Block after block of urban landscape was cratered by bombardment.

Captain John had grown up in a seafaring family from the small harbor town of Pembroke, Wales, the birthplace of Henry VII (at the village's major landmark, Pembroke Castle). It was not far from Swansea. It was said of John's father's side of the family that "all the men and women knew how to handle a boat." And the John family claimed one ancestor who sailed with distinction in the Royal Navy during the Napoleonic

Wars and another who sailed on tea runs in a China clipper to Asia. Captain John had a couple of Ming vases in his home in New Orleans as proof of these expeditions, and at least one other descendant in Wales had a home decorated with a large Japanese cabinet from another of these voyages.

John was raised in a large family with three brothers and sisters, but all the siblings had left Pembroke by the time of his arrival in August 1942. Just who Captain John might or might not have visited upon his return to Wales, or what he thought of the destruction he saw in his native land, is unrecorded.

He didn't have long to stay and contemplate the calamities of the war; he was still in it: on the twenty-fourth the *Contessa* sailed singly and without incident on its homebound voyage to New York.

CHAPTER 6

Walking the Tightrope

It was not easy for Malevergne to find his way home to Morocco. No one in the Vichy administration, it seemed, was in a rush to let him return, and, once again, his profession made him stand out to the authorities. The head of the French navy in Morocco, Admiral d'Harcourt, perhaps not surprisingly, didn't want the river pilot at Port Lyautey back once again in Africa to be tempted to aid the escape plans of all those who, like the Belgian pilots, might wish to find their way back into the war via Portugal or England.

So despite his acquittal, Malevergne could not get the visa that would allow him back to his home, back to Germaine and the children and his cottage in Mehdia. The months passed through summer and into fall.

Meanwhile, Malevergne suffered through a bout with malaria contracted in prison and could not afford quinine. In fact, without a job and stuck in France, he could not afford much of anything. His clothes were threadbare and he had no money to buy new ones. Malevergne was also unable to send anything to help his family in Mehdia, who he knew were suffering as well.

In September, his luck turned slightly. He was able to find office work in Clermont-Ferrand and heard good news from Gannat about Brunin and Paolantonacci, who had finally faced trial: Pao had been acquitted, and Brunin had been sentenced to the time he'd already served in prison. Unfortunately, the Belgian pilots had been given two to eight years of hard labor.

In late November the impasse with his visa was at last resolved. Admiral d'Harcourt agreed to allow Malevergne to reenter Morocco, but with one major stipulation: he could not stay in the Port Lyautey region, including his home in Mehdia.

He received his passport on December 3 and began saying his

good-byes—to Brunin, to Pao, to the people he had worked with over the past couple of months. Malevergne took the train to Marseilles on the tenth, noting the overcrowded train, the lack of heat, and a glacial wind whipping down the valley of the Rhône River.

He shipped from Marseilles to Oran on December 14, 1941, and had to spend a night in that city, during which he witnessed a galling display of Vichy patriotism—a two-hour parade of the province's Legionnaires.

Finally he was aboard the train for Casablanca, December 16—a year to the day since his arrest. Back in Morocco, nearing Port Lyautey, he felt an uneasy mix of great excitement, dread, and caution, knowing that he was about to see his family again but remembering that he would only have a few moments there and that many difficulties of money and continued separation awaited him.

Germaine and the boys were on the quay as the train approached, and they all rushed together and met in a deep embrace. Little Claude, who had been feverish the morning his father had been taken from their home in Mehdia, was now walking and able to call him "Papa." He seemed a little uncertain about his father; Malevergne thought it might be the military coat he was wearing. They sat together on a bench, stymied by their circumstances. So much to say; no time to say it. The reunion passed in whispers and tears. Ten minutes was an instant. Malevergne was soon back on the train to Casablanca and an uncertain future, while Germaine and the boys stayed standing at the station, their waves and faces fading backward from his window.

The country had changed in his absence. It had grown more "German," in Malevergne's estimation. An organization had been created called the Service d'Ordre Légionnaire, a sort of French version of the SS designed to infiltrate and coerce the machinery of its own government. According to Malevergne, "the Legion seems to have adopted the German coarseness, passing alongside us without ever seeing us."

Also grown in counterpoint to the Fascist elements was the organization that he had helped form a year earlier, now commonly referred to as the Resistance. "Born of the idea," Malevergne wrote in a triumphal moment, "that we were not a race of beaten dogs, but patriots and past masters of the art of walking the tight rope until victory. For one who fell, ten would be added."

Malevergne took a room at a hotel not far from the German Armistice Commission on the Boulevard de la Gare and reported, as requested, to the office of d'Harcourt, who did not deign to receive Malevergne yet allowed all the appropriate bureaucratic papers to be issued to him.

Malevergne soon discovered that he was being followed by police, at least during his first days back in Morocco. This did not stop him from becoming reacquainted with old friends and fellow travelers over dinner at the Brasserie des Arcades. The officers following him took seats in another room in the same restaurant. "There was nothing for them to do except to take a table, too," Malevergne commented. So the two groups dined agreeably in their separate stations, ignoring each other to the best of their abilities.

Thankfully, Malevergne was able to get a pass to visit Germaine and the boys for Christmas Eve and for a few days after the holiday. The simple joys of being once again with his family made him think of others not so fortunate, left behind in Clermont-Ferrand, including Brunin. But he couldn't dwell in melancholy. There was work to be done.

Soon after the New Year, Malevergne was back in Casablanca, where he was able to find a job with an old friend, Charles Chenay, who owned a fish cannery in the city and was sympathetic to the role that Malevergne was about to chart for himself. Because it was winter, there was not much to do at the factory, except to educate himself on the canning business. Malevergne was given a salary of 1,500 francs a month and told by Chenay to "arrange your time as you like. I know you well enough to know that you will not abuse this privilege."

Chenay spoke this caution with a knowing smile.

★   ★   ★

Home again in Morocco, René Malevergne settled into something of a routine. He leased a room with a nosy but kindhearted landlady named Mina; took his meals at the Bouef à la Mode on the Boulevard de la Gare, near his home and just down the street from the German Armistice Commission; and began acquainting himself with some local "patriots," including Lucien Garbieze, the director of a small manufacturing enterprise that made vegetable fiber from palmetto leaves.

Garbieze knew far more about Malevergne than Malevergne knew about Garbieze, and soon he would ask to meet with the river pilot at Malevergne's new office at the cannery. There Garbieze confided to Malevergne that "he had followed my odyssey closely" and that, knowing how Malevergne had "suffered in the flesh and spirit from the Nazi invasion," he would love to "count me among his friends." Malevergne understood the underlying meaning of this language and knew that by agreeing to be Garbieze's friend, he was committing to the Resistance. Nonetheless, agree he did.

Malevergne's new job with Chenay required him to periodically check on the arrivals of fishing boats at local ports so he could purchase sardines for the fish cannery. Because of this, he was granted an ongoing pass to a number of Moroccan communities, excepting Mehdia and Port Lyautey. Soon he began reporting on what he saw there to Garbieze and the Resistance.

Every evening between six and eight, Malevergne would go to the Regent Hotel in Casablanca for drinks and gossip. Garbieze kept a secret radio from which he could get news of the outside world, primarily from the BBC. He came to these gatherings and shared in whispers. The radio also offered a different perspective on circumstances in Morocco. The group learned, for instance, that the principal reason for a nationwide shortage of fuel was that the German Armistice Commission was appropriating its use for the homeland.

As the weeks and months passed, Malevergne was informed that his knowledge of the coasts of northern Morocco was of particular interest to his new friends. He soon found out, through his old compatriot

Paolantonacci, with whom he'd been reunited, that the intelligence he was passing along was winding up in the offices of an American in the city, a Colonel Dave King. He also learned that he'd been given a code name by the Americans—"the Shark"—and that vague plans were in the works for a possible invasion of Morocco.

Malevergne began to assist the Americans in smuggling arms and communications equipment. He and others also started to collect and pass along information on the depths of ports, locations of sandbars, landing sites, and Vichy defenses. They noted the characteristics and cargoes of ships leaving the harbor in Casablanca. They picked up port gossip coming from the crews of Axis-controlled ships, checking for the routes they planned on taking to escape Allied surveillance.

Through the spring and summer of 1942, the pace of activity of the underground picked up considerably. Malevergne's work pass continued to allow him access to a number of ports, and he was even able to sneak off to Mehdia for an evening with his family in the cottage by the River Sebou. He was also asked to hide at least one refugee in the process of escaping Casablanca in his room, away from Mina, the nosy landlady.

Then, toward the end of summer, he was introduced to a man from the Resistance named Colonel Lelong, who was intensely interested in what Malevergne knew about ports and landing areas, particularly in northern Morocco. *Is there anyone who knows more than I about the area around Port Lyautey?* thought Malevergne. Something was going to happen soon, he realized, and he would most certainly be a part of it.

Several days later, the sounds of the French battleship *Jean Bart*, stationed in Casablanca harbor, unlimbering her guns, resounded in the morning air, waking the city and continuing through the day. The warship was simply testing its weaponry, but everyone knew it was doing so with the prospect of action to come. Anticipation and anxiety ran through the city like a sizzling current. The confidence of the Resistance grew with the sense that something was in the works and that it would happen soon.

CHAPTER 7

D.C.

The plans for Torch had changed before George Patton put a boot down again in Washington. Upon hearing of the outline for an attack focused solely within the Mediterranean, George Marshall and the U.S. Joint Chiefs of Staff became almost instantly jittery about the possibility of Spain or Germany closing the Strait of Gibraltar and trapping Allied forces within. A port on the Atlantic side of North Africa offered an immediate link to the continent. A line of communication from Casablanca on the Atlantic to Oran on the Mediterranean, despite the distance between the cities, was preferable to no Atlantic base at all. And though Eisenhower had come to side with the British, now arguing that striking with the American force so far to the west in Africa would slow the army's ability to take Tunisia before the Germans, he and they were overridden. At least for the time being. Back on the table again for Patton were plans to lead the Western Task Force, whose central goal would be the taking of Casablanca, rather than leading his task force into Oran on the Mediterranean.

For the next two weeks, the U.S. and British chiefs of staff, as well as FDR and Winston Churchill, engaged in what Eisenhower's aide, Captain Harry Butcher, called "the transatlantic essay contest," trying to decide, once and for all, how exactly to invade North Africa. As the back-and-forth continued in London and Washington, Eisenhower sent a note to Patton saying, "I feel like the lady in the circus that has to ride three horses with no very good idea of exactly where any one of the three is going."

★　★　★

If London appeared half dead to George Patton, Washington was like Grand Central Station in a constant state of rush hour. Uniformed men and women swarmed through the city. When you could find a cab, it usually overflowed with ride-share companions. The War Department had just announced the hiring of three hundred thousand women to civilian positions that ranged from tens of thousands of clerical jobs to driving trucks and riveting airplane wings in factories all over the country. It seemed like half of the new employees had arrived in D.C. over the weekend. There were lines to buy newspapers, lines to get a shave, lines to get breakfast in the morning, lines to get shoes shined.

Parts of the gigantic new pentagonal Department of War building, being constructed between Arlington National Cemetery and Memorial Bridge, were already occupied by some War Department staff, but several months of furious work needed to be done to complete it.

Patton steered clear of both the new construction and offices near his troops' point of departure in Hampton Roads, Virginia. Upon returning from London, he and his staff reoccupied a third-floor loft in the War Department's Main Navy and Munitions Buildings—sixteen identical rectangular buildings that stretched like two octaves of piano keys down the Capitol Mall on the site of what is now the Vietnam War Memorial. They were divided by military branch, with the army occupying the Munitions buildings, and the Navy, the remaining structures.

His naval counterpart, Rear Admiral Kent Hewitt, commander of the Western Naval Task Force, which was to transport Patton and his army to Africa, occupied rooms in the Nansemond Hotel in Norfolk, next door to Hampton Roads in Virginia. The two met for the first time in Washington on August 24, a few days after Patton's return from England. Unfortunately, their immediate feelings toward each other were a far cry from mutual admiration. Patton was brusque and unsympathetic toward the navy's troubles and, as usual, was loud and profane in expressing his opinion. He complained, as he had in London, about the negativity and the pessimism of the navy officers.

A gentlemanly man of fifty-five with prominent ears, hair going quickly from gray to white, and a slight wattle beneath his chin, Hewitt had served in the navy for almost forty years in a career that stretched

back to the days of Teddy Roosevelt's Great White Fleet. He'd won a
Navy Cross for heroism while serving as captain of a destroyer during
World War I and spent much of the time between the wars as head of the
Department of Mathematics at the Naval Academy. He had, according
to accounts, a low-key manner that was like a placid lake to Patton's
pounding surf. Hewitt was not, however, a man to be bowled over by
bluster and rage. Though he stifled his own anger at Patton's peremp-
tory behavior, it was there in spades and, by the end of the meeting, deep
enough to send Hewitt directly to his superior, Admiral King, to say that
it was his opinion that unless Patton were removed from command of
the Western Task Force, the navy should bow out of the operation. King
went immediately to George Marshall to tell him of the contretemps and
to back in his own man in the interservice squabble. While Marshall was
able to cool matters between Patton and the navy sufficiently for them
to carry on their missions without dismissing either Patton or Hewitt, it
was not an auspicious way to begin planning for a monumental invasion.

Meanwhile, in London, the back-and-forth on Torch continued in the
wake of the disastrous Dieppe raid of August 19. Planned and executed
by British forces under Lucian Truscott's mentor, Lord Mountbatten,
Dieppe was designed as a test amphibious assault against German forces
on the coast of France to see how the Luftwaffe and German army would
respond to attack. Unfortunately, Operation Jubilee, as it was called, was
quickly and brutally repulsed. More than half the six thousand troops
sent ashore, most of whom were Canadian, wound up killed, captured,
or wounded. The raid served no greater military purpose than to prove
to all those who might still have doubts that the Wehrmacht was indeed
deeply rooted in French soil and that extricating it would take far more
mules and chains than had been dispatched to Dieppe.

As the American army's newly christened chief expert on amphibious assault, Truscott accompanied the raid as an observer on board a
British destroyer called the *Fernie*. He would later write that "I am not

among those who consider the Dieppe Raid a failure," but he saw and felt the evidence of its bloodiness and destruction. The *Fernie* took hits from shore batteries and brought aboard so many injured soldiers that the wardroom was "carpeted with the wounded." Still, Truscott felt that "German defenses in the West were given something to consider." And the raid "raised questions about just where the next Allied assault would come." The Allies also learned valuable lessons about how to conduct large-scale amphibious attacks, an education that was bound to be helpful in the coming attack against North Africa. Truscott wrote that "it was an essential though costly lesson in modern warfare."

Back in London just the day after the raid, he resumed the role that had been assigned him before Patton's return to Washington. Truscott was to be the Western Task Force's eyes and ears on the continuing command discussions about Torch, which were once again topsy-turvy.

Winston Churchill had just returned from a meeting with Stalin in Moscow and called Eisenhower and Mark Clark to have dinner with him at Chequers to discuss the operation. It was Churchill's strongly held opinion that it was a waste of time and resources to attack Casablanca, leaving Patton's army on the western edge of North Africa hundreds of miles from Rommel. Churchill wasn't worried at all about Spain or Germany attacking Gibraltar and thought that the French in North Africa would mount little or no defense. Churchill felt that the essence of Torch ought to be an attempt to secure Tunisia, between Algeria and Rommel's forces in Libya, before Germany could send forces to the area and establish a beachhead.

Eisenhower tended to agree with Churchill, but another powerful opinion suddenly injected itself into the essay contest at the end of August. From Washington, FDR put forward a plan that would remove British land forces entirely from Torch operations. American troops would land in Oran and Casablanca, transported primarily by the U.S. Navy with some assistance from the British fleet.

FDR's thinking was colored by an American sense that the British presence in the invasion would serve as a provocation to the French and might prompt a resistance that might otherwise not be there. This notion stemmed from the fact that soon after the French surrender to Nazi Germany in June 1940 and the subsequent creation of the Vichy regime, the British had attacked the French fleet in North Africa, sinking or badly damaging five French warships and killing more than a thousand sailors. The bad taste and hard feelings left by this lambasting remained, particularly in the French navy, and Roosevelt assumed that the French in Africa would be more likely to offer stiff resistance if the campaign against France were jointly waged by American and British forces, rather than by Americans alone. Reports coming from a recently installed American intelligence agency in North Africa, the Office of Strategic Services (OSS), tended to reinforce these opinions.

According to Harry Butcher, Eisenhower felt that the "quite desperate nature" of the operation was beginning to sink in. To his mind, the psychological component of the action—trying to guess what the French would do—detracted from areas of expertise he knew and was comfortable dealing with, namely professional preparation and military decision making. If the Allies guessed right, "we may gain a tremendous advantage in this war; if the guess is wrong, it will be almost certain that we will gain nothing and lose a lot. The unfavorable potentialities are vast, including not only the chance of a bloody repulse, but of inciting into the ranks of our active enemies both France and Spain," Butcher wrote. There remained possibilities, of course: "If we can take into North Africa such a strong land, sea, and air force that resistance rapidly can be crushed, TORCH unquestionably would be a good operation." But Eisenhower's general feelings toward the plans were not cheery.

Marshall, too, had begun to worry deeply about the perilous nature of the American invasion. Gone was all sense that the Allies were ready for a direct, cross-channel attack against Germany in 1942. An inexperienced and untested army making an unprecedented amphibious attack on North African beaches would be trouble enough if France staunchly defended her protectorates within the Mediterranean. And defeat in this first American engagement of the war in Europe would be disastrous in profound ways to the nation's spirit and will to fight. Still, it was far better to engage the French in Morocco in this first test, went Marshall's thinking, than to raise the possibility of tangling with the Wehrmacht in Tunisia or possibly even Spain.

Out of these disparate ideas came a compromise put forward by Marshall and the U.S. Joint Chiefs of Staff. On September 2, they proposed a plan that called for simultaneous landings of Allied forces in Casablanca, Oran, and Algiers. Eisenhower named Major General Mark Clark deputy commander in chief of the North African theater with overall command of Operation Torch. Major General Lloyd Fredendall was named commander of the Oran assault, and British Lieutenant General Kenneth Anderson was tapped to lead the invasion of Algiers.

For the Western Task Force under Patton's command and aimed at Casablanca, 34,000 U.S. troops would be deployed for assault, with an additional 24,000 to follow once French Morocco was taken. Oran would see 25,000 American troops landed by naval assault transport, with 20,000 to follow in port. A mix of British and U.S. forces (about 10,000 Americans and the same number of British soldiers) were assigned to the landings in Algiers.

The Western Task Force would sail from U.S. ports aboard U.S. Navy vessels, as originally planned. The Mediterranean forces would sail from Great Britain in a combined British and American convoy. The invasion would take place a month later than had been scheduled, early in November, rather than October, with the departure date of the Western Task Force estimated to be in the third or fourth week of October.

The details of the invasion remained mountainous, but its essence had finally been agreed to and would proceed. Despite the difficulties that lay ahead, it felt good for Patton and his staff to be focused on creating a certain plan for the invasion of Morocco. They could concentrate on the enormous task of putting together an invasion force of some 35,000, expected to be ready to sail across three thousand miles of ocean to attack North Africa in less than two months' time.

Now the planned invasion entered a new phase. Already in Washington and Virginia, Patton and his staff, along with the U.S. Navy, Army Supply Services, and the Army Transportation Corps, had begun the process of assembling the supplies, the troops, and the ships necessary to sail in late October to make an amphibious assault on Morocco in early November.

But what they needed at the moment was more intelligence. What would await them in Morocco? What would it take to land all those troops on that Atlantic shore? What hazards would they find on the beaches in Casablanca, Fedala, Safi, and Port Lyautey? What were surf conditions like? What fortifications awaited them? How many French troops were stationed at the various locales? Where were their reinforcements stationed, and how quickly would they be able to arrive after the invasion? Would the French fight at all?

There were Americans, Brits, and Frenchmen already in Morocco collecting answers to these questions and more. In fact, they'd been at the task for months. Now was the time to put their work to good use.

CHAPTER 8

The Apostles

In early 1941, the U.S. State Department signed an economic pact with General Maxime Weygand, the military commander of Vichy forces in North Africa. The accord, negotiated by the chief American consul in North Africa, Robert Murphy, unfroze French assets in the United States and allowed the French government to buy cotton, sugar, tea, petroleum, and other essentials in the States and ship them home to North Africans. While the agreement drew criticism from American allies, it helped the Roosevelt administration maintain a continued connection with the French government in North Africa. Those ties, went the thinking of FDR and Robert Murphy, might someday serve as a means to avoid conflict between the two nations in the inevitable battle between the Axis and the United States; or to even help convince Pétain and Weygand to join forces with the Allies against Germany.

There was an ulterior motive in the agreement for the United States. French officials agreed to allow twelve American vice-consuls into the port cities in North Africa where these goods were to be unloaded. The expressed purpose of these postings was to observe the shipments and their distribution and to make sure these same goods weren't being subsequently shipped out again to Axis powers. In fact, the twelve vice-consuls were recruited and selected by American intelligence organizations and, with the knowledge and blessing of the president himself, sent to North Africa to spy. While their cover assignments were with the Department of State, in fact they were the first wave of a group of agents who would eventually work within the newly founded OSS, whose boss was Colonel William Donovan, based in Washington. While in North Africa, they did their State Department assignments under the supervision of Murphy; the military work, which would soon be the major portion of their duties, was overseen by Colonel William Eddy, Donovan's man in Tangier.

Franklin Roosevelt had asked Donovan, a World War I Medal of Honor winner, to form an agency that would essentially spy in foreign lands on behalf of the executive branch. Initially called the Coordinator of Information (COI), the OSS was created to gather intelligence and help coordinate the chaotic systems of spying that existed within the federal government leading into the war. At the time, each of the service branches, along with the FBI and the State Department, had its own intelligence division, and there was little cooperation or shared knowledge passed among them.

Donovan, a lawyer who'd worked as a U.S. attorney in New York and for the Justice Department in Washington, had traveled widely in Europe between the wars, meeting with a number of heads of state, including Adolf Hitler. Nicknamed "Wild Bill" from his football-playing days at Columbia University, Donovan quickly began recruiting officers to his agency, and one of his earliest choices was Eddy, another highly decorated World War I veteran, who was also a scholar and academic.

Eddy was the son of Presbyterian missionary parents. He was born in Syria and grew up speaking Arabic and English. He returned to the United States for his college education and was at Princeton when World War I began. Eddy enlisted and served in a Marine Corps intelligence unit, where he won a Navy Cross, two Silver Stars, and a Distinguished Service Cross for action at Belleau Wood and elsewhere. He was also wounded in the leg and suffered a subsequent infection to his hip that caused him to walk with a severe limp for the rest of his life.

Between the wars, Eddy took his PhD from Princeton and then returned to the Middle East as head of the English department at the American University in Cairo. In the late 1920s he took a job teaching English at Dartmouth College before assuming the post of president of Hobart College, which is where he was in December 1940 when he volunteered to return to the Marine Corps.

Despite the scholarly turn that his career had taken, Eddy maintained an affinity for the Corps and service. When he rejoined the Marines, he was posted first to Cairo to serve as the naval attaché to the U.S.

delegation there; but he was soon recruited by Donovan, who sent him to Tangier, where he assumed supervision of the twelve consuls—nicknamed the "Twelve Apostles"—who had arrived in North Africa earlier in 1941 and were already working in Oran, Casablanca, Algiers, and Tunis.

The consuls were a highly educated group, many from the privileged class, most with cosmopolitan backgrounds and a facility for foreign languages. Ridgway Knight was a Harvard Business School grad who spoke fluent French and a smattering of Italian and German. He'd run Pierre Cartier's jewelry business on Fifth Avenue after college and was expected—by Cartier himself—to wed Cartier's only daughter. Instead, Knight married someone else, bought ten thousand cases of Château Mouton Rothschild champagne (1929) and entered the wine business with a friend. He had his pilot's license and tried initially to enlist in the Army Air Force but, due to poor eyesight, wound up at a naval recruitment office. There his résumé caught the attention of someone in intelligence, and soon enough he was flying off to Lisbon, then Tangier, and then a posting in Algiers.

John Crawford Knox, a graduate of Groton, Harvard, Oxford, and the French military academy at Saint-Cyr, had joined the French Foreign Legion in the 1920s and served with it during the Rif wars in Morocco. He, too, was posted to Algiers.

Carleton Coon and Gordon Browne, who both worked under Eddy in Tangier, had explored Morocco in 1939 as field scientists for Harvard University. Coon was a noted anthropologist; Browne, an archaeologist. Both spoke French and Arabic and were well versed in the history, geography, and culture of the various regions of Morocco.

Sent to Casablanca initially were a handful of spies, including W. Stafford Reid, a 1915 graduate of Yale and veteran infantryman of World War I; Kenneth Pendar, a former antiques dealer, who was soon sent on to Marrakech with Franklin Canfield; and the head of the Casablanca office, David Wooster King, a native of Connecticut who, like John Crawford Knox, was a former member of the French Foreign Legion.

King enlisted in the legion early in World War I, before the United States entered the conflict. He had left Harvard and signed on to the fighting as an infantryman in 1914 and was twice wounded fighting with the French. King suffered a serious eye injury and was almost buried alive in a trench. He wound up the war serving as a lieutenant in the U.S. Army but wrote an account of his experiences in the legion in the 1920s called *L.M. 4086* (the designation of his unit).

King was almost fifty years old when he arrived in Casablanca in 1941, but his feelings toward Germany continued to be governed by his experiences in World War I. Like the Free French, he referred to Germans with the pejorative term "les Boches." He and Reid took up residence in a beautiful villa outside the city in the Casablanca suburb of Anfa and began their double duties as consuls checking on the shipments allowed by the Weygand-Murphy accord and spying on the Vichy forces and Axis influence and presence in the city.

Casablanca was a kind of model city of French colonialism in 1941. Designed and constructed by the first French governor of Morocco, Marshal Hubert Lyautey, the port of Casablanca had helped grow a small native community into the largest economic center in northwest Africa in less than thirty years. The new city that had sprung up on the shores of the ocean was modern and well planned, with European architecture and an efficient infrastructure. According to Kenneth Pendar, "The city was neat, white and shiny under the hot blue African sky." It reminded him of a seaside resort community in Florida. The American consulate looked like "a Federal building in Miami."

Tidy and white though the city may have been, the war brought to Casablanca a sense of anxiety, apprehension, and outright fear that added some cloudiness to that African sky. Its proximity to Europe—less than two hundred miles from the Strait of Gibraltar—linked it so closely to the Continent that it became an entrepôt for European refugees. French, Belgian, Dutch, and Polish émigrés flooded the city, looking for avenues of escape and raising tensions all around. The sense that conflict would come to Morocco had been in the air for months, but just what form it would take was an open question. An Allied attack on Vichy North Africa was always a possibility, but so was a German takeover of the region. The trust between Nazi Germany and Vichy France was hardly deep. And there was already a Nazi presence in the city: something called the German Armistice Commission, whose agents essentially spied on everyone from their would-be allies, the Vichyites, to the Arab and Berber natives of Morocco to the newly arrived "vice-consuls" at the American consulate.

King and Reid quickly landed their first French agent, who delivered information about the port and its naval guards. In fact, there turned out to be no shortage of refugees and *colons* willing to volunteer their services with good and bad information.

They also began the process of striking out into the city and around its harbor to observe and collect information on their own. Pedaling around the area on bicycles during the midday lunch break, they made acquaintances with French dock workers and began mapping the geography of the port and its defenses. They also kept a close eye on the activities of the French dreadnought *Jean Bart,* a 35,000-ton battleship that was the pride of the French navy and the principal defender of the Casablanca harbor.

Late in the year, Colonel Eddy arrived in Tangier and began to oversee their work. Eddy passed along an order from Donovan that King, Reid, and the rest of the Apostles create a clandestine string of radio stations through North Africa in order that American intelligence could continue to disseminate information throughout the region in case of a diplomatic break with Vichy or the advent of a military action. By March 1942, King and Reid had theirs up and running in Casablanca.

The vice-consuls also solidified their informant chains. They were able to find two agents who supplied them with decoded copies of German Armistice Commission and Spanish consulate cables; an agent working at the Casablanca airport gave them information on the arrivals and departures of Axis officials; another gave them airplane counts and maps; while other agents tracked the movements of ships and cargo in a number of North African ports.

Contacts were also made with tribal leaders in the Rif Mountains and Muslim leaders in the Arab centers of Fez, Meknes, and Marrakech. Weapons were promised to these groups in the event of an Allied invasion. In turn, the Moroccans were asked to organize revolts if and when the fighting came.

In addition, resistance and sabotage plans were mapped out with would-be squads of French Resistance fighters, with goals of blowing up bridges, cutting power lines, and even kidnapping the members of the German Armistice Commission in Casablanca on the day of the invasion.

The OSS agents were not without their detractors. As newcomers to Africa and the world of espionage, Eddy, King, and the rest of the Apostles were often viewed as rank amateurs, particularly by their Continental counterparts. The British felt that these Americans were bumbling their way through systems and connections that had been established and nurtured through years of hard work by their own intelligence forces. Prior-existing U.S. intelligence agencies, most particularly the army's G-2 unit, questioned the need for an organization like the OSS. The European command, meanwhile, was at times befuddled by an excess of information from an excess of intelligence sources.

Last, the Gestapo, experienced and brutal players at the game of espionage, had a particularly contemptuous view of the newcomers. The American agents at the consulate "represent a perfect picture of the mixture of race and characteristics in that wild conglomeration called the United States of America," wrote a Gestapo member in Casablanca to offices in Berlin. "We can only congratulate ourselves on the selection of this group who will give us no trouble. In view of the fact that they are totally lacking in method, organization and discipline, the danger presented by their arrival in North Africa may be considered nil. It would be merely a waste of paper to describe their personal idiosyncrasies and characteristics."

Regardless of the assessment of OSS members' capabilities by their European and American counterparts, both the War Department in Washington and Allied headquarters in London turned out to be intensely interested in their activities and their reports on the activities of the French in the late summer of 1942. As Operation Torch was being agreed to by the Joint Allied Command in July, Bill Eddy was in high demand. He flew to Washington in late July and back to Tangier; to London at the very end of the month and then again back to Tangier; finally to London twice more in the month of August.

In Washington, Eddy was invited to a dinner party with General George Strong, the head of army intelligence, General Doolittle, and General George Patton just prior to Patton and Doolittle's trip to London. Eddy was there to present a report on the situation in North Africa, and to some extent it was a tough audience. He was given a warning by Strong—no friend of the OSS—to offer straight talk with no unwarranted assessments of capabilities. "Stretching of the facts might lead later on to huge loss of American lives," Strong told him. For the party, Eddy donned his full dress Marine Corps blues, including his chestful of medals. His arrival in the beribboned uniform, in conjunction with the pronounced limp, prompted Patton to say in an aside, "The sonofabitch has been shot at enough, hasn't he?"

For all the pressures, Eddy gave an impressive performance, describing the French Resistance in terms of numbers, organization, leadership, and capability during the coming invasion. Eddy's report was so thorough and detailed that it prompted all of his subsequent travels in August. By the time of his last visit to England in the planning stage of Operation Torch in early September, he was being asked for his opinions on such delicate matters as the presence of British troops in the invasion and the supreme question: what would the French military do when the Allies struck?

Eddy advised that British forces be included in the campaign only for the purpose of fighting Germans and Italians and that the French know that they were there "only in transit" to Tripoli and Sicily. "The essential point is the assurance to the French that there will be no occupation and annexation of French territory by the British." Of the French military response, he wrote: "We can count on the submission or active support of the French Army as we must also count upon the determined resistance of the French Navy and of the aircraft under the Navy's control."

To help counter this "determined resistance," Eddy volunteered his agents in Morocco to perform some of the sabotage that they'd already been planning in Casablanca and elsewhere. This included those plots to destroy bridges and power stations, as well as plans to eliminate the German Armistice Commission through assassination.

He also recommended that a Frenchman, who for months had been helping in the Tangier office, be summoned to London to offer assistance in planning the invasion of Casablanca. Carl Clopet had for years worked as a salvage tug operator in Casablanca. He was a hydrographer who, according to Eddy, "knows every rock and buoy and wreck, as well as being an expert on the very treacherous swell which is perhaps the chief hazard for any landing party."

Clopet would soon be off to London. Nor would he be the last expert on a Moroccan port suggested by Eddy to the Joint Command. It turned out that Dave King in Casablanca had recently recruited another Frenchman for the OSS. His code name was "the Shark," and, like Clopet, René Malevergne knew every rock, buoy, and wreck at the entrance to another port in Morocco, at the River Sebou. Depending on where the final plans for invasion might lead Allied forces, "the Shark" could be an invaluable aid to the cause.

CHAPTER 9

The Hazards of Port Lyautey

For General Lucian Truscott, it felt like high time to get back to the States. His assignment was rapidly shifting from planning to operation, yet here he was, still stuck in England, mapping out the invasion as the clock continued its inexorable countdown to the action itself. He was now definitely to have the command of the northernmost of three amphibious assaults on the Moroccan shore, but his troops would be sailing from the United States. Not only had he not even laid eyes on the soldiers he would be commanding, but they hadn't yet been decided upon. He didn't even know what troops he would be leading. This was no small thing for a man whose reputation had been built on his ability to train soldiers.

And there were still huge problems to deal with in the overall amphibious planning for the Western Task Force. At the Allied headquarters, Truscott gathered together a group of American and British officers to tackle those issues and send along recommendations to Patton in Washington. Along with Truscott, the group including two U.S. Army majors, Pierpont Morgan Hamilton and Theodore Conway, and three British members of the team drawn from Mountbatten's staff: Major Robert Henriques, Lieutenant-Commander R. de ("Dick") Costabadie, and Wing Commander John Homer.

One of the thornier issues of amphibious assault on Morocco was quickly elucidated by the members of the group from Lord Mountbatten's team. In November in North Africa, practicable landing conditions for an amphibious strike within the Mediterranean could be counted on four days out of five. On the Atlantic side, however, the odds were exactly reversed: out of five typical days in November on the Moroccan shore, only one offered decent weather for landing an amphibious army. Not only was the pounding surf on the northwest corner of Africa an impediment, but suitable beaches and ports were scarce. A largely man-made harbor at Casablanca was the best landing site in the area, but the French navy anchored there made a direct assault on the city a hazardous operation at best.

A few widely scattered ports north and south of Casablanca presented possibilities for attack. These included Fedala, a few miles north of Casablanca; Safi, about 130 miles to the south; Port Lyautey, which lay a dozen miles up the River Sebou, 80 miles north of Casablanca; and Rabat, which lay about halfway between Port Lyautey and Casablanca.

Patton's initial plan, put together in Washington, called for the Western Task Force to be divided into three forces. The largest, a division-sized expedition headed by Patton himself, would point toward Fedala, the center point of the three-pronged attack, with the assault and taking of Casablanca as its main objective. A second group, the one designated for Truscott, would land at Rabat with two battalion combat teams and one armored battalion. The smallest of the three groups would land at Safi to the south and include one combat battalion team and one armored battalion, whose tanks were to provide support for the taking of Casablanca.

This plan went to the Supreme Allied Command in London with a copy to Truscott for comment and consideration in the first week of September. To Truscott's mind, the attack on Rabat was a mistake. Intelligence had informed him that its port was in disrepair from lack of use—sandbars had built up around it. It was also the residence of the sultan of Morocco, the spiritual and political leader of the nation's native population. An attack against Rabat might be seen as an assault on the Muslims of Morocco and impair efforts at quickly winning over the country as a whole.

Truscott and the others in his group felt that invading Port Lyautey, to the north of Rabat, offered both strategic and tactical advantages. Not only would an assault away from the home of the sultan offer fewer political complications, but the airport in Lyautey was the newest and best in the region, built with the only concrete runways in northwest Africa.

From the outset, the army's Twelfth Air Force, along with Patton, Eisenhower, and most of the Allied command, believed that the quick capture of a northwest African airfield was of crucial importance to Operation Torch. With an airport in hand, the army could catapult single-engine, P-40 fighters from carriers attached to the convoy in order to neutralize the French air force and aid in Patton's assault on Casablanca. Port Lyautey's was a quality airfield just two hundred miles from Gibraltar. If it were quickly captured, the U.S. Army Air Force (USAAF) and the Royal Air Force (RAF) could also fly bombers in from England. Gibraltar would be more secure; the path into and out of the Mediterranean would be safer.

It was this argument that held sway. The plan for attacking Rabat was scrapped and a sub–task force named Goalpost, a reference to Truscott and Patton's polo-playing interest, was established with a primary focus of taking the airport at Port Lyautey as quickly as possible after D-day. Truscott would lead this wing of the assault.

Despite the work of the operatives in Morocco, intelligence remained a problem in both London and the United States. Useful photographs for the invasion were so rare that the American public was actually asked to provide general vacation snapshots and film footage from foreign travels in the hopes that images of North African locales would turn up and help to fill gaps in the general understanding of the area. In fact, the principal reason Truscott and his contingent, itching to get to Washington to prepare for the invasion with their troops, were kept in London was that they were waiting for photographs of the Atlantic Coast to come from British reconnaissance planes. British intelligence was, however, in Truscott's words, "extremely reluctant to undertake new photographic missions for fear of disclosing our intentions to the enemy."

Regardless of what those photos might tell, it was almost dead certain that the basic objectives of Goalpost would remain constant. The first of these "was to capture and supply one or two air fields whence our aircraft (which are to be flown into Gibraltar as soon as the situation permits) can support our forces in the south [i.e., Patton's force] who will be operating against Casablanca." The aim of the northernmost portion of the three-pronged attack on Morocco, wrote Truscott, "should be to have one air field available for use by our aircraft not later than nightfall on D-day."

The first combat mission of Truscott's infantry (whoever they were) was to "capture, hold, and supply" the airfield at Port Lyautey "for the use of aircraft, to be flown in from Gibraltar." The second goal of the mission was to capture and hold Port Lyautey itself.

The success of the operation as a whole depended upon the neutralization of French aircraft. Getting American planes into the skies as soon as possible would not only deter the French from entering the fray but would aid Patton's assault on Casablanca. Furthermore, if Gibraltar were subject to heavy Axis air attack in response to the North African invasion, it would be vital to have African air bases for its defense and as an outlet for aircraft stationed there already.

There were obstacles to both the taking and the supplying of the Port Lyautey airstrips, to be sure. Intelligence had described the field as lying within an inverted loop of the River Sebou on well-protected terrain. There was high ground to the south in the form of a ridge that ran parallel to the seacoast. A marsh marked the airfield's western edge, and a second ridge lay to the northeast of the Lyautey field. The width of the series of runways was about five thousand yards.

A lagoon, about three and a half miles long and a mile south of the river, ran parallel to the coast toward Rabat. It was fringed by steep cliffs that fell down to the beach into soft white sand. Steep sand dunes and shale slopes marked the north entrance to the river, along the ocean, and they stretched within the interior to about three quarters of a mile. Farther inland, to the north, there was more high ground with rough grasses but a commanding view of the southern bank of the river, suggesting that a landing to the north of the river could provide a quick means of assault on airfield defenses.

The most formidable barrier to supplying the airport was the course and shallowness of the river. A sandbar at the mouth of the Sebou had a depth of seventeen and a half feet at high-water peaks and a mean depth of just thirteen feet at low tide. Bringing cargo up the river for the field would require shallow draft shipping and would have to be done within the blessing of a high tide. The river itself was said to have a depth of only seventeen feet. In addition, the French had recently constructed a chain boom across the Sebou that would have to be cut in order for traffic to flow by.

All this was to say nothing of the problem, already pointed out by members of Mountbatten's staff, of the hazardous and pounding conditions of the Moroccan surf at that time of year. In the back of everyone's minds was the report that the Atlantic offered just one in five days in November when its pounding assault on the northwest African shore calmed enough to make an amphibious landing feasible.

Nor was it to mention the press of time that everyone agreed was crucial for the success of the operation. The quicker Torch was completed, the better it was for the inexperienced American army. Any delay in taking Morocco would invite what Marshall, Eisenhower, and Patton feared most: an attack by Germany or Spain on Gibraltar, and through Gibraltar to North Africa. They wanted to take the airfield in a single day.

Because of the land and river obstacles to the airport and the speed at which it needed to be grabbed, initial discussions on taking the field centered on the possibilities of using parachute troops and sabotage as a means of quickly circumventing obstacles. Also put forward by Truscott himself was a novel idea: using commando forces on a ship that would steam up the Sebou River soon after the invasion force struck. A small unit of specially trained infantry would be delivered at the airfield by whatever vessel was chosen for the mission, there to strike quickly and efficiently at the French forces guarding the strips, á la raiding groups that Truscott had helped organize in England.

While this last idea seemed speculative in London, it would gain more currency in Washington as time passed and the countdown to invasion neared. It was, after all, the very sort of small, surprise attack that Truscott had been learning at the side of Mountbatten in London for months. Why not employ it here, in conjunction with the larger amphibious assault on Port Lyautey?

Of course, such an attack would rely heavily on the navy's ability to navigate the treacherous shoals at the entry to the Sebou River, to say nothing of the difficulties of sailing up the shallow river to its inland port. And it would have to be done in haste and presumably under the extremely dangerous conditions of amphibious assault. To mount a commando raid on the airfield under those circumstances would require someone deeply familiar with the passage.

But hadn't the OSS guy in Tangier, William Eddy, just informed the command that the river pilot at Port Lyautey was in league with the Allies? Wasn't he supposed to know every rock, buoy, and shoal on the River Sebou? Would it be possible to get him out of Morocco to London to help with the planning of the invasion?

CHAPTER 10

"I should like to embrace you"

The idea of extricating René Malevergne from Morocco to England had first been proposed by William Eddy to Torch commanders back in late August. Enough interest in the possibility was exhibited in Washington for Eddy to mention the operation to Dave King in Casablanca, probably via radio upon his return to Tangier.

Meanwhile, the plans for sub–task force Goalpost were being formulated and rushed to completion in London and Washington through the early weeks of September. Between Truscott's team and George Patton in the Munitions buildings in Washington, the idea of using a commando team against the airport grew sounder. The necessity of getting the help of the river pilot in the operation also ripened. But it appears that it was on King's and Eddy's own initiative that the plan moved forward.

The prompt came in mid-September, when Gordon Browne and Franklin Holcomb, a Marine Corps captain and assistant to Eddy in Tangier, arrived by chance in Casablanca. Holcomb had accompanied Browne on a trip to Fez, Taza, and Marrakech, where Browne had been taking photographs of the Taza corridor, a historically important pass that had presented an avenue over the Rif Mountains between east and northwest Africa. Holcomb held a diplomatic pass through his work at the American consulate in Tangier, which allowed him the freedom to drive between Spanish and French Morocco. When he and Browne turned up in Casablanca with a Chevy, an attached trailer, and a valid passport, it looked to King like an opportunity.

Ever since Eddy had alerted him to the possibility that Malevergne might be needed for the invasion, King had been contemplating how he might get the river pilot out of Morocco. By September the port of Casablanca had become impossible as a means of escape. The idea of transporting Malevergne in the Chevy with Browne and Holcomb as the purveyors of his escape seemed natural to King. He quickly wired Eddy to get permission for the action and soon had his response: go ahead, Eddy told him, but make sure Malevergne was placed in the baggage compartment. Sometime soon after, Dave King sent Lucien Garbieze to Malevergne's office at the fish cannery with a simple request: *The Colonel would like to see you, he said.*

That evening, another friend of the Free French, Monsieur Rey, picked up Malevergne at his hotel and drove to a little square not far away. They waited there briefly, smoking cigarettes as the evening sun drifted out over the ocean. An automobile with diplomatic plates from the U.S. consulate soon arrived, and Malevergne and Rey were whisked out of Casablanca to the south, in the direction of the suburb of Anfa. There they found themselves pulling into the driveway of an expansive villa. Moments later, the two were escorted to a nicely appointed waiting room, where they were joined by a man whose name Malevergne knew quite well by now: Colonel David King of the OSS.

King was a tall, lean man with a wiry frame and tense disposition that suggested to Malevergne that the American was somehow ill-suited for the sumptuous comforts of the villa. He was an outdoorsman, whose "face was weathered as if he had spent years exposed to the desert winds," Malevergne later told his diary. He also had a facial tic—that old war wound near his eye had obviously damaged nerve and muscle.

Sitting in the waiting room together, eyeing one another through the experiences of two wars, the aging patriots from far-flung corners of the globe must have wondered at the curious ways of a world that had brought them together to plot an escape from Morocco; but that's how things worked, and King was the sort of man who got quickly to the point: "We need you, Monsieur Malevergne," he told the Frenchman. "Have you decided to leave?"

"I ask only for that," Malevergne said. King told him that he would be contacted in the near future, and Malevergne told the American that he wanted to get the permission of Garbieze and his fellow resisters before he left; he had grown deeply loyal to them over the past few months.

King agreed but emphasized the critical nature of what was to come. "This is more important," he said bluntly.

The deal was sealed with a glass of whiskey. It was Malevergne's first in a very long time, and he savored it.

King himself drove the Frenchman back to town and dropped him and Rey off in a safe spot, not far from where the journey to the American villa had begun.

"Old friend, this time I think it is on," said Rey to Malevergne, as they watched King drive away.

There were things to do before he left. On Sunday, at the request of his old friend Paolantonacci, Malevergne traveled to the civil prison in Casablanca, where Pao's twenty-year-old daughter was detained. Her name was Anna, and she had been condemned to ten years of forced labor for her work with the underground. She seemed to Malevergne to be holding up well, though it might have been simply a brave face because she also told him that a brutish guard had been assaulting her.

"Count two months after my departure," he told her by way of encouragement. Meaning the invasion was coming. Help was on the way. "I don't think she gave my prophesy due credit," Malevergne subsequently told his diary.

The following week he visited Germaine and the boys in Mehdia. He warned his wife that he was going away, that this would be the last visit for quite some time; he took a little coffee, and then he left at three the next morning, with the children still sleeping. He refused to say good-bye to them—a little superstition that he felt would ensure that he would see them again.

As he cycled back through the forest toward Rabat and Casablanca, Malevergne heard horses and, for a moment, thought of fleeing. Then he reconsidered, climbed calmly off his scooter, and soon found himself facing four native Moroccan policemen. Trying to look convincingly lost, he asked in Arabic for directions to Sidi Taibi and thanked them profusely when they pointed out the route.

Back in Casablanca, he found out that the Resistance was not quite ready to let him go. He was sent on a final mission to a village northeast of Port Lyautey, which he duly visited by means of the train and his bicycle.

Chenay, his old friend and boss at the cannery, also had a job for him: he asked Malevergne to accompany a fishing boat to Agadir, to the south of Casablanca, which he did, returning to Casablanca by way of Marrakech.

All the while, he anxiously waited for word of his departure from the Americans.

Given the heartache he had felt upon saying good-bye to Germaine and the boys on his last visit to Mehdia, it felt a little wrong to go see them again, but he couldn't resist, and he made yet another trip home. Once again, Malevergne took his leave of the family as the children slept.

Finally, the moment came. He was wanted at the villa. Malevergne visited the office of Chenay. Of course, he couldn't tell him the truth. Malevergne said simply that he was tired of sardines. He was going to look for work elsewhere in Morocco.

Chenay gave him his final wages and thanked him for his work. Wished him well in his new pursuits. His secrets were safe. With his last check, he paid off Mina, the landlady, and bade her adieu. They had grown fond of each other over his eight months in the hotel. To her, he said he was off to Marrakech.

"It isn't your birthday today, is it Monsieur Malevergne?" she asked him.

An odd question. "No, why?" he responded.

"Because I should like to embrace you," she said.

They hugged. He took his suitcase and headed toward an uncertain future.

CHAPTER 11

Snatching the Shark

To Gordon Browne, the argument over whether to hide the Frenchman in the trailer or the trunk of the car was growing old fast. Here were the four of them—Browne, Dave King, Franklin Holcomb, and René Malevergne, the French river pilot who was the reason they were all gathered here—standing by the garage of King's lush villa on the outskirts of Casablanca, waiting to embark on a cross-country trip that would lead to Tangier if they were lucky, the Moroccan prison in Rabat if they weren't, and time was fast ticking away. They wanted to hit the border between French and Spanish Morocco just after sunset so as to obscure, as best they could, any search of the Chevy and its attached trailer; yet they couldn't decide whether or not the trailer was the equivalent of a car's trunk.

Holcomb, Browne's traveling companion, was young and accustomed to following orders to the letter. He was not simply a captain in the Marine Corps and assistant to Colonel Eddy, but also the son of the nation's top marine, Corps Commander Thomas Holcomb. Holcomb's contention was that because Eddy had ordered Malevergne to be placed in the "baggage compartment" of the Chevy, the trailer was off limits. The patently obvious fact that Malevergne, standing in their midst with a slightly baffled look on his face, was a bit too rotund to fit in the Chevy's trunk didn't seem to matter to the marine.

Dave King was plainly losing patience with this reasoning. As head of OSS operations in Morocco, it was he who had located Malevergne, he who had planned for and arranged this means of escape from Morocco for the Frenchman. A World War I hero whose combat experiences included being buried alive in a trench, King had a reputation for getting things done with alacrity. He made his argument through clenched teeth to Holcomb: *If a trailer is not a baggage compartment, then what is?*

Despite the fact that he was the junior officer here and out-experienced, Holcomb remained adamant. He'd already achieved something of a legendary status within the world of American espionage in North Africa for his hardheaded toughness. Soon after he had arrived in Tangier to assume his post as assistant to Eddy, a group of Italian thugs had accosted him in the street. In the ensuing brawl, Holcomb had "upheld the highest traditions of the Corps," according to one observer, meaning he roundly thumped his attackers. In those early days of the war, when any sort of incident that exhibited American pluck was worthy of attention, President Roosevelt himself got wind of the story and suggested that Holcomb be immediately promoted from lieutenant to captain.

Of course, the booya spirit required to pummel a fistful of Italian Fascists did not necessarily convert to diplomacy, which is why Gordon Browne chose this moment to enter the fray.

"How badly do they want this man?" he said, indicating Malevergne.

"Badly," said King.

"Then what's the argument?" Browne asked.

Quickly, they made a nest for Malevergne in the two-wheeled trailer attached to the Chevy. About the size of a chariot, it was hardly bigger than the trunk. And with two empty fifty-liter gas drums occupying the great majority of space in the trailer, it looked like it would take a pair of crowbars to squeeze "the Shark" inside; but somehow he managed to fit into a space between the cans of fuel. They'd laid a heavy Moroccan rug on the floor to give him a modicum of comfort. Browne, King, and Holcomb tossed a couple of gunnysacks over his body. Then they took a tarpaulin and covered the entire trailer, gas, and hidden Shark. It was nearly four o'clock in the afternoon when Browne and Holcomb headed out of the garage and into the city of Casablanca with a last reminder from King: *Make sure he gets some fresh air once in a while.* An asphyxiated river pilot would not do anyone much good.

*   *   *

While it was unlikely they would be stopped, the sight of two Americans in a Chevy hauling a trailer through the streets of Casablanca was still unusual enough to draw attention. Both Browne and Holcomb assumed casual poses in the front seat of the car—windows down, arms resting nonchalantly on the doors—as they navigated their way from the south side of the city to the north and out into the countryside. Malevergne, in the trailer—"this minuscule box" is how he remembered it—was crammed in with his knees up under his chin, fearful that if he moved even a little bit, he would knock against the trailer gate, send it flying open, and fall to the pavement.

Anfa, where King's villa was located, was built in the hills south of Casablanca. The city itself occupied a flat plain through which the trio traveled to reach the northern suburbs. French Morocco was about the size of California and populated by around eight million people, primarily Muslims of Berber descent. The road between Casablanca and Tangier ran near the coast and, until reaching the mountains in Spanish Morocco, was sixteen feet wide and laid with macadam—a fact that helped cushion Malevergne in the trailer and eased his worry about bouncing out.

He owed this relatively smooth travel at the start of the trip to the man who gave his name to the port of which Malevergne was the pilot. Marshal Hubert Lyautey had arrived in Morocco in 1907 to quell rioting that had broken out among the native populations. Moroccans had attacked a group of French laborers who were building a new railway through an ancient cemetery in Casablanca.

It was just one of a number of tensions and disputes that had been building between Moroccans and French colonists since the late nineteenth century, when the swapping and partitioning of African lands had begun among European nations. France, which had already assumed control of neighboring Algeria and Tunisia, cast its eye on Morocco in the northwest corner of the continent in the last quarter of the century.

Morocco maintained a shaky independence through the end of the century, loosely governed by its sultanate, which had been established in Fez way back in the seventeenth century. The Alaouite dynasty became even shakier in the early years of the twentieth century under the rule of Sultan Abdelhafid, whom native Moroccans considered little more than a pawn of French interests.

European horse-trading in North Africa grew intense during these years, primarily through the prodding of Germany, whose colonial aggression in the region prompted France, Great Britain, and Italy toward agreements that would solidify already established interests. Libya became a protectorate of Italy when the Italians agreed to let France dominate in Morocco. Similarly, France agreed to let Britain control Egypt in exchange for keeping hands off its interests in Tunisia, Algeria, and Morocco.

The French had already established and were developing a number of commercial ties in Morocco. Wool and tea were among the chief exports of the country. The process escalated in the wake of its agreements with the other European powers. As French entrepreneurs, workers, and colonialists began to descend upon the African nation, there were a number of clashes with local residents who felt, quite rightly, that their land was being usurped by Europeans.

The troubles that began in 1907 and prompted the appointment of Marshal Lyautey to the region turned out to be a giant step toward making the sultanate of Morocco an official protectorate of France. That happened in 1912, when the sultan had his arm twisted into signing a treaty with the French government in Fez. At the same time, France made an agreement with Spain, which allowed that country to maintain interests in a sliver of Morocco long controlled by the Spanish, just across the Strait of Gibraltar from Spain. Thus the sultanate was divided into two protectorates, French and Spanish Morocco, each of which would turn out to be more linked to its European protectorate than either was to the other. Tangier, located in Spanish Morocco, was left an open city.

Lyautey was named to the post of first resident general of French Morocco. He encouraged an influx of French and European citizenry to the nation, and they came in droves. The city of Casablanca, a modest port on the Atlantic ocean with a population just over ten thousand, ballooned by 1920 to a modern city of 110,000. Lyautey encouraged and supported civil talent. Education, health, and transportation systems in Morocco were built up or modernized and became widely admired. Aside from constructing the coastal highway system upon which the Americans and Malevergne were now traveling, Lyautey also built the artificial seaport (which would be named for him upon his death in the 1930s) on the River Sebou on the road to Tangier. He also oversaw the construction of the airfield adjacent to the seaport and had it paved so that it became the only concrete-based strip in North Africa.

The native population, however, was far from quiescent at these drastic changes. Tribes in the mountainous regions of north Morocco called the Rif had maintained some degree of autonomy throughout the colonization process. When Spain encroached on these territories in 1921, the Berber tribes in the region organized under the leadership of a Spanish-educated journalist named Abd el-Krim. In a stunning defeat for the European power, just three thousand native fighters routed an army seven times as large, killing eight thousand Spaniards and chasing the remaining thirteen thousand back to the safety of Spanish Morocco's coastal communities.

The southern portions of the Rif extended into French Morocco. The colonial powers there were made uneasy, to say the least, by the presence of a rebellious force just to the north and established a series of outposts along the southern edge of the Rif. These were periodically attacked and taken over by the forces of Abd el-Krim, which only added to French disquiet. By 1925 the French government, military, and colonial administration had had enough. Marshal Henri Philippe Pétain, the hero of World War I, was sent to Morocco with a large French army that, combined with the Spanish forces that joined it, created an army of 250,000. Soon they were in the field, chasing the Berbers of Abd el-Krim in a brutal ten-month campaign that included the use of mustard gas against the tribal

forces. In 1926 Abd el-Krim and his forces surrendered, effectively bringing an end to the war of the Rif.

Dissent among native populations did not die, but its form became
more political than militaristic in the years leading up to World War II.
A nationalist movement evolved, but its weapons were primarily edito-
rials, petitions, and other means of nonviolent suasion of French colonial authority. But French commercial, agricultural, and civil influence in
Morocco continued to grow as more and more *colons* arrived in North
Africa from France, looking for opportunity.

It's doubtful that any of this Moroccan history was on the minds of
Browne, Holcomb, or Malevergne as they cleared Casablanca and
headed north out of the city toward Rabat. For the men in the Chevy, the
principal concern was the health of their passenger in the trailer, specifically, the damage the carbon monoxide he was inhaling might be doing
to the Shark's brain. They stopped soon after they hit the open road
north of the city to check on him. "Tout va bien—pas trop de monoxide," Malevergne told them when asked how he was. As if to reward him
for the answer, Browne and Holcomb decided it would be safe to let the
Frenchman ride in the backseat of the Chevy, at least until they neared
the Spanish Moroccan border. With his head down and a couple of rugs
piled on top of him, René Malevergne assumed a more comfortable position in the car itself as they continued on their trek.

It was half past five when they went through Rabat. From beneath
his rugs, Malevergne could hear the noise of the city, could feel the starts
and stops and intensity of the traffic. There was little conversation between the travelers, but the Frenchman could tell they'd cleared the city
when the sounds of the road lessened. Now he was in his home territory,
the forests south of Mehdia, the route that he'd bicycled just a few days
earlier after visiting Germaine for a final time. He buried himself beneath
the rugs once more as the car neared Port Lyautey.

North of the River Sebou and Souk el Arba du Rharb, the three
men paused at a wide spot in the road and shared a tin of ham, bis-
cuits, and some fruit juice that King had supplied for the journey. They
were about twenty miles south of the border and decided to stop here to
let the setting sun catch up with their plans for arriving at the fron-
tier after dark. It was also a good time to review what lay ahead, since
Malevergne was headed back into the trailer, probably for the duration
of the trip.

To the pair of young Americans risking freedom to haul Malevergne
out of Morocco, he must have seemed a somewhat unimpressive prize for
the Allied cause. A short, middle-aged Frenchman with a ready smile and
amiable manner but little to recommend him in terms of appearance—
and what else had they to go on, given the language barrier?—as a crucial element to the war effort. Yet here they were, in the middle of hostile
Morocco, about to enter the most dangerous part of the journey to bring
this little guy to the powers that be. Oh, well. Have some more ham.

The word from King was that the French border-control officer was
one of his contacts and would be tipped off to help expedite their crossing. But the border had both French and Spanish officers, and there could
be no certainty of what might happen with the Spaniard. A little bit of
baksheesh might be helpful, but who knew?

Beyond the crossing, within Spanish Morocco, were five checkpoints
on the highway to Tangier. This was a rough and mountainous path,
and it would have been nice to be able to pull Malevergne from the
jouncing trailer every now and again along the road; but Browne and
Holcomb knew the specific locations of just four of the five stops. They
couldn't risk putting the Shark in the backseat if there was a possibility
they might bump unexpectedly into a team of Spanish *Regulares*—the
native Moroccans employed by the Spanish army—at that one unknown
checkpoint. So they prepared Malevergne as best they could for a trailer
trip all the way to Tangier.

While Holcomb held the diplomatic passport, which he'd been given
through his work in the attaché office, the Chevy belonged to Browne,

who was driving. It was a fairly well-known vehicle at stops on the road between Tangier and the various sites in the French Moroccan interior that Browne had been studying for several years. He was a Harvard-trained archaeologist who spoke Arabic and had studied the Moroccan interior for several years before the war with well-known anthropologist and fellow OSS agent Carleton Coon. Browne's studies were his cover. They'd allowed him and Holcomb the trip to Taza prior to landing in Casablanca. The trailer and gasoline drums were also familiar to the authorities. Traveling through the interior of Morocco was not like traveling Route 66. There weren't Sinclair stations every ten miles; it was necessary to haul your own gas. Unfortunately, as it turned out, Browne and Holcomb had exhausted the supply in the trailer and were near to exhausting the supply in the Chevy itself.

As he and Holcomb once again prepared Malevergne's nest in the trailer, covered the Shark with the gunnysacks, and tied the tarpaulin over all, Browne rehearsed in his mind how he would casually describe the work he'd been doing if he were asked. Just another exploration into Moroccan history.

It probably helped that, except for an athletic build through the chest and shoulders, Browne had the look of a scholar: wire-rimmed glasses, quizzical cast to his eyes, thinning hair slicked back on his head to reveal a broad forehead. He remembered how once he and Coon, his usual companion on these road trips, had been asked by Eddy to gather typical Moroccan stones found on the highway to bring back to Tangier. The idea was that some U.S. Army explosives expert would craft plaster of paris models of these rocks, pack them with powder and projectiles, and set them out as booby traps for Vichy or Nazi vehicles happening down the road. The only problem was that the stones on the French Moroccan roads were pretty easily avoided. It was Coon's idea to collect a far more prevalent road hazard: mule turds, which they subsequently gathered and placed in the very trailer now occupied by Monsieur Malevergne. They drove them back to Tangier on these same roads and past these same checkpoints. Oddly, no one inquired about their purpose.

*   *   *

The terrain near the border above Larache was more rock than dung, and Browne and Holcomb felt bad for the poor Frenchman being pounded in the trailer. Unfortunately, there was little they could do to help, except try to avoid the ruts in the road. That was easier said than done, now that darkness was descending over Morocco. They pulled to the side of the road one more time just to ask how he was doing, and once more Malevergne called out, "Tout va bien—pas trop de monoxide."

A moment later, the Chevy's headlights illuminated the border offices and the barricade separating the protectorates. Browne took a deep breath and let it out slowly, trying to calm a racing heart. He and Holcomb could see the guards rousing from a quiet early evening to see who was coming down the road. A dog started barking as the car approached, and Browne braked slowly, feeling the jolting push-push-push of the trailer on his own back as they came to a creaking halt.

Both Holcomb and Browne climbed out, stretched, and were greeted by the French officer and his dog. Holcomb already had their passports out and in hand as he climbed from the car, and together he and the Frenchman walked into the station. The Spanish guard stayed outside with Browne, walking around the car and trailer and asking what was beneath the tarpaulin. Browne rapped on the empty cans and gave him the usual answer: gasoline for their explorations into the Moroccan interior. He tried to maintain an air of nonchalance, stretching and bending like a man near the end of a long car journey, as the guard, followed by the old dog, a pointer with a whipping tail, made a circuit around the vehicle and its haul. Then, with an approving nod of his head, the Spaniard veered off toward the office to join the French officer and Holcomb.

Browne stayed with the car, bending his legs, stretching his back. Still the long-distance traveler unwinding at the end of a hard journey. He focused on the three men standing in the light of the office and lit a cigarette, watching them looking down at his and Holcomb's papers.

Full darkness had come to the scene. It was so quiet now that he could hear the dog's light footsteps on the hard-packed road. Maybe it was the fact that they stopped that made Browne turn his head toward the trailer, just to make sure the Frenchman remained safely hidden. What he saw there made him take a quick, frightened suck of air.

The old dog was poised in a perfect point aimed right at the curled body of René Malevergne beneath the tarp. Browne took an anxious glance at the office to see if anyone was spying the same thing he was. The heads of the three men inside continued to bow over the passports. Browne made a low, guttural sound, a kind of hissed "get" at the dog, but the pointer didn't move a muscle. He looked back again at the office and then squatted down, searching for a good, stinging pebble to chuck at the dog. He quickly found one at his feet and made a nice sidearm throw, as if he were skipping a rock on a placid lake. The gravel caught the dog squarely in the ribs. Unfortunately, the pointer was only temporarily distracted. The dog took a couple of quick prances and glanced briefly over at Browne, as if he were noticing him for the first time. Then back he went to his overriding duty: pointing out that something peculiar was tucked into this trailer.

Kicking the dog, giving it a shove down the road, would surely make the sort of yelping commotion that Browne didn't want, but he was sorely tempted to do just that. He stood up from his crouch and glanced once again into the station. They were still ignoring the vigilant mutt outside.

It was then that Browne remembered the ham inside the Chevy. A little scrap of meat, a little juice left over in the tin, might do the trick. He opened the back door of the car, eyeing the dog, still standing at attention. Browne quickly found what was left of their roadside meal and pulled it out, hoping the scent of good American tinned ham would be a treat the pointer couldn't resist. Slowly he waved the tin in the air in the direction of the dog, and slowly the pointer's nose and eyes rose toward him. Browne remained focused on the dog and his lure, resisting a temptation to look back at the guardhouse. A second later, the dog's jaw dropped and Browne saw his muscles relax. The pointer was his or, more precisely, the ham's. He set the tin down for the dog, who immediately left his post and headed over to more closely inspect the good smell. Soon his tongue was lapping at the four corners of the tin, slurping up whatever drop of juicy fat it could.

Not only was the Frenchman forgotten, but the guards themselves were appreciative of his generosity toward the old dog. They smiled and thanked him for treating their companion.

The pointer at the border turned out to be the most alarming moment on the way to Tangier. All five checkpoints in Spanish Morocco were gone through without incident. Back in the trailer Malevergne noted that Browne was driving with what seemed to be an achingly light foot on the gas going up and down the hills. It was only later that he learned that the Chevy was nearly out of gas and that, to preserve what was in the tank, the Americans were coasting down every mountain on the way to Tangier. Despite the pace and despite being knocked about in his nest, Malevergne maintained a sense of humor and spirit the whole way.

"We passed all the controls without undue difficulty," Browne would later write in his report of the trip for OSS offices in Washington, "including the sometimes tough one at the International River. I drove slowly over the bad spots, every jounce, and there were big ones, hurting me mentally as much as it did Malvern [sic] physically. We pulled up finally and arrived at Holcomb's house on the hill behind Tangier, opened up the trailer and helped Malvern out. We asked him how he liked his journey. He replied, 'It's all right for the "type sportif."' "

CHAPTER 12

Romping

Oblivious to her coming role in the great operations being hatched in London, Washington, and Morocco, still just a made-over banana boat from New Orleans drafted into service and doing her duty for the war, the *Contessa* was once again at sea, again heading for Bangor in Northern Ireland with a contingent of 190 troops, now in the company of convoy HX 208 out of New York, at the same time René Malevergne was making his way out of French Morocco.

She had landed back in Brooklyn in early September from her initial transport voyage and made a quick turnaround. Fifty-some ships sailed in this new convoy in eleven columns of five, stretched out to a distance of about six and a half miles. They steamed at an average of ten knots for the first two days, then dropped to a snail's pace of eight knots to accommodate the slowest ship in the convoy, which was soon ordered off to Halifax when she proved incapable of keeping up.

Commodore Lennon Goldsmith of the Royal Navy headed the group from the *Cairnvalona,* which, he was disgusted to report, was the only ship in the convoy to smoke badly, due to a "filthy load of coal obtained from a colliery that wasn't likely again to get the business of the Royal Navy anytime again soon."

Aside from an assortment of essentials for the population of Great Britain, ranging from steel to grain and molasses to timber, the convoy carried a number of supplies that would be used in the upcoming and still secret—to those who were carrying the goods—invasion of North Africa. A number of tankers carried various forms of fuel, ranging from paraffin to highly combustible airplane gasoline. As it traveled, the convoy was escorted by a rotating group of four destroyers, which relieved one another at three intervals through the course of the journey. Aside from the *Contessa,* only three other ships were transporting troops.

A week into the voyage, Goldsmith received an order to steer his convoy forty degrees to starboard. Unfortunately, the ships were in a thick fog and had to be guided by sound signals. "The result," Goldsmith reported, "would have been laughable if it had not been so painful." Perhaps not realizing there was at least one former officer of the Royal Navy in the contingent, Goldsmith illustrated something near contempt for the commercial captains in his group. As an explanation for the chaos that ensued from this attempt at redirecting the convoy, Goldsmith reported: "All Masters of merchant ships sleep soundly every day after their lunch. Any sudden awakening brings them on deck almost blind and completely sodden. One blunderer is apt to disorganize the convoy entirely."

Later in his report, Goldsmith confessed that trying to get so large a convoy to change course in the midst of thick fog presented a serious and vexing problem. While sound commands worked in theory—the signal was simply repeated from one ship to the next behind it, down a column of eleven vessels—in practice it was like playing the parlor game "Telephone." There was no certainty whatsoever that the ship at the tail end of a line stretched out for six and a half miles could repeat what had been said at the beginning. "I lost none of the Leaders of the Columns," Goldsmith reported, "but the repeating ships in no single case repeated the signals. The young mates on watch may not have heard—they may well have been far astern of station." By the time the fog lifted in the wake of the forty-degree maneuver, Goldsmith discovered that twenty ships in his convoy were no longer there.

Among these was the *Contessa.* In his report at the end of the voyage, the commander of the armed guard unit on board, Lieutenant William Cato, told briefly of losing the convoy. The only allusion Cato made to the difficulties described by Goldsmith was when, in that same report, he requested "at least two Signalmen when traveling," plus additional personnel for keeping good lookout when traveling singly.

★   ★   ★

The basic contingent aboard the *Contessa* was a group of longtime Standard Fruit Company sailors, primarily based out of New Orleans, who had sailed with her north to New York back in June and were now transporting their second load of troops across the Atlantic to service in Great Britain. Another group of seamen, mostly deckhands, had signed up through the maritime unions in New York for the individual voyages to England and back. In all, the crew numbered sixty-nine sailors, counting the captain.

The *Contessa*'s crew exemplified the global economy of the day. Eventually there would be Filipinos, Danes, Estonians, Spaniards, Portuguese, Mexicans, Peruvians, Belgians, Brazilians, Finns, an Australian, and, soon to come on board, a group of Arabs from the Gulf of Aden. In terms of age, sea experience, and international flavor, the merchant crew could hardly have been more different from the fourteen-member naval armed guard that was ostensibly protecting them within the convoy. These were young U.S. Navy recruits, most in their late teens and early twenties, many of whom had never been at sea.

Adding to the sense of disparity was a traditional discord that existed between the U.S. Navy and the merchant fleet. To put it bluntly, the U.S. Navy command lacked respect for its merchant marine counterparts. It's also fair to say that merchant seamen, a far more independent breed of sailor than was found in the U.S. Navy, tended to be "resentful of the gold braid," as naval historian of World War II Samuel Eliot Morison put it.

Morison, whose sympathies lay decidedly with the U.S. Navy, described the difficulties faced by the commander of armed guard units, usually an ensign or junior-grade lieutenant: "These lads had an unusually difficult task. They had to train the men to become a well-knit gun crew and maintain naval discipline in the unbuttoned atmosphere of a merchant ship, without any superior officer to support them or

C.P.O. to help them. They had to achieve a working relationship with the master and officers of the vessel, and at the same time prove a 'good guy' to the merchant seamen in order to obtain their assistance in passing ammunition, or as substitutes for bluejackets in case of casualty."

The navy was far from alone in its negative assessment of the merchant marine. The popular perception was that these crews were composed of outcasts and slackers, when they weren't fellow travelers and communists recruited from around the globe. Rather than adding color and an international flavor to the enterprise, the multinational cast of characters on a merchant ship simply represented the dregs of many societies, not just America. One only had to wander down to some dockside tavern in any harbor town from Norfolk to New Orleans to get a sense of the riffraff and rough customers. And the maturity of the group— what might seem like solid job experience and accrued wisdom to a merchant crew—was generally viewed as another example of commercial shipping's willingness to take all comers, including those far over the hill.

For their part, merchant seamen were generally happy to have some form of defense units on deck but could hardly feel a deep sense of camaraderie with the boys with the firearms. The merchant marines were wage earners whose past relationship (prior to the war, at any rate) with their ship, its owners, and the demands of their labor had been a different beast from the relationship of seaman to command that was found in the U.S. Navy.

Hard-won union fights through the 1930s had improved the lot of most merchant seamen by the time World War II began. Able seamen (ABs) were earning twice as much at the end of the decade as they'd earned at the start (up from about $32.50 per month to around $82 in base pay). But the relationship between ship owners and crew was always somewhat adversarial, which could make the chain of command in the merchant marine more complex than it was in the U.S. Navy.

On the sea, a good ship's master maintained discipline and controlled a vessel with the same mastery, whether in the navy or the merchant service. But like the ordinary seamen, he served the ship's owner, its cargo, and his own interests, not the interests of a nation. In other words, money mattered. Due to his lengthy experience, the quality of ship at his command, and his duties as an ambassador to Standard Fruit's paying steamer clients, Captain John was a well-paid ship's master. He earned in the neighborhood of $450 a month, while typical merchant masters earned a hundred dollars a month less.

As a licensed officer, John was represented by the Master, Mates, and Pilots Association (MMPA). There were also unions representing engineers, cooks and stewards, and radio operators. The two largest unions, representing both deck and engine departments, were the Sailors' Union of the Pacific (SUP), based on the West Coast, and the National Maritime Union (NMU), centered on the East Coast. All had emerged from the Depression and labor wars of the 1930s as well-run, well-advised organizations with their own newspapers and pamphlets produced by accomplished writers and with millions of dollars in the bank. They were also thought to be lairs of communists and sympathizers with the Soviet Union.

At the start of the war, and through the first few months of the "Second Happy Time" for German U-boats, there was a movement to have the U.S. Navy assume command of all merchant marines. Morison suggested that at the root of this movement was a lack of trust in the merchant seamen due to the basic economic, rather than patriotic, relationship that existed in the merchant service: "Any ship in which a bluejacket serves is his ship, his country's ship, to be defended with his life if need be. But to the union-indoctrinated merchant seamen the ship is the owner's ship, his class enemies' ship, to whom he owes nothing and from which he is morally entitled to squeeze all he can. The navy principle 'Don't Give Up the Ship' did not appeal to merchant seamen."

While Morison acknowledged that the NMU had done a far better job than the U.S. Navy in "abolishing the color line and encouraging Negroes in every way" (it was claimed that 20 percent of all merchant seamen were African American) and that it scrupulously policed against "performers"—the term given to drunks, brawlers, and other sorts of troublemakers aboard—and avoided strikes during the course of the war, he never fully bought into the idea that the merchant marine should be independent from the navy in times of war. He would write later that it was his "emphatic opinion that if and when another war occurs, the merchant marine should either be absorbed by the Navy or man an auxiliary service under military discipline, like the Naval Construction Battalions, the famous Seabees."

The idea of a takeover was bandied about by honchos in the U.S. Navy as early as February 1942 and reached the desk of the president that spring, but FDR never sanctioned it. Instead, the convoy system was instituted, along with the assignment of the naval armed guards to the ships of the merchant marine. Just how the guardsmen and the merchant seamen would blend together was a work in progress in the middle of September as the *Contessa* set off from New York Harbor on its second trip across the Atlantic.

The war and its massive shipping needs brought with them a demand for merchant seamen as well. Despite the dangers of U-boats lurking seemingly everywhere in the North Atlantic, union halls in port cities like New York were filled with men looking for berths. Skilled seamen, however, were at a premium.

A few years earlier, in 1938, the U.S. Coast Guard had instituted a school for merchant marine cadets at Kings Point on Long Island (two others would eventually be built at Pass Christian, Mississippi, and San Mateo, California), but its first graduates didn't emerge until 1942. It took four years to train qualified deck and engine officers. These two designations—deck and engine, along with steward—constituted the basic departments of the ship.

The officers in the deck department of the *Contessa* included chief, second, and third mates. The chief mate was second in command to John and was in charge of cargo operations and seeing to the safety and security of the ship. The second mate was the ship's principal navigation officer.

Unlike an army quartermaster, who is charged with distributing supplies and provisions, a merchant marine quartermaster usually steered the ship under the command of the watch officer on the bridge.

Serving beneath the officers in the deck department were a dozen ABs, who were unlicensed but able to communicate in navigational terms with officers and to serve as helmsmen and lookouts. The part of the crew most apt to be rotated in and out of particular voyages were the ordinary seamen, called "utility crew" on the *Contessa* lists.

The steward's department on the *Contessa* was overstaffed compared to a typical peacetime trip. On the September voyage, as on the previous journey to England in August, the ship held an extra 190 mouths to feed in the form of the troops being transported to the war effort. The *Contessa*'s dining and food-preparation facilities were busy and cramped operations centers. The *Contessa* carried three bakers, a butcher, six messmen, a pantry chief, and six stewards, along with the chief steward and his two assistant stewards. They did a seemingly perpetual ballet of food preparation and service for the length of the trips.

The engine department was charged with overseeing the maintenance and operation of the ship's engines. Aside from chief and second engineers, the *Contessa* had third and fourth engineers to oversee the constant attention necessary to maintain the ship's power. The *Contessa* carried four boilers pumping steam to four quadruple-expansion engines. These could produce 5,600 horsepower at her top speed of sixteen knots. Sailing at that rate for a full day, the *Contessa* swallowed almost three hundred barrels of oil.

The chief engineer was in overall charge of all engineered equipment on the vessel, including boilers, main engines, refrigeration systems, electrical systems, and secondary engine units like pumps and windlasses. The second engineer served a supervisory function, overseeing the donkeyman, the firemen, the wipers, and the oilers, who toiled over the machinery itself.

The engine department was without doubt the most technically sensitive operation on the ship. Hot, cramped, loud, and often dangerous, this area was the beating heart of the ship. Like that organ, it was located right in the solid trunk of the *Contessa*'s body. When working smoothly, the ship's engines thrummed in a familiar rhythm of pistons and cylinders, crankshafts and rods. While modern ships have a bank of computerized sensors to inform the crew of trouble in the engine department, those who worked around these gigantic machines—almost 150 tons apiece and as big as a pickup truck—used their eyes, ears, nose, and touch to determine if a problem had arisen or was in the making. Servicing the machinery was a full-time occupation for many hands. Oilers walked around in fifteen-minute rounds with a can of oil in their hands to make sure shafts and pistons were well lubricated; firemen made sure the pressure was up but not too high. And every few minutes someone had to stick his hand into a space between the top of the engine and a pounding piston attached to a huge rotating cylinder as it hit the bottom of its cycle. That hand had to get back out before the engine cycled the piston back up, or it was, simply put, a mass of flesh and crushed bones. It was the only means available to test the temperature of the space to make sure it wasn't overheating. "That wasn't no fun neither," was the understatement of a sailor assigned the task on a Liberty ship's reciprocating engine.

It was September 26 when Captain John's ship emerged from the soup to discover that she was once again on her own. But by now the *Contessa* was so near her destination in Northern Ireland that John ordered her to "romp," the terminology for continuing the voyage on her own. Traveling at an increased speed of fourteen knots, without the strictures of the convoy surrounding her, she was able to make her harbor and deposit her troops by September 28 with no untoward incidents.

That soon changed, however, after she set out for Avonmouth, just outside Bristol, her destination in England. While sailing across the Irish Sea, Cato ordered the gun crews on the *Contessa* to open fire on what turned out to be two British bombers, which appeared low on the horizon and flew within a thousand yards of the ship early on the twenty-ninth. The very next day, two more friendly bombers appeared around noon, coming from the north and again flying within a thousand yards. Once more, the nervous gun crews on the *Contessa* took potshots. Thankfully, in both instances, no hits were made on the targets.

On the thirtieth, the *Contessa* arrived at Avonmouth and dispensed with her cargo. Cato reported one more interesting bit of news regarding her stay in Bristol: "Attention is called to the show of hostility between the negro troops at Bristol, England and the Naval gun crews from ships in port there," he wrote later. "Several naval gunners have been severely injured." Cato offers no details of these "hostilities," nor does he mention whether any of the *Contessa*'s crew was involved.

Just eight days later, the *Contessa* was done with her business in Great Britain and once again at sea, sailing home for a much-needed and highly anticipated rest in New York. Counting up the trips she'd made early in the year in the Caribbean, plus the initial trip to pier 1 in Brooklyn and the back-and-forth journeys between New York and England, Captain John noted in his log that this was the ship's twelfth voyage of the year.

Her thirteenth would be the most memorable.

PART II

CHAPTER 13

Hollywood

*Casablanca, city of hope and despair located in French
Morocco in North Africa—the meeting place of adventurers,
fugitives, criminals, refugees lured into this dangerous oasis by
the hope of escape to the Americas . . .*

OPENING NARRATION OF THE TRAILER FOR THE
WARNER BROTHERS MOVIE CASABLANCA

In August 1942, Warner Brothers Studios in Hollywood was beginning the editing of and preparing the marketing campaign for a war movie that had finished shooting late in July. *Casablanca* had begun its life at Warner the previous December, when a play called *Everybody Comes to Rick's* crossed producer Hal Wallis's desk the day after Pearl Harbor. A melodrama involving an expatriate American who owns a café in Morocco, the story emanates from the sudden arrival at Rick's Café of a woman with whom owner Rick Blaine had an affair in Paris. The play interested Wallis because its themes revolved around the war in Europe and questions of what Americans should do and think about it. Blaine exemplified a certain kind of national attitude about the conflict. As it seemed more and more likely that the United States was going to be drawn into world war for the second time in the century, his cynicism about the ways and means of global politics fit neatly into the smaller universe of Casablanca—a city swarming with a host of spies and scoundrels, as well as European refugees desperate to escape the ever-expanding clutches of Nazi Germany.

It's only when his former lover from Paris, the beautiful Ilsa Lund, shows up at the café with her husband, a heroic Czech underground fighter, that we learn that Rick has a more human side. Or at least had one in the not-too-distant past when the two met and fell in love as the war approached France. The tensions between the lovers, the exotic setting in North Africa, and the moral and political dilemma placed in Rick's lap—will he or won't he give the couple two letters of transit that will allow Ilsa and her husband, Laszlo, to leave Casablanca, and will he or won't he choose sides in the coming war?—suggested to Wallis that there was a film in this play, and he quickly authorized Warner's story department to buy rights and assign scriptwriters to the work. Never mind that that key plot device, the letters of transit signed by Charles de Gaulle, were a remarkably fanciful means of escaping Morocco, and that, in fact, holding any papers signed by de Gaulle was more likely to get a person thrown in the Rabat prison with René Malevergne than grant him passage to Lisbon. That was an inconsequential matter to Wallis. He ordered the rights purchased and quickly renamed the project *Casablanca,* after a place few people in the United States could find on a map but that, Wallis thought, would suggest another recently made popular film called *Algiers,* starring Charles Boyer and Hedy Lamarr.

Wallis asked a pair of brothers, Julius and Philip Epstein, to do the script for the movie. They specialized in turning plays into films and had recently done so for Frank Capra's movie *Arsenic and Old Lace.* Capra had just been hired by the federal government to produce and direct a series of documentary films called *Why We Fight* and had asked the Epstein brothers to come to Washington to help him with their writing. All of which meant that though the Epsteins had agreed to write *Casablanca* for Wallis, they had to take a break in the middle of the job to head to Washington to work for a month with Capra. During that interim, Wallis hired another Warner writer, Howard Koch, to work on the *Casablanca* script.

After some fishing around for a director, Wallis settled on a Hungarian immigrant named Michael Curtiz, who had arrived in Hollywood from Austria, where he'd directed scores of films in the silent era. To the acting community in California, he was known as an autocrat, prone to treating his cast and crew like petulant children; but he'd had a number of successes in Hollywood (including a string of Errol Flynn features:

The Charge of the Light Brigade, The Sea Hawk, and *The Adventures of Robin Hood*). He had Wallis's respect and, perhaps more important, made movies that "were brought in on time, rarely went over budget, and almost always made money."

A veteran contract player at Warner, Humphrey Bogart, was signed to play Rick Blaine, the café owner. Bogart had twenty years of acting experience, eleven of those making movies in Hollywood; but he had only recently become a star at the studio, with the release of *The Maltese Falcon.* Casting him as Rick Blaine was one of the simplest aspects of Wallis's job. Bogart exuded the sort of electric combination of barely stifled passion and lip-curled cynicism that described Rick Blaine. Rumors that Ronald Reagan was considered for the part were just that. Wallis never seriously considered anyone but Bogart.

Ingrid Bergman, in contrast to her costar, was one of the freshest faces in Hollywood. Just twenty-six years old when she was hired to play Ilsa, Bergman had been signed to a contract by David Selznick, the producer of *Gone with the Wind,* after he saw her in the Swedish film *Intermezzo.* She was a "radiant" beauty, to use the word most frequently employed to describe her performances and presence. Bergman, however, was also more than a little uncertain about her role in *Casablanca,* both before and during filming. Wallis made inquiries of Selznick about hiring Bergman for the role of Ilsa in April (Wallis had to pay $25,000 to Selznick to "borrow" Bergman for his movie), but to the actress there seemed to be nothing terribly special about the script. It seemed like a standard sort of melodrama, and she desperately wanted to play the role of Maria in *For Whom the Bell Tolls,* which was soon to be cast. She didn't want to be occupied shooting a mediocre movie if it would mean losing her chance at being a part of the filming of the highly anticipated adaptation of the Hemingway novel.

The set of *Casablanca* actually shared the trait the Warner Brothers marketing department attributed to the city of Casablanca. It was, in fact, "a meeting place of . . . refugees." Ilsa's Czech husband was played by the Hungarian actor Paul Henreid. Peter Lorre was an Austrian born in Hungary. Claude Rains was the British actor who played Captain Renault. And Conrad Veidt, who played Major Strasser, the Gestapo agent shot at the Casablanca airport by Rick Blaine, had left Germany with his Jewish wife in 1933. Half a dozen other actors in the company with lesser roles had likewise fled German oppression in Europe.

Made with alacrity within the framework of the Hollywood studio system of the day, *Casablanca* nonetheless had more than its share of difficulties during production. In part due to the changes in scriptwriters, the movie had gone through an unusual number of drafts and rewrites over the course of the spring and summer of 1942, with additions and changes made all the way through the shoot. There were still gaps and unanswered questions in the plot that were being filled as shooting began in May and wound down in July. Even as the crew prepared to film the crucial airport scene, Bergman had not been given the pages that would tell her just where, and with whom, her character was going to wind up. Would she stay with Rick in Casablanca or head off with her husband, Laszlo, to continue the fight for freedom in other parts of Europe? Bergman, who was a perfectionist, predisposed to nervousness, and preoccupied by her interest in the casting of *For Whom the Bell Tolls,* kept asking Curtiz and the writers just who it was that she was supposed to be in love with, her husband or Rick Blaine.

In the original play, Blaine gets the girl. Ilsa stays behind with him in Casablanca. But Wallis and the writers recognized immediately that that sort of ending wouldn't cut it with the film audience. Only through this act of selflessness, insisting that Ilsa leave, would filmgoers see Rick's commitment not just to Ilsa but to greater causes. "I'm no good at being noble," he tells her, "but it doesn't take much to see that the problems of three little people don't amount to a hill of beans in this crazy world."

In August 1942, as the editing on his film was beginning, Hal Wallis had no better idea than the next Hollywood producer exactly where or when the United States was going to enter the war in Europe. But as head of production at Warner, he did happen to have this movie nearly in the can, and North Africa was already proving to be an important locale in the war's evolution. Wallis also had a feel for the patriotic sensibilities of the nation. He knew that his audience would want an ending to the movie that would offer some hope and certainty in what felt like desperate times. Unfortunately, the rough cut that he'd just viewed had more ambiguity than he wanted to see.

Wallis was a man who involved himself in every aspect of moviemaking, from choosing stars to suggesting the briefest of cuts to film editors as his movies neared completion. He was known for writing reams of memos to staff, detailing his wishes. It was a practice encouraged at the company, which printed an advisory on all its stationery: VERBAL MESSAGES CAUSE MISUNDERSTANDINGS AND DELAYS. (PLEASE PUT THEM IN WRITING.) Though the rule came from the head of the studio, Jack Warner, not Wallis, Wallis himself was habitually disposed to oblige.

As Wallis reviewed the last scenes of the film, he felt that it needed "a good punchline," one that was in keeping with both the narrative of the movie and the mood of the nation. Wallis was not the sort of film producer who was interested in shades of gray, which is what he felt he was seeing in the close. He wanted *Casablanca* to end with a clear-cut moral.

In the final scene, Blaine has just insisted Ilsa leave on a departing airplane with her husband. He follows that heartrending moment by shooting a Gestapo agent who has come to the Casablanca airport to prevent the plane from taking off. After this jolt of melodrama, Rick is seen walking off into a foggy early morning with Louis Renault, the French police officer who ought to be arresting Rick for the murder of the German agent. The question was what to do with these two world-weary figures, who have spent the movie parrying each other in a kind of cynical fencing match. What should they say to each other now? What does this archetypal American character say to this archetypal French character, given the complex circumstances of their two nations' geopolitical postures, and given the artistic and moneymaking demands of Hollywood movie production?

The final scene had been filmed a few weeks earlier on stage 1 at Warner Brothers Studios in Hollywood, for reasons of frugality and the restrictions of war. The location was supposed to be an airport in Morocco, but not much attention was paid to making the details specific. In fact, no genuine planes were available for use by Warner or any other studio at the time. All had been drafted into official business by the Department of War.

Instead, the company prop department created a wooden cutout of a twin-engine plane that turned out to be considerably less than a full-size replica, even in single dimension. To hide the artifice, the set was liberally fogged and the mock plane was placed as far back on the stage as was possible without completely obscuring it.

In contrast to the actors and sedan occupying the foreground of the shot, the cutout, perhaps not surprisingly, lacked depth and proportion, despite the steaming dry ice and distance from the camera. To give the scene a little more verisimilitude, an assistant director decided to hire a handful of little people—midgets—to portray mechanics. Dressed in light-colored coveralls, they were directed to look busy around the plane, checking under the faux fuselage and plywood wings of the cutout, as if preparing it for flight. Meanwhile, the actors were to project high drama before the camera.

But what should Rick say and do next? The script called for the two of them to walk off into the Casablancan fog, with Renault telling the gendarmes who have accompanied him to the airport "to round up the usual suspects." He will let Rick go off to the Free French garrison in Brazzaville, in the Congo. But the day of shooting, someone suggested that Renault should go off to Brazzaville as well. He'd just been made something of a heroic figure himself by failing to arrest Rick, and what would happen to him in Casablanca if he didn't leave? In the ever-changing circumstances under which the film was shot, that revision was instantly accepted.

To Wallis, the two of them going off together felt right. This was how this story should end, both from a narrative point of view and from the audience's point of view: the American and the Frenchman should end as allies, shouldn't they?

But on August 7, 1942, Wallis sat down to type a note to the editor, Owen Marks. He wanted to add one more line, however, he still wasn't exactly certain what that should be. He decided to have Bogart record a voice-over for two possibilities, and Marks would need to cut in the one chosen. The first choice Wallis crafted, "Louis, I might have known you'd mix your patriotism with a little larceny," was in keeping with Rick's wise-guy character, but there was something too cynical about it, Wallis thought, something that thrust a viewer backward in the movie, toward a sense of who these characters were at the start of the film, not the way they had evolved. So Wallis ultimately decided to use the other line he jotted down for Rick to record: "Louis, I think this is the beginning of a beautiful friendship," which, of course, was the coda that would ultimately be placed in the movie.

Had it been phrased in the form of a wish rather than a belief, this last line would have resonated thousands of miles away, in the halls of the Munitions buildings in Washington, at Allied headquarters in London, and at the offices of the American legation in Tangier, as well as among many elements in Casablanca itself.

But as much as they might have hoped that Operation Torch would somehow constitute the beginning of a beautiful friendship, the people planning the invasion of North Africa were involved in war, not the creation of a movie. Only time would tell if Rick and Louis would walk off together into the Casablanca night as allies.

CHAPTER 14

Tangier to Gibraltar to England

U ncoiled from what he called "his casket"—the trailer hauled by
Holcomb and Browne through the hills of Spanish Morocco—to
be deposited here, at the doorstep of the American consulate
in Tangier, René Malevergne found himself standing before yet another
sumptuous villa occupied by U.S. spies. He was soon shown to a soft bed,
where it was easy to assume he was in safe hands. Malevergne fell into a
welcome sleep, awakening refreshed and ready to continue his journey.

The next afternoon, someone from the American consulate—a tall
man with a sympathetic air, according to Malevergne—brought a fistful
of British passports and a change of clothing for what was envisioned as
a straightforward, albeit disguised, voyage to Gibraltar under a forged
passport. The clothes were ill fitting, and the pile of passports had
no faces or builds that resembled his. It was the first indication that
Malevergne's trip out of the Spanish zone might be a little more complex
than envisioned.

On September 29, the second day after his arrival in Tangier, he met
for the first time with Colonel William Eddy, the chief architect of his
exfiltration from Casablanca. As he had when he had met Patton back
in Washington in July, Eddy wore his dress uniform for the occasion.
Malevergne had dinner with Eddy and noted the colonel's limp from
those old war wounds, as well as the fact that Eddy spoke a "rude
French." Eddy explained how he'd picked up the language in the war,
apologizing for the fact that "I speak [French] like a soldier."

Malevergne immediately liked Eddy's "comforting sensibility." The
fact that Eddy brought up the issue of a salary also pleased him, not for
mercenary reasons but because it showed a sensitivity to Malevergne's
circumstances. The $280 a month for his work for the Americans was
more than fair, Malevergne thought. And Eddy won more points when

he volunteered to provide Germaine and the boys six thousand francs a month while Malevergne was away.

Though Eddy could not offer specifics on what Malevergne was going to be doing in the service of the Americans, he told the pilot for the first time that he would be working with the U.S. Navy, that from Gibraltar he would head on to London and from London probably to the United States. Eddy told Malevergne that he would send a letter, by way of diplomatic pouch, to Gibraltar, and that Malevergne was to take the letter to London, where it would serve as a form of accreditation to the Allied command. He also promised to send a telegram to what Malevergne called "the intelligence section of the American Navy"— more likely OSS offices in Washington—telling the agency of the pilot's arrival in Tangier. Finally, Malevergne was asked to compose a series of postcards to his wife, implying that he had left her for another woman. These were later mailed by Holcomb from various cities in Morocco as a means to disguise Malevergne's whereabouts to the French authorities, who presumably would be on the lookout for him. Malevergne makes no mention of whether or not Germaine was prepared to receive these notes, whether or not any actually arrived in Mehdia, or what her response was if they did.

Eddy and the staff in Tangier soon decided that the subterfuge involving the false passport should be scrapped. It was determined that sending Malevergne to Gibraltar by standard means, guarded only by transparently phony documentation, was impractical and dangerous. Option number two, however, turned out to be no cakewalk either.

On September 30, Malevergne, swimming in the oversized garments he'd been given at the American consulate, was taken to yet another grand villa—it seemed all of these spies had lovely homes—decorated with African hunting trophies and ancient weapons and owned by an Englishman named Grim. Malevergne had little time to appreciate his surroundings. That evening around 8:00 p.m., Monsieur Grim drove him down the hills of Spanish Morocco to the Mediterranean coast. There the Frenchman was deposited at the darkened offices of a steamship company and into the hands of an anonymous guide, who immediately told Malevergne that the valise in his hand, in which he was carrying his shaving kit, would have to be disposed of.

In a light rain, the man led Malevergne silently along a road running parallel to the beach. The Shark quickly understood why he had to get rid of his toiletries: they soon came upon a surveillance zone, where the valise would have surely given him away. Malevergne and his guide were let through and continued in silence to a distant spot on the road beyond the checkpoint, where the blackness of the night seemed almost total and all that could be heard was the lapping of the sea along the beach.

From the darkness a silhouette emerged and walked slowly and wordlessly toward and past them. They paused as the man turned around and came back in their direction. With careful deliberation, he pulled a white handkerchief from his pocket: the signal that they worked for the same cause. The gesture prompted Malevergne's companion to speak to the man in a soft-toned Arabic. The two conversed briefly before the guide who had brought Malevergne to this rendezvous quickly and wordlessly disappeared.

With his new companion, yet another anonymous escort who didn't bother with introductions, Malevergne crossed the road and headed toward the beach, where a boat lay at the water's edge. They pushed it into the surf, and Malevergne was directed to stretch out in the bottom of the craft as his guide took the oars. There was nothing to look at but the cloudy sky above. He listened to the creak of the oars in their locks and felt the glide of the boat grow smoother as his guide gained a rhythm to his stroke. After a quarter of an hour of rowing, the Moroccan boatman paused and looked down at Malevergne. In Arabic, he asked Malevergne for a payment in order to continue.

Malevergne was no novice when it came to this type of character. He'd seen plenty around the docks and harbors of Casablanca and Port Lyautey. He wondered how many involved in arranging this man's help had already been hit up for a payment. *I don't have any money,*

Malevergne told him in Arabic, *but if you'd like me to row, I would be happy to.*

The escort was apparently a man used to being told no. He made no further mention of money and, resigned to the task at hand, started rowing once more. As appeasement, Malevergne offered him a cigarette, which was accepted, and the journey continued for another quarter of an hour.

Then, in the darkness, they heard the sound of a motorboat approaching. The Moroccan lit a lantern in the rowboat as the powered craft neared and idled its engine. There was a bump as the gunwales jounced off each other. It was indicated that Malevergne should leave one boat for the next, and so he was passed off once more, with his second guide telling this third one that Malevergne had no money. Apparently that wasn't cause to turn around, as Malevergne was crammed into the hold of his new transport, which stank of salt and rotten fish. He listened in his cramped position—only slightly more spacious than the trailer hauled by the Chevy from Casablanca—as the motor whined and they left the rowboat behind, heading rapidly out into the strait. In half an hour's time, he was allowed out of the hold and came up to see the lights of Tangier off the stern and the lights of Tarifa, in Spain, off the bow.

"The boat is very small," Malevergne later told his diary. "It is a big canoe with a motor and bit of decking fore and aft. A small roof . . . over the motor protected it from bad weather. The cleanliness on board was doubtful. On the port side, a man slept [in a curl]. I gathered he was the only member of the crew other than the owner at the tiller."

A squall hit the boat as it neared the Spanish coast, and the lights of Tarifa suddenly disappeared in the storm. Unfortunately, the engine died too. The owner indicated to Malevergne that he needed to fix it, but the crew member, if that's what he was, remained curled in sleep. For unknown reasons, the captain was loath to wake the curled man, so Malevergne volunteered to take the rudder while the helmsman ducked beneath the covering on the motor to see what he could do. Thirty minutes later, the engine kicked in and the man emerged, indicating by gesture to Malevergne that the spark plugs had gotten wet.

Soon the storm abated. The clouds began to lift and once again Malevergne could see the lights of Tangier off in the distance. They put Tarifa on the port side of the little boat, and very soon the famous rock of Gibraltar loomed ahead of them. It was one o'clock in the morning of October 1.

A British officer named Morris welcomed Malevergne at the port and escorted him to a home in town, where Malevergne was shown to a room where he slept soundly until nine in the morning. Upon awakening, he was told that he would have to stay in the house through the day, because of "too many suspicious elements" out in the streets.

Bad weather prevented Malevergne's immediate departure for London. He whiled away the day, "a prisoner once again" in the house in Gibraltar. Malevergne was still in the oversized outfit that had been given to him in Tangier, and Monsieur Morris asked him if he would like a more comfortable set of clothes. *Merci.* When the British officer returned with new clothes and the news that he would be flying out to London early the next day, Malevergne asked Morris if a letter, the one from Colonel Eddy describing who he was to the proper authorities, had arrived in the diplomatic pouch from Tangier. Morris's answer seemed evasive to the Frenchman. He hemmed and hawed before finally saying that the letter would accompany Malevergne in the plane to England and that it would be given to him when he touched down. "I do not like this method of proceeding," Malevergne told his diary, "but what can I do about it?"

In the middle of the night, he boarded a plane for Great Britain, and at daybreak on October 3, René Malevergne spied the southern coast of England. Maybe it was simple fatigue that dampened his excitement, maybe it was his French predisposition against the British, but he remained nervous about the letter and generally suspicious of the people in whose care he was escorted.

At the airfield in Eton, two English officers and a young French lieutenant greeted him. As he was being whisked from the runway, Malevergne was asked if he knew a Colonel Lelong, a leader of the Resistance in Morocco. Yes, he told them, he knew Lelong. Then you will see him in two hours, he was told. But again, Malevergne was uneasy. Where were the Americans? he wondered. Where was the letter? Why was he being kept in British hands?

He was taken to lunch and then a hotel, where yet another British officer arrived, "very tall, dry and rigid." The officer told Malevergne that he would have to wait three or four days at the hotel, during which time "several high-ranking officers will come to talk to you."

By this time Malevergne had had enough. His own tone turned as dry and rigid as the British officer's. "I shall tell you nothing until I see Colonel Gruenther, adjutant to the official representative of the American Government," he said. Eddy had given Malevergne Gruenther's name in Tangier. Though he was incorrect about the recently promoted general's rank, the river pilot got the essence of his point across to his British hosts. He wanted to see the brass and he wanted to see him now.

Unfortunately for him, "the brass" was far more ambivalent about greeting him.

CHAPTER 15

Needs and Wants

The heat coming from George Marshall's cable to Eisenhower's command in London was almost palpable. Aside from the one Eisenhower received, copies singed the fingers of General Mark Clark and Eisenhower's recently appointed chief of staff, General Alfred Gruenther, as well. It was dated October 2 and read:

> It is reported here by Eddy under date September 29th, Tangier, that Chief Pilot Port Lyautey has been smuggled out of Morocco enroute to London and Washington. Since such action is not only changing the tempo of operations in North Africa but will inevitably cause widespread comment and rivet attention on this particular area to the possible prejudice of any operations therein, information is requested as to whether or not you were consulted by O.S.S. and whether such action had your approval.
>
> Marshall

In other words, the head of the Joint Chiefs wanted to know, whose harebrained idea was this?

The fact of the matter was that no one in London knew that René Malevergne's extrication was in the works, nor was it sanctioned by the command. Eisenhower sent a cable back to Washington telling Marshall as much. He had not been consulted by OSS or anyone else on the matter, despite the fact that his orders to the OSS had explicitly stated that they were to do nothing in Morocco without his approval. He would not have sanctioned the action if he'd known about it. Of course, that raised the question, Why hadn't he known?

The problem, thought Eisenhower's aide Harry Butcher, was that there were just too many different intelligence services at work in late September. Army G-2, naval intelligence, the British agencies, including Special Operations Executive (SOE, a spy organization formed in 1940 by Churchill)—Butcher confessed to his diary that he and others in London were still trying to differentiate between the OSS and the OWI (Office of War Information). And the man on Eisenhower's staff who presumably should have been the first to know of a request like this, Al Gruenther, could easily be forgiven. He was new enough to the post to be just learning all the players in the operation.

Gruenther had been sent to London from Washington at about the same time as George Patton in early August, but he'd come with a steep learning curve. Gruenther had been stationed that summer in San Antonio, Texas, where he'd been decidedly out of the loop. In fact, it wasn't until ten minutes before his flight to England that Marshall's secretary, General Walter Bedell Smith, informed him that Operation Torch even existed.

When Gruenther landed in London, the first person he met with was Eisenhower, who asked him how much he knew about Operation Torch. Gruenther's understated response was, *Very little.* That didn't prevent Eisenhower from immediately thrusting his new aide into the thick of things. The next morning, Gruenther found himself sitting in a meeting with officers from the British command, who, Gruenther would later relate, were less than impressed with his acumen.

Soon after he arrived, Gruenther met Eddy, who was in London early in September. In fact, it was to Gruenther that Eddy sent his recommendation that Carl Clopet, the hydrographer from Casablanca, be sent to London to aid in Torch planning. The mention of Clopet was contained in a long list of recommendations from Eddy to the combined chiefs. That catalog, however, apparently did not also include mention of René Malevergne.

Clopet eventually arrived in London, but between Eddy's last visit to London and Marshall's cable, there was no news of Malevergne in Eisenhower's office. And Gruenther, who was charged with coordinating the various planning details of Torch as they pertained to Eisenhower's office, as well as making sure none of those secrets leaked out, was plenty busy with other spillage.

The Malevergne escape turned out to be only one of a number of moments when the planned invasion of North Africa might have been broadcast to the enemy. There was, for instance, the story of the officer from Eisenhower's staff who was flying to Gibraltar from London carrying plans for Operation Torch. Anyone carrying such classified information was supposed to keep it in a weighted bag so that it would sink if the plane went down over the ocean. In fact, that was what did happen in this instance—the plane was attacked by the Luftwaffe and went down in the Mediterranean—except the officer had apparently decided a weighted bag was too cumbersome. The officer's body washed ashore with the plans in his pocket, where they were subsequently discovered by Spanish authorities. Apparently, however, water damage made the papers illegible.

On another, even stranger occasion, a box full of maps of the North African coast, intended for use in the invasion, fell out of a truck and tumbled onto the streets of London on a windy evening. An army detail was detached to make sure all the maps were picked up, but Gruenther was left wondering if they'd all been retrieved in the breeze and, if not, what would the person assume who found a map of the North African coast on the streets of London? And what might he or she do with such a curious item?

London soon traced the order for extricating René Malevergne back to the offices of General George Patton in the Munitions buildings in Washington. Whether Patton's offices had received notice from the OSS

(presumably by way of Eddy and perhaps Donovan) about King's opportunity to get Malevergne out of Casablanca via the Chevy and its
trailer and so ordered the action, or whether they had given tacit approval to the extrication after it was carried out in Morocco, ultimately
did not matter. Patton and his command *did*, in fact, approve of the action after the fact, if not before, and Malevergne was now in London.
What's more, there was little time to bemoan the execution of the deed.
Beyond Marshall's cable and a subsequent hubbub with Eisenhower's
staff, it was spilled milk and, on the whole, typical for such an unwieldy
and hasty operation.

Since the basic idea of an invasion of North Africa had been approved
at the level of the commanders in chief of the United States and Great
Britain only in late July, and the outline for that invasion, including the
final locations where troops would land, had been agreed to only in
the first week of September; and since the date for the invasion had been
set for approximately the first or second week of November; and since
this was a first collaboration of the war involving two great nations, with
their separate armies, separate navies, separate air forces, aimed at two
separate invasion locations on the continent of Africa in two different
oceans, it's obvious that the possibilities for error were bountiful. That is
to say nothing of the hundreds of ships involved and the more than one
hundred thousand troops to sail in one convoy from the shores of England, and another three thousand miles across the Atlantic. In addition,
one hundred thousand seamen were to man the ships in these separate
convoys. The Western Task Force alone was the largest single convoy
ever to embark from the United States with the intention of amphibious assault against a foreign power. And it wasn't as if the U.S. Army
was well versed in this sort of operation: the last time it had sailed from
American shores with the intention of a direct assault on an enemy had
been during the Spanish-American War.

Added to these difficulties was the fact that planning for the invasion was being conducted in cross-Atlantic fashion, with Eisenhower, Mark Clark, and the European high command settled in London; Patton and his Western Task Force staff, including Lucian Truscott and company, now back in Washington; Doolittle and the Twelfth Army Air Force split between Washington and England; and Admiral Hewitt and the U.S. Navy Western Task Force command stationed at the Nansemond Hotel in Norfolk, Virginia. Meanwhile, the OSS and other intelligence operatives were working out of North Africa, Washington, and London; army transportation and supply commands were stationed in Washington, New York, and Norfolk (with separate divisions based in England organizing the "inside" invasion within the Mediterranean); and the War Shipping Administration, which controlled and understood where Allied transport and cargo shipping was at any given moment in port or on the high seas, was in Washington. Oh, yes, and the U.S. Navy as a whole was trying to wage war against Japan in the Pacific, just as the demands for its men and supplies were now escalating in Europe.

It wasn't until early September that the organization, assembly, and equipage of the two task forces of Operation Torch began in earnest and haste. Quickly it became apparent that there would be a battle for resources between the force sailing from England and Patton's force sailing from the United States. The task force from Great Britain got the jump on the western forces by sending to Washington on September 8 a massive request for 344,000 tons of matériel. Not only would this requisition from one wing of the invasion alone strain the limits of available convoy shipping, available army troops, and available supplies, but it would seriously tax the navy's ability to supply escorts for the shipping. Furthermore, closer examination of the request revealed that much of the matériel was duplicated in shipments that had already been sent to England. It turned out that many of the supplies sent earlier in the year were buried so deeply in British warehouses that it was more practical to ship the same items to the UK a second time than to find them in storage and repack them for the invasion of North Africa.

Under the circumstances, Patton and the Western Task Force needed to hustle to finalize plans for the invasion, so that they could raise their hands and shout, "Us, too!" as the goods and transport were being divvied up. All of their requests needed to be coordinated with the U.S. Navy and the Mediterranean task force within the fluid context of a larger strategy that had only just been agreed to. In other words, the invasion of Morocco was now a certainty; all Patton and company had to do was make it happen in two months' time.

Personnel and training were also crucial factors influenced by the loud tick of the invasion clock. Because the operation in Morocco was an amphibious assault, it would have been logical that marine units, who were the American troops most highly trained in just such a style of combat, should have been called upon to serve; but the Corps was tied up in the Pacific, where the battle for Guadalcanal had just been undertaken, so the inexperienced U.S. Army would be landing in the surf of Morocco.

Nor were the three thousand navy and coast guard personnel needed for landing the troops in the Western Task Force particularly well versed in the exercise. As Samuel Eliot Morison put it, "It would have been desirable to select young men, who were used to lobstering, fishing, and other small craft work." The problem was, they weren't there. "So as frequently in this war, the Navy had to make boat sailors out of raw recruits who had never seen salt water."

That wasn't all: In a progress report to Eisenhower in early October, General James Doolittle estimated that 75 percent of the Twelfth Air Force was either untrained or partially trained. Adding to these difficulties for the air force was the fact that the one nearby airfield controlled by Allied forces prior to the invasion—the British base at Gibraltar—would be used by the Royal Air Force to supply support for the "inside" invasion force in the Mediterranean, which meant that air support for Patton's Western Task Force would have to be provided by carrier-based planes within the convoy.

Unfortunately, in the fall of 1942, the U.S. Navy was hardly brimming with aircraft carriers. The Japanese had sunk the *Lexington, Hornet, Wasp,* and *Yorktown* and wreaked havoc on the *Saratoga* and *Enterprise,* which meant that there was only one large carrier in the Atlantic fleet, the *Ranger*. As a consequence, four tankers had been converted into a new class of carrier for use in the European theater and the Western Task Force. Altogether these five carriers and quasicarriers could haul about 250 bombers and fighters to the theater. But again, training was an issue. The pilots were so inexperienced that the Navy decided not to have them practice carrier landings on the voyage across the ocean for fear of losing lives and aircraft.

For all of these difficulties, lack of shipping remained the single biggest hurdle for Operation Torch preparations. There simply weren't enough vessels to carry cargo, transport soldiers, and provide escort to both the Western Task Force and a portion of the Mediterranean. This was in addition to shipping supplies to England for the "inside" assault. Particulars like the number of combat and service support troops were still in flux, but getting hard figures was essential to determine the type of shipping required for the operation. How many troop carriers were needed? How many cargo ships? How many landing craft? How many escorts and carriers? All depended on numbers that were still being figured out, still being totaled. And because ships of all kinds were in such demand, time was needed to occasionally transform vessels from what they were into what was needed. For instance, twelve ships had to be converted into combat loaders to help carry infantry for the Western Task Force. This involved providing troop space on the ship as well as more quarters for navy personnel sailing the vessel; installing davits for the landing boats that would be attached to the transport; adding armaments; and increasing the capacity of the ships' booms for loading cargo.

The demands of keeping the secrets of Operation Torch from the wide world were a mighty strain too. Only the highest Allied commanders and the planners of the invasion were supposed to know the destinations of the forces involved; but given the very nature of the operation—the long-anticipated entry of the United States into the war against the Axis—and the fact that there were a limited number of options for attack, it was not surprising that guesses about where the invasion might occur occasionally hit the mark. In the third week of September, for instance, Eisenhower and Marshall were made extremely nervous by an intercepted cable sent from United Press offices in London to United Press offices in Washington that advised its American counterparts to prepare to cover a story out of Casablanca, rather than Dakar. (A young reporter out of Houston, Texas, with a moon-shaped face punctuated by a mustache, Walter Cronkite, would soon get the assignment.)

The fact that the OSS was so heavily involved in planning operations didn't inhibit other intelligence agencies, American and British, from continuing their work, which, perhaps not surprisingly, led to difficulties regarding where information was coming from and by whom it was being sent. More headaches for General Alfred Gruenther and many others.

Even de Gaulle and the Free French forces in England, notoriously loose lipped, were being kept in the dark about the exact nature of the attack. Again, maintaining this silence was not an easy proposition. Truscott recalled stopping by to see Eisenhower before flying home to the States on September 19. While there, he witnessed de Gaulle's chief of staff stopping by to deliver a message from de Gaulle to Eisenhower. "General De Gaulle understands that British and Americans are planning to invade French North Africa," said the courier. "[The general] wishes to say that in such case he expects to be designated as Commander in Chief. Any invasion of French territory that is not under French command is bound to fail." According to Truscott, Eisenhower merely thanked the officer, who saluted and walked briskly away.

Given the haste with which Torch was concocted, the lack of experience of its fighting forces, the sheer size of the enterprise, and the possibility that plans for the attack would be given away before the operation was begun, it was no wonder that knees began knocking in both London and D.C. as the run-up to invasion began. No wonder, either, that a strong hope remained that the French would offer little or no resistance to an invasion from their former Allies and potential "friends." As Morison put it, the Western Task Force "resembled a football team forced to play a major game very early in the season, before holding adequate practice or obtaining proper equipment."

Even George Patton, in a note to Eisenhower in September, suggested "the picture" of invasion was "gloomy," though he added, with typical brio: "Rest assured that when we start for the beach we shall stay there either dead or alive, and if alive we will not surrender. When I have made everyone else share this opinion, as I shall certainly do before we start, I shall have complete confidence in the success of the operation."

Meanwhile, in the Soviet Union, Stalingrad was under murderous assault from the Luftwaffe, even as fierce door-to-door fighting was waged on the ground. Wave after wave of bombers swept over the city, dumping their payloads on targets against a tattered and withering Soviet air defense. Street fighting was more evenly matched but even more gruesome. The Russian army had turned every street, every block, even the sewers, into bloody, labyrinthine battlefields, exacting a steep price on the Wehrmacht for every inch of ground.

Internal pressures were also being brought to bear on Allied leaders. In early October, FDR's 1940 presidential election opponent, Wendell Willkie, returned from a 33,000-mile global tour of battlefronts, including a stop in Moscow. His call for the quick opening of a second front received wide and extensive coverage. While he claimed that "Germany will never conquer Russia" and that "the United Nations had the power and resources [to win the war]," the question that concerned Willkie was "How soon will we win and at what cost in human lives?"

The *Times of London*, the British Labour Party, and Stalin himself were likewise clamoring for the rapid opening of a second front; and while Roosevelt, Marshall, Eisenhower, and the British command knew the moment was on its way, a deep sense of anxiety pervaded headquarters in London as well as Washington. Eisenhower wrote to Marshall in an early-October report on Torch progress that was otherwise optimistic: "As you can well imagine, there have been times during the past few weeks when it has been a trifle difficult to keep up, in front of everybody, a proper attitude of confidence and optimism."

CHAPTER 16

Meeting Gruenther

Al Gruenther was in his early forties, balding, sharp featured, and blessed with a wide, accessible grin and deep smile lines in his cheeks. He greeted René Malevergne soberly, however, when the Frenchman finally got his wish of seeing the "adjutant of the official representative of the American government." Gruenther was surrounded by a cordon of British officers and a translator who put the Frenchman immediately on his guard. Malevergne was eager to tell his story directly to the American, and he proceeded as best as he was able to present his bona fides to Gruenther. "Colonel," he said, again getting the rank wrong, "Colonel Eddy wrote a letter when I left Tangier that was to have been given to me at Gibraltar to serve as an introduction to you. Monsieur Morris, who handled this affair, assured me that the letter would follow by diplomatic channels and that it would be in London at the same time as I. Where is that letter, Colonel?"

Of course, Malevergne couldn't have known that Gruenther had just been upbraided in a cablegram by the head of the Joint Chiefs of Staff about his presence in London. He couldn't have known that his name—or, more accurately, his occupation as the river pilot at Port Lyautey—was being bandied about at the highest levels of command; or that there was still some uncertainty about whether or not he was who he purported to be. There was also the question of what to do with Malevergne if he was indeed a river pilot from Morocco. In this context, Gruenther's first question of Malevergne, "Do you know Monsieur Clopet?" made perfect sense. To Malevergne, however, it was an annoyance. He immediately sensed that his identity was doubted. "Monsieur Clopet is the director of a tugboat company at Casablanca," he answered forthrightly. "He is one of my friends."

Gruenther seemed not entirely satisfied with this answer, which

further confused Malevergne. Gruenther adjourned with the British officer who'd accompanied the river pilot to the meeting, and the two talked
for several minutes. The world of cloak-and-dagger dialogue, whispered
asides, and secrets was profoundly discouraging to Malevergne at that
moment. Again, perhaps it was his French background, but he couldn't
help but feel that the British were the source of the suspicion surrounding his appearance here. He felt that if he could just talk to Gruenther
outside the company of his English escorts, all would be made perfectly
clear. But it wasn't going to happen. At least, not yet.

When Gruenther returned from his tête-à-tête with the British officer,
he had abrupt and hard news. "Monsieur Malevergne," he said, "a general will visit you tomorrow morning at your hotel. Then, your mission
accomplished, you will return to your point of departure."

Gruenther would not entertain further discussion. He turned on his
heel and left Malevergne astonished by this turn and, once again, in the
company of the British. Malevergne returned to his hotel "profoundly
discouraged." There he obsessed about the missing letter from Eddy and
the maltreatment that he continued to assume was based on a British perception of who he was and what he was doing in London. "I was sincere
when I agreed to serve the Americans," he told his diary. "I did not base
my agreement on the approval of the English. . . . I do not understand
why they seem to want me to serve the English."

The *Contessa* arriving in Havana Harbor in 1939
(Standard Fruit Company photo)

The Western Task Force en route to Morocco, late October 1942
(courtesy of the National Archives)

General George Patton (l) and Admiral Kent Hewitt (r), sharing a light moment on board the *Augusta*, en route to Morocco, late October 1942 (courtesy of the National Archives)

General Lucien Truscott (r) in North Africa (courtesy of the National Archives)

Entrance to the River Sebou (courtesy of the National Archives)

Casablanca harbor (courtesy of the National Archives)

First P-40s to take off from the USS *Chenango*, headed for the Port Lyautey airfield (courtesy of the National Archives)

Scuttled French trawlers at a crucial bend in the River Sebou (courtesy of the National Archives)

Aerial view of the bend in the Sebou and the Lyautey airfield
(courtesy of the National Archives)

René Malevergne (white trousers) receives the U.S. Navy Cross
(courtesy of the National Archives)

Malevergne receives the Silver Star from General Lucien Truscott
(courtesy of the National Archives)

René Malevergne and family: wife Germaine and sons René and Claude (courtesy of the National Archives)

CHAPTER 17

SOS

Lucian Truscott's group, including Mountbatten's Englishmen—
Henriques, Costabadie, and Homer, along with Truscott, Hamilton, and Conway—had finally made their way to Washington
to oversee the organization, training, supply, and final planning of the
Goalpost invasion force in the third week of September.

Once there, Truscott and company set up shop in offices cheek
by jowl with Patton's headquarters in the Munitions buildings. Much
needed to be done. While the overall shape of the sub–task force's role
was pretty clear now, gathering all of the elements needed to undertake
the mission represented a microcosm of the same difficulties inherent in
Torch as a whole.

The troop list for Goalpost included forty different units of various
shapes and sizes, including, according to Truscott, "infantry, artillery,
armor, aviation, antiaircraft artillery, tank destroyers, engineers, signal
and medical troops, prisoner of war interrogators, counter-intelligence
and military government personnel." The Goalpost commander had finally learned where the bulk of his nine thousand troops would be coming from—the assault troops were from the Sixtieth Infantry Division,
which would be joined by an armored battalion combat team from Patton's old Second Armored Division—but these and the various other
units involved were scattered in army bases across the country. The infantry and armored combat units were at Fort Bragg in North Carolina,
but some of the engineers were in Richmond, Virginia, parts of the medical units were in New Jersey and California, and the air force units were
sprinkled in California and Virginia. By the beginning of their second
week in Washington—less than a month now from when the convoy was
scheduled to depart—Truscott and his team had no idea where in the

United States they might find half a dozen units that were on their must-have list for sailing to Morocco.

Working hand in glove with the general, as he had for months now, was Major Ted Conway, a former *New York Times* reporter. Conway had been sent to England in late April with Truscott to learn the ins and outs of commando warfare under Lord Mountbatten. To Robert Henriques, they were similar in more than just their duties. Conway was "another Truscott," thought Henriques. A man who defeated his expectations of what an American soldier should be like. He didn't "look and act tough." He wasn't "ruggedly efficient, brash, full of pep, all bustle." Instead, as with "the best of the professionals, Truscott and Ted . . . had what was in fact a 'West Point' manner, just as distinct as the 'Oxford' manner of the twenties and thirties but exactly the opposite." Their style "was a negation of mannerisms. Unless they had something to say they very pointedly did not talk. Unless there was need for propulsion, they made a point of not driving themselves or anybody else. Until it was appropriate to do so, they did not emanate personality. They were scrupulously realistic, quietly efficient, so highly trained and so confident that, when they were ignorant, they never thought of hiding it. But when you saw these people in command of troops and on the battlefield, as [Henriques] did later and often, they were certainly as good soldiers as anything the allies could produce, and a good deal better than most."

The other American aide that Truscott had brought with him from England, Major Pierpont Morgan Hamilton, was a forty-four-year-old international banker born with a silver spoon in his mouth. Lean and dapper, Hamilton was erudite, cosmopolitan, and an impeccable speaker of the French language. He had spent the years between the wars earning a bachelor's degree, and then a master's degree in business, from Harvard, before taking a job in banking in Paris, where he polished his French for seven years. Hamilton's bloodlines were decidedly upper crust. His surname came from his great-great-grandfather, Alexander Hamilton of Founding Father fame; his first and second names were derived from his grandfather, J. P. (John Pierpont) Morgan, the legendary financier.

Educated at Groton prior to World War I, Pierpont Hamilton had served as an airman in the war. He rejoined the service four months after Pearl Harbor and was quickly placed on active duty in the Army Air Force. Major Hamilton was sent to England and, like Truscott and Conway, attached to the combined operations staff of Lord Louis Mountbatten as an intelligence officer. With Mountbatten, he helped plan the Dieppe raid and then returned home with Truscott to work on Operation Torch.

The weeks of working together under Mountbatten had made Conway, Hamilton, and the trio of Brits already quite familiar with one another by the time they arrived in Washington. There they continued their collegial duties under Patton and Truscott on sub–task force Goalpost.

Robert Henriques arrived in Washington to find a city that "was not unqualified fun for anyone in British uniform." Not only had amenities in the crowded capital failed to keep pace with the hordes of newly arrived war workers, but he found a general sense among Americans, often stated bluntly to him, that the United States was being called to duty to save Great Britain and the Allied powers from yet another European mess, as it had in the First World War. " 'Again' was the savage adverb," Henriques wrote, and he heard it on more than one occasion. As in: "Again 'our boys' were to be 'sacrificed' to save Europe."

Neither was Henriques completely sold on the mission to which he was assigned. Like most of the British high command, he thought Americans were too concerned about an Axis attack on and through Gibraltar. Like them, he sensed that the fight should be carried out inside the Mediterranean. Morocco was a waste of time. The Germans were unlikely to defend the country, feeling that its distance from the more serious upcoming battles east of Algiers made it strategically unimportant ground. In general, he thought Operation Torch was "a bad, mad gamble which the American Chiefs-of-Staff decided to take because it was the view of their Intelligence Chiefs that the French would not fight."

Yet Henriques was more than willing to concede the fallacies of the British perspective as well. He understood, for instance, why the British were being wholly excluded from the Moroccan invasion and limited in their role in the Mediterranean invasion. He agreed with the American perspective "that the French did not like the British" and admitted that "while the British knew this to be true—and did not themselves like the French—they resented the Americans saying it."

Henriques's expertise was in planning and attention to detail. He had a reputation for obstinacy and steering relentlessly through bureaucratic roadblocks, and he was there to provide the continuing background on prior British amphibious assaults to the Americans through Truscott's staff. He went about his business with diligence and speed, as he had to, given the fast-dwindling time at hand and the fact that he was about to be given a daunting task.

A week after Truscott got home from London, he left the Washington offices of his sub–task force to go to Fort Bragg, North Carolina, and prepare the soldiers whom he'd been assigned for Goalpost. These were assault troops from the Sixtieth Infantry Regimental Combat Team of the Ninth Infantry Division, headed by Colonel Frederic J. de Rohan; and an Armored Battalion Combat Team of the Second Armored Division, under Patton's old World War I friend Lieutenant Colonel Harry Semmes. Yet another hiccup awaited Truscott at Fort Bragg: he discovered that no provisions had been made for him to have a regimental staff, which meant that he was forced to call on Conway and Hamilton to join him in North Carolina, leaving Henriques and the rest of the Mountbatten contingent to continue with the preparations for invasion in Washington.

It was in this same week that Truscott learned positively that there would be no paratroopers available for his use in attacking the Port Lyautey airport for Operation Torch. Patton and the combined chiefs of staff, however, had enthusiastically endorsed his idea of using Army Rangers for the same goal, and a company of seventy-five was delegated to the task. Now all that was needed was a ship to deposit these soldiers at the airport.

It fell to Henriques, near supply sources in Washington, to find one. He went first to the navy and then to the War Shipping Board. He was told, according to his own account, written much later, that "every available ship in the allied pool which was capable of sailing the Atlantic had long ago been enlisted for the TORCH assaults," but he remained persistent. Truscott had an October 14 deadline by which he needed to present to Patton a final plan for sub–task force Goalpost. Just three and a half days prior to that day, Henriques finally found the ship he'd been looking for.

The USS *Dallas* was a World War I–vintage destroyer of the Clemson class, 314 feet and about 1,200 tons, with a top speed of thirty-three knots. She was a four-piper, the nickname given to destroyers that sailed with four distinctive funnels running along their midships; but she also had another distinguishing characteristic and another nickname. The *Dallas*, like others in her class, lacked a raised forecastle, which gave her profile a distinct sheer strake running from stem to stern. It earned her that second nickname: she was both a four-piper and a flush decker.

Far lighter than the newest World War II destroyers being put to sea by the U.S. Navy, she displaced about half as much water as the Fletcher class of destroyers. The *Dallas* had run coastal patrol duty from Argentina to Nova Scotia from mid-1941 to March 1942. Then she'd served as escort for a couple of convoys to Iceland and Northern Ireland before settling into duty, once again, patrolling the U.S. Atlantic coast from New York to Cuba from April to the first week of October. She was docked in Philadelphia awaiting her next duty when someone from Truscott's staff—probably Henriques—discovered her. Captained by Robert Brodie and with a crew of about one hundred, she was not a ship that had been scheduled to see much action in the war. Her day, for the most part, had come and gone. But rid of her masts and superstructure, she might be just light enough and speedy enough to navigate the River Sebou with a detachment of Army Rangers. And she had some firepower to defend herself as she sailed up the river: four 4-inch deck guns, one 3-inch antiaircraft weapon, twelve torpedo tubes, and two stern-mounted depth charge racks. So the *Dallas* was called to Norfolk and prepared for sailing.

She would not be the last unlikely ship needed for Goalpost.

The man who was ultimately responsible for coordinating the supplies and transportation of the countless requests like Henriques's was General Brehon Somervell, head of the army's Services of Supply (SOS) branch. Somervell was a 1914 graduate of West Point who began his career in the Corps of Engineers. Like Patton, Somervell served in Mexico in the chase' of Pancho Villa before World War I, but his bent was engineering and logistics, in which he quickly became a rising star in the army.

Between the wars, his talents won him a succession of important planning and engineering posts within the Army Corps of Engineers, culminating in his appointment by Franklin Roosevelt to head the Works Progress Administration (WPA) in New York in 1935. There he oversaw the construction of LaGuardia Airport and proved himself capable of coordinating vast projects with thousands of workers, millions of dollars, and scores of components.

His skills were put to further use in his next large work: the construction of the Pentagon, beginning in 1941; but that same year, he made a political enemy of Senator Harry Truman, who was conducting hearings on War Department spending and felt that Somervell was typical of a certain type of army officer "who didn't care anything about money." Truman's difficulties with Somervell did nothing to prevent the general's rise in War Department esteem. His promotion to major general and head of SOS was carried out in early 1942 over the heads of several higher-ranking officers.

Somervell was made aware of Operation Torch soon after the combined chiefs of staff named North Africa as the destination for the U.S. entry into the war in late July. Though he and the SOS had been anticipating a cross-channel invasion of Europe, he wrote to Eisenhower that he and his operation were growing so accustomed to "changing horse in mid-stream" that "we are getting a bit used to it even if their tramping around does muddy up the water a good deal." For more than a month afterward, he and SOS had to essentially improvise planning, as they lacked such rudimentary details as the location, timing, and size of the invasion. While the outlines of the operation became clearer after the September 5 decision to definitely include the Western Task Force, along with the Mediterranean invasion, nothing was simple about Torch.

The matter of finding troops and supplies, transporting them from locales across the country to ports, primarily in the Hampton Roads area of Virginia, on the East Coast, and then making them ready for shipping to North Africa fell to Somervell and his people. His people included the head of the army's Transportation Corps, Major General Charles Gross, a West Point classmate of Somervell's whose principal job was to find the shipping to transport all those supplies and soldiers to the shores of North Africa.

As with Patton's Casablanca operation and Truscott's sub–task force, Somervell's job was made immensely more complicated by the demands from England for duplicates of supplies that had already been shipped but were now lost in warehouses across that "sceptered isle." In addition, the U.S. Navy was constrained by a lack of ships available to serve as escort for both the necessary supply convoys to England and the upcoming gigantic convoy to North Africa.

Despite the requests from England, the focus of Somervell's U.S. command was the Western Task Force, and it was hardly less demanding. With commanders like Truscott and his staff changing requests and ordering equipment piecemeal, confusion and contradiction reigned within the supply chain. Not knowing, for instance, whether Truscott's command would need paratroopers for its assault on the Port Lyautey airfield or Rangers wasn't simply a tactical matter; each unit had different supply needs, and the supply needs affected cargo requirements; cargo requirements affected shipping needs; shipping needs affected navy escort demands, as well as the capacity of ports in England and, soon, ports in North Africa, to handle the unloading of all the matériel streaming into their docks.

Since late August, arms, ships, and personnel had been streaming into the Norfolk/Hampton Roads area. The railroads, the piers, the cities, and the waterways of the region were teeming with cargo, machinery, and men, waiting for the signal to begin loading the ships; but it wasn't until September 29 that that order arrived, and even when it did come, the confusion persisted. Troop commanders continued to order special equipment, and basic information about the task force, like schedules, cargo specifications for ships, unit assignments, and which items should accompany which units, remained hard to find during the loading process. There were troubles with freight coming from inland suppliers and manufacturers, as well. Some railcars were inadequately marked or mismarked. And the simple swamp of matériel in the port made the assignment of supplies to individual ships an immensely complicated process even without the last-minute changes.

Regarding those abrupt changes, Somervell decreed to his staff what he considered the most expeditious manner of dealing with them: if General Patton endorsed the request, SOS was to supply it.

All the while, the clock was ticking on the invasion plans, not only on operation levels, but political as well. September slipped into October, the first week of October slipped into the second, and while plans started to become somewhat clearer, there were still special needs that were emerging until the very end.

CHAPTER 18

Amphibians

As of early October, just a month from D-day in North Africa, many of the army troops engaged in Operation Torch had yet to train in amphibious assault. Out in Chesapeake Bay at a recently opened facility called Solomons Island, a center had been established by the navy to provide just those sorts of exercises for the Marine Corps, which was training for island invasions in the South Pacific. These were the first such training grounds in the country, and they provided a lengthy stretch of beach for landing vehicles to practice maneuvers. Of course, none of those beaches presented the sort of crashing surf that was likely to be faced on the shores of Morocco; nonetheless, as soon as the first ships of the Western Task Force were loaded with men and supplies, they sailed off to this nearby training center, where they would disembark and get some sorely needed practice landings.

These were troops from Patton's central division of the task force. He was there at Solomons Island, along with Admiral Kent Hewitt, to observe the exercises on Hewitt's flagship, *Augusta*. His squabbles with the navy had grown no less intense in the weeks following his first meeting with Hewitt. The most recent contretemps centered on how the ships ought to be loaded. Patton hated the notion that the navy was "attempt[ing] to issue orders to me." While the army was interested in packing its cargo so that matériel first needed on the beaches of Morocco would be last stored in the ships' holds, the navy had its own way of doing things and wanted to load according to the best utilization of space. Patton's mood was not improved by the performance of the navy during the amphibious assault exercises at Solomons Island. "The timing of the landing by the Navy was very bad," he wrote bluntly, "over forty minutes late to start with, about all we can hope for is that they do better next time."

As Patton's force was being trained at Solomons, thirteen more ships, comprising what was labeled the "X" force of the Moroccan invasion (Truscott's Sixtieth Infantry troops) and the "Z" force (commanded by General Ernest Harmon and headed toward Safi, the southernmost site in the Western Task Force attack), were readied for shipping. They would follow Patton's troops to Solomons for the same sort of amphibious exercises.

At the same time, Truscott's final plan for sub–task force Goalpost was due in Patton's offices in Washington on October 14. Truscott presented it in person and found Patton in a far more sanguine mood than he'd been in just days earlier. To Patton, the gathering and approval of these final plans was an indication that the die was cast; all that was left now was to load the ships and sail into battle. As he wrote to a friend that same day, the fourteenth: "I have now reached the situation which you and I have felt many times before—after the ponies have been shipped for an important match, one's worries seem to disappear. I believe that we have done everything humanly possible and that this expedition contains the best trained troops of all arms this country can produce."

Truscott can be forgiven for being less accepting about the state of affairs, since he and Harmon and their troops had yet to do their amphibious training. In fact, he had to hustle to get back to Norfolk in time to oversee their exercises at Solomons Island.

There he found an operation in full flourish. Ships were loaded by civilian stevedores, under Army Transport rules and supervision (in a couple of instances, up in New York, the navy did the packing and got it wrong, and the ships had to be unpacked and reloaded, much to the chagrin of the Army Transport team at the Port of Hampton Roads), into vessels sailed by U.S. Navy personnel. The standard order of loading, as per Patton's orders, involved packing combat vehicles and ammunition and supplies so that they could be gotten off the ships first. C, D, and K rations were also loaded into the vehicles. The troops carried other meal rations on their persons.

Combat vehicles needed to be prepared for the surf off of French

Morocco, so elaborate efforts at waterproofing vehicles were under-taken, including covering electrical equipment, raising exhaust systems beneath the vehicles, and creating sheet-metal housings on the backs of the tanks to prevent their engines from being disabled by submersion. All of this work needed to be done near the piers because the elaborate sys-tems erected to protect the vehicles also caused them to quickly overheat and break down, which meant they couldn't travel far to be unloaded.

As with every step in the process of organizing Operation Torch, there were hiccups along the way. Because the loading scheme linked weaponry to troops, it was thrown off every time one type of combat unit was sub-stituted for another in the process, or if there was a shift of one unit from a particular ship in the convoy to another.

A new handheld rocket launcher that would eventually gain wide renown in World War II, the bazooka, was issued to troops just two days prior to launching. Ammunition was supplied and packed with the weapon, but it was discovered only later that instructions on how to use the launcher had been crated separately.

The commanders of the various sub–task forces, including Truscott, established "war tents," guarded by MPs, which held battle information and to which officers began reporting to be given their missions. It was here that at least two of Truscott's two commanders, Colonel de Rohan and Colonel Semmes, were first told where Goalpost was headed. Beneath the tent were papier-mâché relief maps of the landing beaches surrounding Mehdia; there were silhouette photos of the hills surrounding the beaches, taken from the sea in gray light so that commanders could get a sense of what they might see as they were attempting to precisely land their Land-ing Craft Mechanized vehicles LCMs in the early-morning hours off the coast of Morocco.

Truscott's X force finally got its opportunity to practice amphibi-ous assaults in the next few days, but once again there was a problem. Colonel Demas T. Craw, who had been assigned to Truscott's sub–task force as a commander from the Army Air Force, had been placed on a ship where the captain had refused to lower any nets or craft, claiming that his crew had no training in the exercise and were simply incapable of doing it.

Craw was a no-nonsense tough guy who had been around the block already in the war. A veteran of World War I and the chase of Pancho Villa in Mexico, after the First World War Craw had gone off to West Point, where he excelled at athletics, most particularly boxing, but finished 271st in a class that barely broke 400.

He became an enthusiastic flyer after graduation and wound up transferring from the infantry to the Army Air Corps, where he served in rather ho-hum circumstances until the war in Europe began. In 1939 he was assigned as an observer to the Royal Air Force in Egypt, and much to his delight, he was able to fly twenty-two missions against the Axis before the war began.

Craw, who was of Greek descent, got assigned to Athens in 1941 and stayed there, trying to aid the British, after Axis forces occupied the land. There he became involved in an incident that made the newspapers back home: a fender bender with an Italian major, who took umbrage at the fact that Craw, who was in civilian clothes, was less than humble about the accident. The major ordered two privates accompanying him to hold Craw while he cuffed the American colonel. When Craw was released, he proceeded to deck the Italian major with a single punch.

The upshot of the incident came when the American minister in Athens demanded and received from the Italian legation an apology from the major to Colonel Craw, delivered before the assembled staff of the American consulate. It was said that the major was still sporting a black eye when he read his "I'm sorry."

Sent back to Washington after the war began, Craw was assigned to command the air section of Semmes's tank force, an assignment that brought him to this moment off Solomon's Island. As seen, he wasn't the type to take no for an answer.

Craw contacted Truscott, who arrived on the ship to try to reason with the recalcitrant captain. What Truscott discovered was that the captain was at wit's end. He had been given this convoy assignment with a ship that he claimed was in no shape to sail, crewed by half-trained men who simply did not know how to lower a boat to practice an amphibious assault. None of his officers had any experience either, yet here they were, expected to take part in exercises in preparation for an invasion that would simply be suicidal, according to the captain, who refused to take responsibility for what was to come.

Truscott calmly explained the bottom line here: In fact, the captain's circumstances were not unlike those of many others who were preparing to sail in the convoy of the Western Task Force. If he refused to participate in these exercises, Truscott told him, "navy authorities would have no difficulty in finding some officer willing to do his best under the circumstances."

The training proceeded with the captain's assistance, if not his goodwill.

CHAPTER 19

Monsieur Prechak

Though he was glad to be in the company of the American staff officer once again, Malevergne still felt an iciness coming from the British assembled in Gruenther's office on his second visit. Surprisingly to him, this meeting came just a day after the first. Again it seemed to him that the air was filled with rigid formality. He was asked to explain the circumstances that brought him to London, and Malevergne, feeling as if he were somehow doubted, proceeded to tell the gathering of his journey in the Chevy and its trailer from Casablanca to Tangier. The letter from Eddy had apparently arrived here after all, because one of the officers made mention of it.

Despite the British lack of warmth, Gruenther had had an apparent change of heart about René Malevergne's circumstances. Or at least someone in the command had. Whether this came on the heels of news that George Patton was behind his escape from Morocco and still wanted him in Washington or simply through discussions about what to do with the Port Lyautey river pilot at headquarters in London didn't matter. Eisenhower's chief of staff was far more accepting of the Frenchman the second time around. He even offered Malevergne a ride back to the hotel after the meeting.

The constant presence of an interpreter had inhibited Malevergne from the moment he touched down in England. Though his English was not very good, he felt that he could convey his sentiments and desire to assist the Americans if only he were given an opportunity to speak alone with the general. That moment finally was afforded him in the ride back to the hotel. "Colonel," Malevergne said in a confidential tone, soon after they were alone. "English methods are not pleasing to me. I will say nothing in their presence." Malevergne thought that Gruenther's eyes lit up at this slight castigation of their hosts, that a bond had been formed between them. Unfortunately, he understood little of what the general said in response. However, he told his diary later, "his handshake on parting was significant."

Perhaps even more significant was the loosening of restrictions on Malevergne after the car ride. The interpreter disappeared, and though the Shark continued to be vetted by officers from the combined staffs, he soon understood that he was not going back to Colonel Eddy in Tangier. Instead, he was taken to a home in the English countryside and told that he would soon resume his trip on to Washington. From Washington, presumably, he would head back to Morocco. Though he continued to be visited and quizzed by headquarters staff, Malevergne was able to relax and actually appreciate what were, for him, given the circumstances of these last two years, quite sumptuous surroundings, replete with beautiful English gardens.

There in the country, Malevergne learned that he was to be given yet another identity for his future travels. He was no longer the Shark in this clandestine world, but Viktor Prechak. How this name was arrived at no one bothered to tell him. Soon after, however, as if to confirm his baptism, from George Patton's office in Washington came a letter referring to him by that name and informing anyone viewing its contents that "no difficulty should befall M. Prechak."

So now Victor Prechak waited for word of his next journey, this time to Washington.

CHAPTER 20

Looking for a Ship

The phones at the office of Colonel Cyrus J. Wilder, executive officer of the Port of Hampton Roads, were ringing, one colonel after the next, from the late morning onward on October 17. After Brigadier General Kilpatrick, who was commander of the port, Wilder was the go-to guy at that three-ring circus that was Hampton Roads in mid-October 1942. All the loadings and requests; all the coordination of supplies; the ordering of troops and ships and longshoremen, went through his offices. So it wasn't surprising that the desperate-sounding calls coming from the headquarters of the Army Air Force—first a Colonel Gordon and then a Colonel Howe—were routed in his direction. Each of them had essentially the same straightforward request: they needed more airplane gasoline to be shipped with the convoy.

The problem was, as Wilder immediately pointed out to them, the convoy was scheduled to head out in just five days. Wilder wasn't sure where the gasoline was supposed to come from if the Army Air Force didn't have it itself. Even more important, he didn't have a clue as to how it was supposed to be shipped. Every spare tanker and cargo ship on the East Coast was accounted for and already employed in the effort to supply the convoy.

Gordon and Howe had tossed more clinkers into the request. It turned out that the air force didn't want just any sort of vessel: it needed one that could haul a couple thousand drums of gasoline, was fast enough to keep up with the convoy, and, oh, by the way, had at most a seventeen-and-a-half-foot draft. For what reason they needed these specifications they could not say; but to make the point that nothing about their request was frivolous, they said that it had the endorsement of the highest levels of the task-force command and if Wilder had trouble accommodating them, they would take the matter up the chain of command of the SOS. Starting at the top, that meant General Somervell; followed by the chief of transportation, General Charles Gross; followed by Wilder's boss, General Kilpatrick; followed by Wilder himself.

Precisely how this request was born is uncertain, but it came with a deep sense of urgency. Probably someone in the Army Air Corps doing calculations on the needs and requirements of the Port Lyautey airfield in the first hours after it was taken by Allied forces determined that in order to aid General Patton's assault on Casablanca, planes flying onto the field would need gasoline. While Truscott and his staff had mapped out a means to take the airport quickly with the help of the destroyer *Dallas* and the team of Army Rangers who would be collected on its decks; and while the Port Lyautey airport would be open for arrivals as soon as it was in Allied hands, the problem lay with subsequent departures.

The army P-40s, which were to be the first planes landing at Port Lyautey to aid Patton's assault on Casablanca, were land-based planes being launched from the converted carrier *Chenango*. The *Chenango* was the only ship carrying planes in the Western Task Force's northern group—Truscott's sub–task force. Prior to the war she had been the *Esso New Orleans,* an oil tanker. The ship had been transformed so that it could carry planes but was only able to launch them, not bring the P-40s in. Once those planes set down in Port Lyautey, without access to more fuel they would essentially be as land-bound as emus.

The captains and majors doing the calculations on the gasoline requirements of the P-40s, and where fuel was coming from, no doubt hurriedly took their concerns to the colonels. The colonels passed them on to the commanders, who wound up sending them back to the colonels with make-it-happen speed. If these planes were useless due to lack of fuel, the whole airfield would be useless. The plans for using Port Lyautey as both a base to support Patton's invasion of Casablanca and a solidifying anchor to control the air above northwest Africa were in jeopardy. So, too, would be the focus of Truscott's sub–task force Goalpost. All had suddenly become dependent on getting a vessel that seemingly didn't exist up a river that no one but an unknown French river pilot knew how to navigate.

Enter Colonel Wilder at Hampton Roads, who knew only that the ship and the gasoline were needed for the convoy. Like everyone else who was not a part of the invasion strategy sessions, he had no idea what its purpose was, nor where exactly it was going.

Regarding the gasoline, Wilder got busy and got lucky. After several fruitless calls, he got in touch with the navy and asked its supply depot in Norfolk about the possibility of drumming enough gas to meet the air corps's needs, and one other thing, might they have a ship available? He got half a loaf. While the commander at the depot had the gasoline and agreed to drum it for him, the navy was not ready to take on any extra cargo in its convoy. Nor did it have a ship available to haul it. In other words, if the army wanted to ship more gasoline, it would have to find its own means to do so.

Wilder contacted the War Shipping Administration, which managed and theoretically knew the whereabouts of all U.S. convoy and merchant shipping. The WSA quickly informed Wilder that every available vessel on the East Coast was already invested in the Western Task Force or steaming supplies to England or the Soviet Union. Furthermore, as the navy had already indicated, the convoy didn't have the time to wait for another ship to be found, let alone to wait to find one with the shallow draft, cargo, and speed capabilities required of this vessel.

Even so, as was indicated by the Army Air Force colonels' initial passing mention that they would bring it to the chief of transportation if nothing happened, this request had the weight of high command behind it. George Patton himself had been made aware of the needs of the Army Air Corps at Port Lyautey, and since its needs were his needs, something was going to happen on the request, come hell or high water. As later documents indicate, the need to locate a ship to haul gasoline up the River Sebou soon went to the highest office in the SOS, as well as the highest office of the Office of Transportation, each contact made under Patton's command, if not his explicit order.

Months after the fact, a writer for the *Saturday Evening Post* envisioned the moment when the need for the *Contessa*'s involvement in Operation Torch was discovered. He saw it as occurring above a large map "where the ranking strategists of the United Nations" were looking over plans that detailed the invasion: an "immense British and American armada carrying troops, tanks, planes and guns . . . to spill the raw materials of victory over Rommel." One key post, an African airfield, needed to be supplied with gasoline to ensure the success of the invasion. The problem was that the field lay "a dozen miles up the shallow, almost un-navigable Sebou River in French Morocco, where known facts about the river were few and best guesses were vague." The river was assumed to have a channel that might be only seventeen feet deep. "Where was a ship big enough to haul the supplies essential for this segment of the invasion which drew so little water she could taxi explosive material through seventeen feet of water without disaster?"

Not only that: If the ship wasn't already in Norfolk or vicinity—and, as the navy and the War Shipping Administration had already explained, it wasn't—this vessel would have to be near enough to Virginia so that it could arrive in time to ship out in less than a week. It also had to be fast enough to keep up with the convoy, sailing at an average clip of about twelve knots to make it across the three thousand miles of Atlantic Ocean to the shores of Morocco in time for the invasion.

While the "ranking strategists of the United Nations" didn't exactly start the search for the *Contessa* overlooking a large map of the invasion, in fact the need began with those strategists, and the search ultimately included the United Nations. While C. J. Wilder waited anxiously in Hampton Roads for news of a vessel that fit the bill, and the Army Air Corps did likewise in Washington, the War Shipping Administration sent word to the offices of the Royal Admiralty across the ocean in England. Had any American shipping recently arrived in Great Britain that might accommodate the needs of this air corps request?

A day and a half later, a cable arrived in Wilder's office at Hampton Roads. Colonel Norman Vissering, who worked with Eisenhower's staff in London in the overseas Transportation Corps, wired that the ship that everyone was clamoring for had been found and was on its way to Virginia. Her name was *Contessa*. She was "a reefer" belonging to the Standard Fruit Company out of New Orleans and capable of carrying over seven thousand barrels of fuel with the draft requirements stipulated by her destination. Vissering wasn't certain about the time of her arrival at the Hampton Roads port, but she had sailed from Avonmouth on October 8 and was very near New York when she'd been contacted by the Royal Admiralty. The *Contessa* ought to be arriving in Virginia soon.

In the middle of a fierce mid-October storm, sailing empty from Avonmouth and bobbing like a cork in the vast ocean, the *Contessa* was in trouble—not floundering, but battered for sure—and Captain William John had a decision to make. Despite her birthplace in the northern seas of Glasgow, Scotland, the *Contessa* was not built for the sort of pounding she had been taking in the North Atlantic over the last two months. The same shallow draft that made her trips upriver to banana plantations in Cuba and Honduras routine was now causing her violent predicament in the ocean. She was riding too high in the rocking ocean.

John knew that he needed to take on some ballast to stabilize her, but the only way to do that in the middle of the sea was to take a big gulp of water—to fill a tank aft of the number four hold with ocean water. The problem was that the bulkhead in that area had been damaged during the installation of her degaussing equipment way back in July—these were the electromagnetic coils installed in ships to ward off the magnetic mines laid by German vessels in the midst of Allied shipping lanes. If John decided to take on water to add ballast to the *Contessa,* there was a distinct possibility the water in the tank could leak between the decks and into the number four hold itself. The pumps in the number four hold, however, couldn't suck the water out because the strainer in the bilges was stopped with cork, placed there as another patchwork mend. There would be no way of disposing of the water once it was taken on board.

Storms at sea are a good prompt to action. Deciding that the gale was a greater hazard to his ship than filling the hold, Captain John gave the go-ahead to let the water in. Soon the added weight helped to stabilize the *Contessa,* and soon after that, the winds finally began to abate after almost a full week of howling.

Sure enough, however, the water that the ship had taken on began seeping into the number four hold, and the crew could do nothing to pump it out. Thank God, they were just two days out of New York and dry dock. Thank God, too, that John and the rest of the crew from New Orleans would soon be seeing friends and family for the first time in six months. In John's case, Bessie had booked a room for them in Manhattan and would be there when he arrived.

CHAPTER 21

The Pieces in Place

By five o'clock on October 17, René Malevergne was in the air on his way to what he assumed would be the last stop before returning to Germaine and the boys in Mehdia.

As the ocean swept by beneath him, Malevergne fell asleep on the plane and stayed asleep till just after midnight, awakening to a thick fog that eventually turned into clouds as black as ink. Newfoundland soon appeared below, and the plane landed to refuel.

By the afternoon, Malevergne was flying over the United States for the first time, and he saw below "a veritable garden with little rivers, woods, lakes and green land." Then New York City appeared, spreading for miles around the bays and rivers out his window below. Despite all that had happened to him, despite the uncertainty of what lay ahead, it was difficult not to feel a deep sense of excitement. He had come a long way from Mehdia.

Finally, Washington emerged out of the fog from his plane window, its streets radiating like compass lines from the monumental buildings at its heart. As he began his descent, René Malevergne took a deep breath and braced himself for his arrival into this new land.

★　★　★

Word came to the *Contessa* on October 19 that she was wanted in Norfolk for what was called "a special war mission." The order arrived via radio from the British admiralty under whose command she had journeyed from New York and from whose port she had last sailed. Captain William John ordered the helmsman to set a course to the south and west, and down the East Coast the *Contessa* steamed.

Nowhere is it recorded what sort of response this news received among the crew, but judging from the fact that many had been at sea without meaningful leave for months, it can be imagined. What they were getting into was a mystery. No one aboard had a clue about the operations being conducted at the Port of Hampton Roads; no one knew what their next journey might offer. On October 21, Lieutenant Cato of the armed guard ordered test shots from the four-inch fifty-caliber guns on board. It was the only indication from anyone on board that the *Contessa*'s trip to Norfolk and beyond might ultimately put them in harm's way.

Of course, "a special war mission" could be almost anything. And in the case of this banana boat, much as John might have loved her, he was hard pressed to guess what exactly she could do for the war effort that could be considered special. Especially given her current condition. Whatever lay ahead, John knew that his ship was in rough shape, and she would need a good, solid week in dry dock before she was capable of sailing again.

Still, it's likely that at some point on the way to Norfolk, John went back to his cabin and inspected the chrome-plated .45-caliber pistol that he'd kept there since the days of the "banana wars" in Nicaragua, just to make sure it was in good firing condition.

Back in April 1931, a group of Sandinistas had attacked a pair of Standard Fruit farms in Nicaragua, killing several employees and at least one of the American marines sent to the farms to rescue the workers. While another pair of marines, along with a contingent of native Guardia Nacional, fought a rearguard action, Standard Fruit sent the *Cefalu*, captained by William John, to their rescue. In the panic and chaos surrounding that river dock in Nicaragua, John loaded thirty refugees on board as the rebels approached, guns blazing. Along with the marines and *guardia*, he took aim with his pistol and fired back as the *Cefalu* pulled away from the dock, escaped the jungle, and steamed back to New Orleans with its terrified passengers. The plant overseer died right there on the deck of the *Cefalu* of wounds suffered in the chase.

Keeping handy an old and highly regarded pistol was one of the few things that Captain William John had in common with the man who had prompted this journey to Norfolk, George Patton. Maybe a devotion to their wives too. John reminded himself as they neared Virginia that he must contact his wife as soon as the *Contessa* arrived. Maybe she could come to Norfolk and greet him there for their long-awaited, and now delayed, reunion.

In addition to finalizing plans for Operation Torch with his staff and continuing his squabbles with the U.S. Navy over Torch preparations, George Patton was beginning to say his good-byes before shipping out with the convoy. It is not surprising, given all that was at stake here and the kind of man he was, that Patton's mood projected a deep sense of destiny. He wrote a long letter to his brother-in-law, Frederick Ayer, with whom he was very close. "All my life I have wanted to lead a lot of men in a desperate battle," he wrote. "I am going to do it; and at fifty-six, one can go with equanimity—there is nothing much one has not done. Thanks to you and B. [wife Beatrice], I have had an exceptionally happy life. 'Death is as light as a feather; reputation for valor is as heavy as a mountain.'"

He visited Marshall in Washington on October 21, before heading off to Norfolk. The head of the Joint Chiefs was likewise in a reflective mood as Torch neared. When Patton mentioned an admiral who was a part of Hewitt's staff, the chief of staff asked, "How old is he?" and Patton told him fifty-three or fifty-four. *Near the same age as us,* Marshall remarked, adding, "My, how old we all are."

Marshall was not the sort of man to wallow too deeply in such sentiments. He also offered Patton some practical advice on dealing with the Navy over the next few weeks. He told his commander "to influence Hewitt but not to scare him."

After the Marshall visit, Patton paid his respects to his great mentor, General John "Blackjack" Pershing, ancient and now nearly blind, staying at Walter Reed Hospital in Washington, D.C. Pershing did not recognize Georgie until Patton spoke, telling the old general that he was on his way to war. He reminded Pershing that he had given the younger man his start way back in Mexico in 1916, to which Pershing replied, "I can always pick a fighting man and God knows there are few of them. I am happy they are sending you to the front at once. I like generals so bold that they are dangerous. I hope they give you a free hand."

Finally, Patton and Hewitt together visited the president, who greeted them in the White House, saying, "Come in, Skipper and Old Cavalry-man, and give me the good news." Still uncertain of the navy's commitment to attack, Patton had hoped that in this last meeting with the commander in chief before the invasion Roosevelt would impress upon Hewitt the need to go through with the landing regardless of conditions. To prompt such an order, Patton said to the president, "The Admiral and I feel that we must get ashore regardless of cost, as the fate of the war hinges on our success." But Roosevelt was not a man who spoke in those sorts of dramatic terms in White House conversation. "Certainly you must," he said simply. That seemed to Patton, immersed as he was in the high drama of the undertaking before him and his army, a kind of casual, throwaway response. Patton noted in his diary later that day that "A great politician is not of necessity a great military leader."

On the morning of Friday, October 23, Patton was with Hewitt again. Together they faced some 150 commanders of the Western Task Force assembled in an army warehouse in Norfolk. Though it had been guessed already by many of those assembled, Hewitt stepped forward and revealed for the first time that their destination was North Africa. For the next four hours they went over the plans for the operation in preparation for joining their troops, who were already waiting on dozens of ships gathered in the harbors of Chesapeake Bay. The last details given were reminders of the proper means of burying the dead and registering their markers. They would sail in the morning for Morocco.

Before the assembly was dismissed, Patton stepped to the front to deliver a few last words. His uniform was crisp and his riding boots were shined to a high gloss. Ivory-handled pistols hung on each hip. None of the naval officers and only a handful of the army men had direct experience under his command. To those who were strangers, he must have looked like—and, with that squeaky voice, sounded like—a dandy. But it was hard to miss his fierceness and intensity. Doubtless a good many were thankful to be led by such a bold figure, and doubtless a good many thought they were viewing a pistol-packing nut. His speech would reinforce both views.

"If you have any doubts about what you are to do," Patton said, "I can put it very simply. The idea is to move ahead, and you usually know where the front is by the sound of gunfire. To make it perfectly clear: suppose you lose a hand or an ear is shot off, or perhaps a piece of your nose, and you think you should go back to first aid. If I see you, it will be the last goddamned walk you ever make. As an officer, you're expected to move ahead."

Patton was no less comforting to the naval officers gathered: "I'm under no illusion that the goddamned Navy will get us within a hundred miles of the beach or within a week of the date set for landing. It doesn't matter. Put us on Africa. We'll walk."

"We shall attack for sixty days," he went on, "and then, if we have to, we will attack for sixty more." Patton paused dramatically before his close. "If we go forward with desperation," he said, "if we go forward with utmost speed and fight, these people cannot stand against us."

That afternoon, Patton went aboard Hewitt's flagship, the *Augusta*, where he was given the privilege of the captain's cabin. In the evening he told his diary, "This is my last night in America. 'It may be for years and may be forever.' God grant that I do my full duty to my men and myself."

Patton also wrote a last letter to his wife, Bea. She had seen him off from Washington the evening before, as he boarded his flight for Norfolk. Now it might be many months, maybe even years, before he saw her again.

"Darling Bea," he wrote, "I must have been considerably upset to have started to leave without saying good-by—I guess I was. It will probably be sometime before you get a letter from me, but I will be thinking of you and loving you."

In the midst of this last note, Patton saved room for one last piece of news that was obviously weighing on his mind and that he'd obviously shared with his wife on the eve of his departure. "We are going to sleep on board [the *Augusta*] tonight and leave this place on shore at 0230," he wrote. And then, as if the knowledge would relax Bea as well, he added, "The *Contessa* finally showed up."

PART III

CHAPTER 22

Dry Dock

For the stevedores and staff at the port of embarkation in Hampton Roads, it was hard to discern the special nature of the banana boat that pulled into the port. In fact, her six months at sea, the last three in the North Atlantic, had given the *Contessa* such a battered appearance that subsequent descriptions of the vessel almost universally described her as long in the tooth and run-down, when in fact the *Contessa* had been a relatively modern ship prior to the war. Long gone was the steamer that had proudly cruised the Caribbean with well-heeled passengers sipping drinks in deck chairs as they were serenaded by musicians beside a mahogany bar.

A pilot had guided Captain John's ship through the submarine net by Fort Monroe at the entrance to the harbor at about the same hour that George Patton and Admiral Hewitt were meeting with the commanders at the army warehouse in Newport News on the morning of the twenty-third. He steered her toward pier X, the same loading facility that had embarked Truscott's sub–task force Goalpost. It was here that the port crew got their first peek at the once-proud steamer.

In an ideal world, the *Contessa* would have been loaded with her cargo and would have turned around and joined the convoy that was about to sail from Hampton Roads. But as soon as he was informed of this outline, John quickly disabused port authorities of the notion. Not only was there simply no way that she could immediately go back to sea, but even if she could, it would have been impossible for her to keep up with a convoy in her current state. After describing to port authorities the measures he'd taken to make it through the almost weeklong storm that he and the crew had just faced in this last crossing, John said the *Contessa* had to go into dry dock for repairs.

At a minimum, she needed rivets tightened and some leaking seams closed; her number four hold had to be pumped out, as did the after-hold, which had been filled with seawater to stabilize her during the crossing; she needed pump repairs and to have her degaussing coils replaced or dried—"baked," in the dock vernacular.

The port authorities would have to make their own assessment of what was needed, but while they did so, the *Contessa* was ordered to stand by at pier X until a space opened up in the Newport News Ship-building and Dry Dock Company, hopefully the next day. It appeared that despite all the efforts to find her and get her to Norfolk, the *Contessa* would not be heading off with the Western Task Force convoy to North Africa in the next twenty-four hours. And Captain John, who still had no idea what his special mission might be, assumed that in the best case his ship would be several days in repair. He granted liberty to a number of his crew, allowing them the time to travel to family and friends who had planned to greet them in New York, or to head into the pleasures of the Hampton Roads Port. He himself contacted Bessie in New York and asked her to come down to Norfolk to the Nansemond Hotel for their long-awaited reunion.

Meanwhile, Wilder let all interested parties—army, Army Air Force, SOS, navy, and War Shipping Administration—know that the *Contessa* was in dock and being inspected.

When the air force received word of her arrival, it added an additional request to her payload: along with the airplane gasoline, they asked that she be loaded with bombs. Like the gasoline, it was determined that munitions were needed to aid in the mission of the P-40s flying support for Patton in Casablanca. The combination of volatile gasoline and high explosives, of course, added to the ship's potential combustibility, but in the midst of all the other activities surrounding the *Contessa,* it seemed just another difficult request that needed filling before she steamed out of the harbor.

Though the ship was sailing at the special request of the army, the navy, by order of the Joint Chiefs, commanded all convoy vessels at sea.

Due to the unique nature of the *Contessa*'s mission, Admiral Kent Hewitt ordered Lieutenant Albert Leslie U.S.N. to take charge of the guard unit on the *Contessa*. He was also to assume the role of cocaptain of the ship itself. Convoy orders would be addressed to him to be passed along to the *Contessa*'s civilian master, Captain John.

Leslie had had a diverse career. A World War I naval vet from Pittsburgh, he had continued in the service after the war, twice sailing around the world and serving, among other duties, in relief efforts in Japan in 1923, aiding survivors of the Yokohama earthquake. He'd moved into the Coast Guard during the late 1920s and served as a boatswain's mate in the fight against rum runners on the Eastern Seaboard during the height of Prohibition. By the early 1930s, Leslie had seemingly retired from the sea to take a position in a Pittsburgh bank, where he'd risen to vice president by the time World War II began. He had reenlisted in the navy as a lieutenant and was assisting with the amphibious assault training on Solomons Island near Norfolk when the assignment to join the *Contessa* came from Admiral Hewitt's office. Some sense of the navy's distrust of the merchant ship and her crew, as well as the dangers of the mission itself, was evinced in the orders given to Leslie. Part of his instructions ordered him to take over the ship if the *Contessa*'s crew refused to obey orders, and to use his heavily armed guard to enforce that command if need be.

It took several hours of inspection for a full assessment of the *Contessa*'s damages and needed repairs. The final count of her leaky rivets reached twenty-five; these and two seams, as well as the degaussing coil, all needed fixing, just as John had indicated. Trouble began when word of the extent of these problems reached U.S. Navy authorities. They were adamant that the *Contessa* not sail with the convoy. They simply could not have a banana boat limping along for this ride, potentially slowing the speed of the whole group.

That news was delivered to Wilder in the form of a Saturday telephone call from the chief of staff of the Amphibious Fleet, Captain Lee

Johnson. Johnson had consulted directly with Admiral Ingersoll, who was commander of the Northern Group. Ingersoll had stated flatly that he would not have her.

It was left to Wilder then to call the army with this latest development. The U.S. Army, of course, had none of the navy's qualms: the *Contessa* would go with the convoy come what may, said General Gross, commander of the army's Transport Division. He asked Wilder plainly if the port could get the ship ready in a reasonable amount of time. Not knowing for certain whether "reasonable" meant reasonable for the army's needs or the navy's, Wilder hemmed. Not the pause that Gross wanted to hear. He ordered Wilder to get in touch directly with General Patton for a final answer. Meanwhile, Gross would try to convince the navy that this ship was desperately needed. Gross further put the screws to his man in Hampton Roads: "If you have the will, you can find a way," he told Wilder.

If Wilder wondered at any point in the process about what made this ship's mission so important to the convoy, he didn't voice his question in a public manner and certainly wasn't going to do so to General Patton. Wilder no doubt took a deep breath before dialing the task force commander at the Nansemond Hotel in Norfolk. He no doubt exhaled deeply when he discovered that Patton had already gone to sea on the *Augusta* the day before. Nonetheless, he continued to try to get in touch with the general through Captain Johnson, who, as fate would have it, was on the *Augusta* as well. Wilder soon discovered that the future of the *Contessa* had already been discussed and determined on that very ship.

In his notes from that wild day, Wilder recorded that at 1725 hours on Saturday, October 24, he "called Captain Johnson who told me that the AUGUSTA had gone and that Patton was on board; that [Patton] had just talked to the Navy Department . . . [He] insisted that the CONTESSA go, even if she had to run alone." Johnson said further that "the Navy would let her go if we could get her out of dry dock by 1000 tomorrow [Sunday, October 25] and have her loose [i.e., loaded with her airplane gasoline and bombs and ready to sail] early Monday morning."

Wilder's night was far from over. He called Gross back just before 6:00 p.m. with word that the navy had acquiesced on the *Contessa*. He was also able to impart the good news that she would indeed be out of dry dock in the morning with fingers crossed that the degaussing coils—baked, rather than replaced outright—would hold up for the duration of the crossing. Now all he had to do was get in touch with the captain of the steamer to let him know that he would be leaving the port sooner, rather than later, and that he might have to make the transatlantic run alone.

At seven stories high, the Hotel Warwick had dominated the Newport News skyline for many years prior to World War II. Built primarily to help entertain businessmen with ties to Newport News Shipbuilding and Dry Dock Company, it had been *the* center of social activities in the city since its construction in the 1880s. Its age was beginning to show by the fall of 1942, but it was here in the still elegant hotel dining room that Colonel Wilder's call reached William John. Captain John was having dinner with his wife, Bess, who had just arrived from New York. Bess was traveling with her brother, William Sigsworth, a thirty-year-old salesman who had emigrated from Wales with Bess's mother, father, and sister thirteen years earlier and lived with the extended family in New Orleans.

Though the Johns were accustomed to absences in their marriage—he was, after all, a man of the sea—they'd never had one as long as this in more than twenty years as a couple. Wilder was the agent of an even further extension. With apologies over the phone, he asked that the *Contessa*'s captain come to the offices of the port of embarkation. They needed to talk about the timing of the special mission on which his ship was being asked to sail. It was important that he come immediately.

A half hour after Wilder's phone call, John was in the colonel's office learning that he would be returning to the *Contessa* in a matter of hours, not days, and that he might have to run her alone across the Atlantic in pursuit of the convoy. Furthermore, his cargo was to be a highly explosive mix of airplane fuel and bombs, to be loaded as soon as she got out of dry dock.

Many years later, his brother-in-law, Sigsworth, would describe Captain John as first and foremost a military man, "accustomed to saying yes when service called." Whether it was this stiff upper lip or some other motive that drove him, John was quick to respond. He let the colonel know "that he was perfectly willing to run free, in fact, anxious to run alone."

But Wilder had something crucial to learn too. There might be a hiccup, Captain John informed him. It turned out the *Contessa* "was short a considerable number of crew, twenty-nine having been allowed time off . . . when [John] thought the ship would be in dry dock five days."

Some had no doubt run up to their homes in New York for a quick visit with family; some were no doubt roaming the wild streets of Norfolk. In either case, Wilder knew, this was not good news.

CHAPTER 23

"Our Worst War Town"

Hampton Roads was officially designated a port of embarkation by the War Department in June 1942, but its history stretched all the way back to the first days of English settlement in the colony of Virginia in the early seventeenth century. One of the largest natural harbors in the world, Hampton Roads is doubly guarded from the Atlantic. Twin capes, Henry and James, named by those first Virginia colonists for the monarch of England and his son in 1607, mark the twelve-mile-wide inlet into Chesapeake Bay. Once inside the bay, the harbor at Hampton Roads is found through a second inlet to the southwest, just a few miles from the ocean. Here fifty miles of sheltered shoreline are available to ships arriving from the Atlantic in a sweeping harbor as fine as any on the Eastern Seaboard.

The area is steeped in American history. Virginia's colonial capital, Williamsburg, just up the James River from the port, piqued the interest of John D. Rockefeller about a dozen years prior to the start of World War II. He began to finance its restoration, and tourists soon followed, visiting the site in substantial numbers in the 1930s. Nearby, too, was Yorktown, site of the siege that ended the Revolutionary War.

At the outset of the Civil War, the federal government torched the ships housed at the navy yard that had existed in Portsmouth since the eighteenth century. Rather than see them in the hands of the Confederate state of Virginia, Union forces abandoned the yard until 1862, when George McClellan's Army of the Potomac began its futile peninsula campaign and reoccupied the region. Naval history was made out on the waters of Hampton Roads that same spring, when the famous battle between the world's first two ironclad ships, the *Monitor* and the *Merrimac,* was waged.

"Hampton Roads" is the name given to both the body of water

that forms the harbor and the metropolitan region that surrounds it. The area is composed of several cities, including Norfolk on the southeast side of the harbor; Virginia Beach, which is to the east of Norfolk on the Atlantic Ocean; Portsmouth, just to the west of Norfolk across the Elizabeth River; Newport News, to the northwest of the harbor in the fork between the James and York rivers, which run from the bay; and Hampton, which lies on the same inlet beside Newport News. Docks, piers, and shipping yards are located in all of the cities in the area.

Hampton Roads was a critical point of embarkation in both the Spanish-American War and World War I. Hundreds of thousands of troops embarked for Europe in the second of these conflicts, along with millions of tons of supplies. The port specialty in World War I was the shipping of horses, mules, and forage, and large corrals for the animals were erected near the docks.

The growth of the Hampton Roads Port began during the First World War and would continue dramatically through World War II. Airfields, specialty training camps for army personnel about to join the American Expeditionary Forces in Europe, and a huge naval training camp sprang up in the area in 1917 and 1918, along with warehouses and supply depots. The navy yard had remained active at Norfolk all these years, and private shipping interests were plentiful as well.

At the beginning of World War I, there was a dispute between the cities of Norfolk and Newport News over which community should house the port of embarkation headquarters. Both cities had fine facilities and were well positioned to house the command; and all of the communities in the region would ultimately house various components of the port; but the winner turned out to be Newport News because of its proximity to interior railroad lines. A similar conflict over placement of the headquarters arose in the spring of 1942, and once again Newport News was named port headquarters. The port commander took control of offices in the Chesapeake and Ohio Railway Company in May; but instead of the "Newport News Port of Embarkation," as the harbor had been designated during World War I, it became the "Hampton Roads Port of Embarkation" during the Second World War.

Despite their experiences in global conflict, nothing could have prepared regional resources for the onslaught of military and civilian personnel that arrived after war was declared in 1942. Employment opportunities in the defense industries brought people from all over the country to Hampton Roads looking for work. Shipbuilders and dry-dock workers were needed, stevedores and clerks. The workforce at the Newport News shipyards jumped from around 6,000 in 1939 to more than 31,000 in April 1943; during the same period at the navy yard in Norfolk, the number of workers escalated from 6,520 to 43,000. The number of military installations in the region jumped from ten in prewar years to twenty-six by war's end. So many construction workers were needed to keep pace with all of the building projects in the area that by the last half of 1942, 34,135 workers had been hired in the construction trades, while only 2,175 had been similarly employed before the war.

Population growth in the area, both civilian and military, was equally phenomenal. For the military, the numbers rose from 15,715 in 1940 to 158,024 in 1943. The civilian population jumped from around 390,000 before the war to 576,000 in 1943. In a matter of months, Hampton Roads had morphed from a manageable group of municipalities into the most congested and overwhelmed metropolitan region in the nation.

Finding housing instantly became a problem. Schools, hospitals, and public transportation were overcrowded. And despite the huge influx of population, there were war jobs that were still going unfilled in the fall of 1942. "Demand is far beyond supply in almost everything bearing upon life in a whirling, confused war town," said a writer in a profile of the city for the *American Mercury*.

There was also an explosion in crime. The city of Newport News saw an increase in arrests from 6,353 in 1939 to an astounding 38,377 by 1942; similarly, apprehensions in the city of Portsmouth jumped from around 5,500 to nearly 25,000. Perhaps not surprising, given the huge numbers of single young men who had come to the region, prostitution was the offense most increased by the war; other related problems like open operation of speakeasies, "nip joints," and gambling houses and numbers running also became prevalent.

Seamen and army personnel heading out for an evening on the town in Norfolk would head down to East Main Street, which, according to at least one account, held the most solid block of beer joints in the world. Jukeboxes played "Pass the Ammunition" and "Der Fuhrer's Face." Miss Rose La Rose, described as "a poor man's Gypsy Rose Lee," danced at the one burlesque joint in town.

The Hampton Roads area had long been in the business of entertaining rowdy sailors on leave from long weeks at sea. From Norfolk to Newport News, these were not cities given to deep blushing. But what happened with the onset of World War II was another matter. The local police were simply swamped by the situation, and even the institution of a large shore patrol, created by the navy in October 1942, did little to alleviate the basic problems. A massive raid of houses of ill repute in the second week of the month, encouraged by military authorities to scare soon-to-depart soldiers away from partaking in the Norfolk nightlife, was only partially effective.

The huge influx of army troops to be loaded onto the transports in early October only exacerbated problems. These 34,000 soldiers were supposed to have been quarantined from the temptations of Norfolk and environs during the process; in fact, thousands escaped the provisions intended to keep them in line. Public telephones near the wharves were disconnected and fences ringed the docks. Military police patrolled the railroads and bus depots, on the lookout for deserters. Though the troops had no idea where they were going, they were pretty certain that the war awaited them on the other end of the voyage, and they were not going to be denied a last fling in the haunts of Hampton Roads.

Of deep concern to local authorities was the fact that jails in the area were proving inadequate to the needs of the police. There were not nearly enough detention facilities, which prompted a revolving-door justice system, through which prostitutes were brought but then quickly released for lack of cells to put them in. Typical of the region's lockup facilities was the one in Portsmouth that consisted of five cells, each with two bunks. During the war, an average of fifty prisoners a day were crammed into these pens, segregated only by gender.

Even so, the Norfolk County Jail was the worst of the worst—so bad that it would be closed during the course of the war by the State of Virginia, which wrote in a report that of all of its jails, Norfolk's was the dirtiest and most corrupt. Money was not returned to prisoners; at least one prisoner was held for fifteen months without trial; and the Norfolk County Police were discovered to be holding occasional all-night orgies with the prostitutes confined in the jail.

A number of national publications sent reporters to the area, some to describe the rampant vice, others to reassure folks back home that despite all the rumors and stories surrounding the Hampton Roads area, things were not as bad as they seemed. In the former category, both the *American Mercury* and *Collier's* magazine reported on what the *Mercury* called "Our Worst War Town" in its headline. Both described as the nadir of the community "stockades" set up outside the city limits containing "girlie trailers," to which visitors were steered by local cabbies who would hang out by their cars smoking cigarettes as their fares were entertained inside. In contrast, the *Woman's Home Companion* reported on the more innocent activities available to the workers, including "dances, movies, sports, roller-skating, the USO, and the YMCA."

Stifling a sense of panic at the news that almost half of the *Contessa* crew was missing, Colonel Wilder tried to rationally assess the circumstances. The good word was that work on the ship, miraculously, would be finished by midnight. She would be out of dry dock and loading would begin as soon as she was moved to pier X. Two thousand cans of aviation fuel, each weighing four hundred pounds, were already drummed at Craney Island and awaited the *Contessa* in loading barges. An additional nine hundred tons of munitions were likewise ready to be stored in the vessel's holds.

The bad news was there were virtually no sailors to be found in this great harbor. The twenty-nine crew members missing from John's original group were either up in New York or out in Norfolk, likely enjoying the gyrations of Rose La Rose down on East Main Street. The just-departed task-force convoy had already sucked up every available hand in the area, and the War Shipping Administration, which Wilder had called soon after he heard the bad news about the crew from John, had no one available.

Captain John had given Wilder the name, number, and address of Standard Fruit's personnel man in New York, but when Wilder called up to the city, the Standard rep was extremely doubtful that any crew there could be contacted in time to sail from Hampton Roads in less than two days. He told Wilder that despite the problems in Virginia, he would have better luck searching for crew members in Hampton Roads than in New York, and he volunteered to fly down to help with the hunt.

Meanwhile, that Sunday morning Wilder entertained a string of calls from interested parties wanting to get progress reports on the *Contessa*. His immediate superior at the Hampton port, General Kilpatrick, checked in, as did the task force's Captain Johnson, who informed Wilder that he was sending the new armed guard commander, Lieutenant Leslie, to the port to see if he could be of any assistance in getting the ship out of port. Wilder neglected to inform Johnson of the missing crew, an oversight—or safeguard—that he would later regret.

At about 11:00 a.m., Wilder got a call from pier X. The stevedores were up in arms about loading the cargo. Safety rules prevented them from stowing both gasoline and munitions at the same time; one mishandled bomb would not simply blast a giant hole in the *Contessa*; it would obliterate the ship, pier X, and probably a chunk of Newport News, as well. The union insisted the gas and bombs be loaded separately. Once again Wilder hit the phones. It took twenty minutes of pleading and cajoling for Wilder to arrange for the navy to declare an emergency situation, which would allow for the contiguous loading.

The Standard Fruit agent from New York arrived and was joined by local Standard Fruit reps, two based in Newport News and one from Norfolk. They scratched their heads, checked their rosters, called other shipping agents, and tried to reach their missing sailors, but by the middle of the afternoon had located just one of the seamen, who would be arriving in the morning from New York.

Lieutenant Albert Leslie arrived too, to see what help he could supply, but, unfortunately, he didn't have twenty-nine seamen in tow, so there wasn't much he could do either.

At a little after 3:00 p.m., Johnson called, steaming. He'd just learned from Kilpatrick that twenty-nine men were missing from the *Contessa* crew. In his public notes, Wilder failed to supply the color of the conversation that followed, but the implication is that it was blue. When he was able to get a word in edgewise, the colonel gave Johnson an update on the search, and it appears that there was some discussion between the two about the possibility of the navy supplying the missing crew members. That hope was shot down an hour later when a lieutenant commander from the naval operating base in Norfolk called to say that no one was available.

The one bright spot in the hunt occurred when word arrived in Wilder's office that a navy tanker, the *Gloria,* had arrived in port and that recruits from it might be had the next morning. But by the end of the day on Sunday, the only additional seaman they could rely on was the *Contessa* crew member coming in from New York and a cadet recruited from the War Shipping Administration. There was some brief talk of "Shanghai-ing" sailors from the *Gloria* to serve on the voyage, but that seems to have been more late-in-the-day desperation than a real option. Sunday, the twenty-fifth, ended as it had begun: with the search for twenty-nine sailors for the *Contessa* still up in the air.

CHAPTER 24

Off to Sea

René Malevergne, traveling as Viktor Prechak, had arrived in Norfolk on the same evening as the *Contessa*, Thursday, October 22. He was immediately taken in a launch out in the harbor to the battleship *Texas*, the flagship for the northern branch of the Casablanca invasion. Its commander was Rear Admiral Monroe Kelly, to whom Malevergne was soon introduced. Afterward, Malevergne was taken to the transport *Susan B. Anthony,* where an upper deck cabin had been reserved solely for him. He was liking the way he was being treated by the Americans.

His first week in the States had been spent primarily in an army camp barracks about sixty miles from Washington. It housed officers in transit, many on their way, like him, to Hampton Roads. Malevergne told his diary that the atmosphere here was "frank and cordial" and that "the living is good." He was surprised to discover that morning reveille was delivered by means of a recording delivered over the camp loudspeaker, rather than by a genuine trumpet.

Much as he appreciated the hospitality shown to him in the camp, he was anxious to get on with his journey and was thankful to find himself flying down to Hampton Roads and then on to his berth on the *Susan B. Anthony.* Waking the morning after his arrival on board, he found himself eyeing the superb harbor that stretched around him and counting the impressive number of ships waiting to sail within. There were ten transports alone moored in his vicinity, along with the *Texas* and several destroyers. All would get under way shortly. By the end of the day, ten more transports would join them, along with an escorting cruiser and more destroyers.

Late in the morning, the *Anthony* began her voyage. Malevergne was shown to the wardroom, where he was excited to see a large map of

Morocco fixed to the bulkhead. He was even more thrilled to see big red arrows on the map pointing directly toward Casablanca and Mehdia. For weeks now, he had lived in a state of high excitement and suspense, feeling that he must be returning soon to Morocco—why else would he be here?—but never had he been told precisely where he was going. Now he could see with his own eyes that he was heading directly home. He told his diary that he wanted to "cry out: 'Friends of Morocco, who have waited so long for this day to arrive; Friends of France, who are still in prison: Your day is at hand. Each turn of the propeller brings us closer to you. The second front is on the way.' "

Malevergne held his tongue. He was already feeling a bit conspicuous on the ship because of his native language and the fact that he was the only person on the ship dressed in civilian clothes.

He waited for more answers about his mission, and on his second day on the *Anthony*, they came. Malevergne was introduced to Lieutenant Colonel Jack Toffey of the Third Battalion, Sixtieth Regimental Combat Unit. Toffey gave the Frenchman his first concrete sense of what lay ahead in the operation. There would be three large attacks on Morocco as a whole: at Mehdia, Casablanca, and Safi. Mehdia itself was to be invaded in three columns; the northernmost would be above the jetty marking the entrance to the River Sebou. The southern column was to land at Lac Sidi Boughaba, near the highway between Rabat and Port Lyautey. The central attack would be aimed at Mehdia Beach and was expected to face the fiercest resistance.

While the battle in the center was engaged, the two flanking forces were to sweep around the conflict and head for the airfield and Port Lyautey. Just what Malevergne's role in the invasion would be remained, for the time being, a mystery to him. It was easy to assume that his piloting skills were wanted, but specifics were not yet made available to him.

At this point, it hardly seemed to matter. He was going home in the company of a great American army. Soon French Morocco would be free once again.

★   ★   ★

If Malevergne had been able to linger a little while longer on the *Texas* after he'd first arrived at Hampton Roads, he surely would have run across a young member of the small press corps that was stationed on the battleship, the United Press correspondent Walter Cronkite, who had been give the Operation Torch assignment by the newspaper syndicate. Cronkite perhaps could have used Malevergne's limited English-language skills to help him translate some of the conversation of his bunkmates. These were a group of radio broadcasters working with the Office of War Information, the recently formed arm of the federal government assigned to disseminate news of the conflict to the free world. The broadcasters were a trio of upper-crust New Yorkers with European roots who practiced their French in the shared cabin, while wearing "fancy civilian pajamas," according to Cronkite. "They were to operate something called 'Clandestine Radio Maroc,'" he would later write. "Their sole function was to broadcast propaganda intended to persuade the army of France's puppet government to desert Hitler and come over to the Allied side."

Cronkite had just completed an assignment covering convoy shipping in the North Atlantic. Prior to his first trip between New York and London, he'd gone to the U.S. Navy offices in Manhattan to get credentials and a correspondent's uniform. At the time, in those first few months of the war, according to Cronkite, the U.S. military "was as unprepared for handling the requirements of the press as it was for meeting the enemy." He was given a green armband with a large letter "C," for correspondent, to be worn on his left arm. The trouble was that soon after donning the uniform and brassard, he felt that something in his outfit was inhibiting conversation with the officers and seamen he was encountering on the trip. The language they used seemed too formal; it lacked the usual color and profanity of military personnel. "The officers in the wardroom that evening seemed to me particularly dull," wrote Cronkite. It was only after being asked one too many times about his religious affiliation ("A sort of jackass Episcopalian," he told one questioner) that it dawned on him that the "C" on his arm was suggesting to everyone who saw him that he was a chaplain.

The confusion was fairly well cleared up by the time Cronkite joined the convoy on its way to North Africa. Though the contingent of reporters on board the *Texas* was small, army and navy public relations staff, along with Clandestine Radio Maroc, had substantially increased the presence of communications personnel in the war, helping to alleviate confusion about who was and who was not a correspondent.

Cronkite settled into his cabin for the voyage, listening to the French chitchat around him. As the *Texas* sailed out of the harbor and into the open sea beyond, the first big wave that hit the ship sent water cascading through a hatch left open above their quarters. Cronkite watched with some bemusement as the aristocratic radio team, soaked and assuming the *Texas* was swamped, raced "halfway across the wardroom to the boats" wearing their fancy civilian pajamas. It was only after they saw the totally calm officers in the wardroom that they realized "all was normal, with no indication that the *Texas* was soon to sink."

On the nearby flagship *Augusta,* George Patton was already beginning to acclimate himself to the voyage. He found the mess on the ship to be excellent and cautioned himself about eating too much during the two-week voyage. Someone had given him a rowing machine so that he could exercise while on board. For reading material, he'd packed the Koran, in order to get a better sense of Moroccan culture, which he'd soon be experiencing for the first time.

The *Augusta* left the harbor at 8:10 on Saturday, the twenty-fourth. Patton's central part of the task force, the largest contingent in the convoy, would sail at a slight northeasterly angle, as if heading for England. The southern and northern groups would head toward Bermuda, on a southeasterly course. A rumor had been purposely spread that they would be heading for Haiti to perform maneuvers in the Caribbean. A third contingent, a covering group composed of the battleship *Massachusetts,* two cruisers, and four destroyers, had sailed from Casco Bay in Maine to the southeast on the twentieth. When all elements of the convoy finally rendezvoused out in the Atlantic on the twenty-sixth, there would be more than one hundred ships steaming toward North Africa.

Aboard the *August* along with Patton was the task force's naval commander, Admiral Hewitt, to whom Patton was finally warming. He told his diary that the admiral "impresses me better" each day.

In the sky above Hampton Roads, two silver blimps, serving as spotters for the vessels below, mirrored the panoply as it sailed slowly and gracefully out through the channel to the ocean.

CHAPTER 25

Uncle Sam Wants You

N ow two days behind the rest of the ships but repaired and fully loaded, the *Contessa* was buttoned up and ready to go the morning of the twenty-sixth. Unfortunately, she still lacked a full crew. With the addition of the one sailor from New York, fourteen crewmen were needed in the engineering department and fourteen needed as deckhands and in the steward's group.

Another hand arrived by way of the War Shipping Administration—an intern from the Merchant Marine Academy; and the *Gloria,* that tanker newly arrived to Hampton Roads, provided some relief in the engineering department. Seven of its crew members, including an engineer and a third officer, agreed to sail with the ship in the convoy. But even this addition was problematic to poor Wilder. Because it was a merchant ship whose crew would be paid at a higher rate than they, the *Gloria* crew members wanted a bonus for sailing with the *Contessa,* and the navy was slow to grant the request. In desperation, Wilder agreed to pay the extra funds without having authorization from the U.S. Navy. By this time, no doubt, he was ready to pay the wages out of his own pocket if it meant getting this ship to sea.

Meanwhile, the calls kept coming. General Gross wanted to know if the *Contessa* had yet sailed. Still waiting on a crew, Wilder told him. Colonel Franklin called with the same question. He got the same answer.

Captain John phoned to let Wilder know that he had one more recruit in hand: his own brother-in-law, the salesman Bill Sigsworth, had agreed to sail with the *Contessa* as a part of the steward's department. According to family members, Bill Sigsworth had always wanted to work at sea but had never had the chance. Well, here it was, the opportunity to sail on a memorable first voyage.

By midmorning, Wilder was joined in his office by Lieutenant Leslie, the new "cocaptain" from the armed guard. Then came four representatives of the Standard Fruit Company: Hall and Ramizel from New York and Weiss and Koontz from Hampton Roads. The irony of the situation was obvious to all of them. Here they were in one of the great shipping capitals of the United States—one of the great shipping capitals of the world—and yet they couldn't find eighteen sailors to fill out the roster of an old merchant ship wanting to sail across the Atlantic.

Whether it was a solution that had been bandied about earlier or came in a flash Wilder does not say, but out of this gathering finally came the answer to their dilemma. In his notes, Wilder does not give the name of the person who said it first but the resolution seems to have been quickly agreed upon: *Why don't we fill out the crew with sailors from the Norfolk County Jail?*

It was, after all, Monday morning in Hampton Roads. The jail was no doubt bursting with weekend drunks and truants. Among the crowds that had been boozing and brawling in the juke joints down on East Main Street and taking cabs out to the stockades to hook up with the ladies in the trailers would certainly be enough qualified seamen to fill out the crew of the *Contessa*. Surely the Norfolk County Jail and the courthouses would have no problem disposing of a few of their overwhelming number of cases if it meant lessening overcrowded dockets and providing assistance to the recently departed convoy.

There was not time for second-guessing the idea; no time for wondering what might go wrong if a group of tipplers from the jailhouse were drafted into this mission. Wilder and company simply proceeded. The county sheriff and a judge needed to be contacted, which was quickly done through the offices of the port. By two fifteen in the afternoon, Ramizel of Standard Fruit was waiting down on East Main Street in Newport News to do a quick survey of fifty inmates hauled from the jail for inspection. Of these he chose eighteen, who agreed to sail with the *Contessa*. They were immediately driven to a navy launch and, in the midst of a stinging sleet storm, were whisked out into the harbor where the *Contessa* was preparing to sail.

A few weeks after the events of late October, one of Lieutenant Leslie's hometown newspapers in Pittsburgh would describe those who boarded the *Contessa* as a "bedraggled crew [who] you'd think were the scum of the earth." But others, including Wilder and the Standard Fruit Company people, understood that most of the prisoners rounded up to fill out the crew "were good seamen" who had been where they were "because most of them had done too good a job of celebrating the end of a hazardous trip."

Among those who joined the crew from the jail were seamen who had worked on Standard Fruit Company ships in the past. Perhaps they had already contacted the Standard Fruit Company reps in Wilder's office to let them know their whereabouts. Perhaps this helped precipitate the solution to the dilemma on that Monday morning. These were a quartet of Arabs—Ahmed Ali, Ali Salik, Ahmed Mohammed, and Said Mohammed—British nationals, originally from ports around the Gulf of Aden, who were brought on board to work as firemen in the ship's engine department. Ahmed Mohammed had served under Captain John on the *Amapala,* while Ahmed Ali had served before on the *Contessa,* prior to John's service as her master.

The inmates also included a trio of Portuguese sailors and a Brazilian who were hired on as able seamen. An Australian named Henry Drummond came on board as a cook's helper. A couple of young Irish sailors were hired as utility seamen, as were a teenaged Finn named John Sutinen and a seventeen-year-old American boy named John Riccio. A handful of others filled out slots as ABs and utility workers.

Specifically what had caused these sailors to wind up in the Norfolk County Jail was left unrecorded but can be easily imagined. None of them assumed a position of status in the command of the *Contessa,* but almost all fit easily into the realm of a merchant ship.

Only four of the ex-inmates were U.S. citizens, and, like the regular crew on the *Contessa,* the majority were well into their thirties and forties. Most knew the cut of a merchant vessel from stem to gudgeon. All were willing to cross the ocean in a banana boat on a "special mission," rather than spend another night in the Norfolk County Jail. But it was only when they climbed on board the *Contessa* that these newcomers learned that they were making a lone run across the Atlantic, outside the protective circle of the gigantic convoy that was already three days ahead of them, and carrying a cargo of bombs and gasoline.

Though Leslie had given his blessing to the idea of hiring this group from the·jail, the U.S. Navy's lack of trust in both the *Contessa* and her regular crew had been exhibited earlier in the orders given to the armed guard commander when he was assigned to the ship. The lieutenant was to make sure the ship's mission was successfully completed "whatever the attitude or actions of her crew might be—and to use [his] judgment as to how best accomplish that should the necessity of my taking over arise." Now added to a mix that the U.S. Navy was inclined to distrust anyway was a gang composed largely of foreign boozehounds and reprobates.

Climbing on board from the launch in the cold, wet sleet, their duffel bags slung over their shoulders, to join the rest of the seamen on board the *Contessa,* the newcomers no doubt felt some sidelong glances. But this was already a heterogeneous lot. Even for a merchant ship, it was a remarkable mix of ethnicities, experience levels, and races. Twenty-six separate nationalities were represented in all. Even the flag the *Contessa* flew—still the Honduran flag of her registry—suggested her mongrel status.

Many, if not most, of the crew were doubtless dedicated to the Allied causes they were serving, but only the navy guard and its officers had actually enlisted in the war effort. The fact that this particular ship had been given a special function and crucial assignment by the commander of the Moroccan invasion, George Patton himself, might have filled some with a sense of pride had they known of that fact. It might have struck others as odd and haphazard, and it's easy to imagine a stray negative thought crossing some minds: *God help us all if this banana boat has been handed a vital role in the first action of America's war in Europe.*

What was planned for the *Contessa* on the other side of the ocean was a mystery to everyone on board except Leslie. All the crew knew for certain was that they were on this voyage together, and if a German U-boat should happen upon them while they were carrying their load, the *Contessa* would first light up the sky and next disappear from the face of the earth.

At ten thirty on Monday, October 26, fully crewed, patched, and loaded, the *Contessa* finally headed out of Hampton Roads with Captain William John at the helm and Lieutenant Albert Leslie at his side. They were slightly delayed at the capes that marked the entrance to the ocean—a pilot was needed to guide them through the minefield that marked the entrance to the bay. After dropping him off, they were soon on their way after the convoy.

CHAPTER 26

Convoy

The Western Task Force, now joined as a vast fleet sailing across the Atlantic from west to east, took its initial tack toward Bermuda to indicate to anyone who might be shadowing that it was likely headed for the United Kingdom. Soon after the rendezvous, however, the convoy took a mighty swing toward the southeast, on a course farther down the African coast than Morocco. The intention here was to suggest a destination of Dakar, which many in the German military considered to be the most likely point of attack if the Americans were going to invade North Africa.

The *Augusta*, with Patton and Admiral Hewitt aboard, was screened by a covey of destroyers. In nine columns of five lines behind the flagship and her consorts were thirty-five transports, with additional cargo vessels and tankers, each separated by about a thousand yards of ocean. Protecting these ships on the flanks were the battleships *Texas* and *New York*. Twelve miles behind this main body of the convoy sailed the air group: one aircraft carrier, the *Ranger,* and four escort carriers—the oil tankers that had been modified to allow them to carry planes that could be launched or catapulted, but not landed. Accompanying this group were a cruiser and nine destroyers. Forty more destroyers served as anti-submarine vessels cruising in both an inner and an outer circle around the convoy. Above it all, planes from the *Ranger* buzzed around the ships, also watching for submarines or any other stray ships that might wander into the group. In all, the convoy stretched over the ocean in an area of almost six hundred square miles.

If Patton's force, having just finished its first amphibious landing practice back at Solomons Island, was as green as grass, Hewitt's U.S. Navy crew was equally fresh to the ocean. On two ships mentioned by Samuel Morison, the escort carrier *Sangmaon* and the cruiser *Brooklyn,* fully half of the "bluejackets" were experiencing their first voyages. Many, if not most, of the officers were reservists who hadn't been to sea in years. Perhaps not surprising, under the circumstances, the assembled ships became "floating school[s] of amphibious operations. On the capital ships and destroyers, officers and chief petty officers studied the parts they had to play, and on board the transports and carriers there were endless lectures, discussions and rehearsals for all hands. Large silhouettes of the Moroccan coast were constructed from contour maps and from data furnished by the Amphibious Force staff; pictures and models of enemy ships and aircraft were studied; the air pilots were so well indoctrinated in Moroccan geography that by the time they arrived they could fly straight to their designated targets."

The soldiers crammed into the transports were likewise encouraged to prepare for battle. Training programs were prescribed, according to Truscott, so that every available moment during the voyage should be "devoted to an intensive training to the end that all men of the command would be conditioned mentally and physically to achieve victory regardless of hostile resistance or privation." The problem was that in ships where every square inch that wasn't occupied by a soldier or a sailor was crammed with the stuff of battle, it was damned hard to find space to exercise or train. As Truscott also wrote, "space is the soldier's medium," and it was at a premium on the ships of the Western Task Force.

Individual units and soldiers found creative ways to train. Patton's friend tank commander Harry Semmes wrote of an officer who felt a need to test the bazookas on board—these were the new rocket-launching weaponry that had been loaded on the transports separately from their operating instructions. After finally marrying the launchers to their directions, the commander proceeded to assemble some troops to fire practice rounds into the crests of waves from the decks of his ship.

On the *Henry T. Allen,* Nick Craw—the tough-guy colonel of Greek descent who'd made a name for himself duking it out with an Italian lieutenant in Athens prior to the U.S. entry into the war—organized two groups of air-maintenance workers to serve as infantry reserve in the invasion. Craw, who was the Army Air Force liaison to Truscott's command, decided that because his personnel weren't going to be busy until the Port Lyautey field was taken and humming with American P-40s, they ought to be armed, organized, and useful to Truscott should they be needed in the assault on the port.

On the *Susan B. Anthony,* René Malevergne tracked the progress of the ship, noting her crossing of the gulf stream by the seaweed that marked the flow and the fact that the ship was now experiencing shirt-sleeve weather. He found a quartet of French-speaking American lieutenants on board and was happy to join in conversations in his native tongue. One of the soldiers, Jacques Bartach, had an artistic bent and started to paint a portrait of Malevergne on the crossing. Bartach also surprised and delighted Malevergne by his ability to quote Racine and Corneille.

Malevergne's conversations with Colonel Jack Toffey continued as well. Perhaps trying to allay the Frenchman's fears, Toffey told Malevergne that the American army "shall do everything possible to avoid bloodshed. We shall not be the first to fire. But I must tell you also that we have no plans for reembarkation." Toffey needn't have worried about Malevergne's sensitivity to what was about to happen in Morocco. He understood, perhaps better than the Americans themselves, what lay ahead. "Most of these soldiers do not understand that in order to save the French it will be necessary to engage in a cruel and stupid war against them," he wrote in his diary.

Malevergne studied the maps of the region around Port Lyautey that were on board the *Susan B. Anthony* and added detail about the terrain. Toffey thought his "G-2 information was invaluable." Malevergne worried over certain plans that he became privy to while on board. He learned, for instance, that the Americans were hoping to land artillery to the north of the jetty marking the entrance to the River Sebou. Malevergne knew that landscape to be extremely sandy and laden with dunes that would make a crossing difficult. But he was told the amphibious force had the means necessary to haul even the heaviest guns over the terrain, so he simply noted his reservations.

A week into the trip across the Atlantic, General Truscott came aboard the *Susan B. Anthony* for a briefing, and Malevergne was invited to attend. Afterward, Truscott and Toffey spoke with Malevergne in private and for the first time described his mission in detail. When they reached Mehdia Malevergne would embark on a destroyer whose job would be to force open the estuary and steam upriver. At the Port Lyautey airfield, the ship would land a contingent of commandos, who would quickly subdue the French Moroccan force there and open the airfield to American air traffic. It would be Malevergne's job to pilot the destroyer to its destination.

Did Malevergne have any objections to this plan? No, he told the general and Toffey. There was, however, one thing that bothered him. "My civilian clothing," he told them, "it does not fit this type of operation." Immediately, Truscott gave the order to equip Malevergne with the uniform of a first lieutenant. "We hope that you will do it honor," the general told him as he left.

It was Toffey, not Malevergne or Truscott, who later noted that by wearing the uniform of the United States Army, the Frenchman was subjecting himself to the possibility of being executed as a spy, should he be captured on his mission.

Over on the *Augusta,* George Patton worried "that I should be doing something but there is nothing to do." His relationship with Hewitt continued to improve, and he cracked open the Koran and read sections including "Three Harbors," "The Raft," and "The Sun is my Undoing," which he describes in his diary as "pretty sticky."

He worked the rowing machine some and jogged in place at the dresser in his cabin—three hundred steps—and started to worry that he might not get in a fight at all. Messages from intelligence sources had been arriving that intimated that the French army and air force would not put up a fight. He wrote to Beatrice that he hoped they would, "for it would sort of pull the cork of the men—all steamed up to fight and not have to." He admitted that "also it would be better for me to have a battle," which was no doubt an unnecessary postscript for his wife.

Two days out of Hampton Roads and about halfway between Bermuda and Nova Scotia, a strong wind blew up from the southwest, pounding the ships in the northern group of the task force as they headed west to east across the ocean. Among those getting rocked were the old four-piper destroyer, the *Dallas,* and René Malevergne's *Susan B. Anthony,* which were tossed by the swells pounding against the starboard stern. "Only the *'Texas'* does not budge," Malevergne recorded in his diary. "She is like a rock, and sheds the swells that break upon her."

By midmorning, the total convoy began forming. First came the group from Maine, led by the second battleship in the armada, the *Massachusetts*; soon after came the southern group from the task force, sailing from the southwest in the wake of the *Texas* and her entourage. George Patton and Admiral Kent Hewitt's central group would round out the convoy the following morning, painting an impressive panorama across the horizon. On board the transport *Allen,* trailing just behind the *Texas,* General Lucian Truscott was moved by the sight of the gathering ships.

"A great convoy at sea is a magnificent sight," he would later write. "One thinks of stately swans gliding across some park lagoon, or of waterfowl in precise formation winging their way against leaden skies, or of a great herd of cattle undulating across western plains under watchful eyes of guardian cowboys. But none of these matches the grandeur of a convoy at sea in war time. Forward of us was the battleship *Texas,* broad of beam, bristling with guns, a symbol of power. We followed at a distance of perhaps half a mile. Behind us spaced at similar distances followed other transports. Off to the right, or starboard, there was a similar column; beyond it another, another, and still another. . . . To the rear as far as we could see the formation extended—transports, cargo ships, aircraft carriers, tankers—all with white waves curling back beneath the bows, and a shimmering wake trailing out behind. And everywhere the tossing of signal flags and the incessant blinking of signal lamps as the ships communicated one with another. Now and again far out across the tossing blue waves polka-dotted with white caps, one caught glimpses of the sleek destroyers speeding along like outriders protecting a moving herd. No sound but that of wind and waves and the faint hum of driving motors. No smoke by day, no lights at night, and the faintest indication of either brought a quick reprimand from watchful eyes."

By and large, the two services were joined as one for the crossing, but each branch obviously had its own worries. Of deep concern to the Navy was the difficulty of navigating some three thousand miles across the ocean, not just to reach three specific points on the long and twisting coastline of continental Africa but to find these areas at a scheduled hour in the dark of an early morning. And, of course, that was to say nothing of the fickleness of the weather and the difficulties of negotiating the subsequent embarkation and landing of the craft carrying Patton's army to the shores of Morocco; nor did the two services need to be reminded, once again, that these amphibious landings had been practiced by army and navy together for the first time just weeks earlier.

There was also the fear throughout the voyage not only of discovery but of attack. Karl Doenitz's wolf packs were continuing to wreak havoc among the merchant convoys plying the Atlantic from the Murmansk run down to the shores of South America. Truscott, for one, was thinking of how the "grim possibility" of "the loss of a transport with an assault battalion" would disrupt the plans for the whole invasion. By his calculations, if one battalion were lost, the attack would need to be seriously revised, but it could go on. If two were lost, "the plan would not be practicable."

Doenitz had actually devised the strategy for attacking a convoy of this size at the very end of World War I, when he realized that by sending

U-boats in packs "the more favourable would become the opportunities to each individual attacker." While individual submarines could and did cause much damage at the advent of World War I, when the convoy system was put in place in 1917, "the oceans at once became bare and empty; for long periods at a time the U-boats operating individually, would see nothing at all; and then suddenly up would loom a huge concourse of ships, thirty or fifty or more of them, surrounded by a strong escort of warships of all types."

A pack of submarines, however, strung out over a span of ocean and working in concert once a convoy was located, could wreak maximum havoc on Allied shipping. "In the darkness of the night sudden violent explosions and sinking ships cause such confusion that the escorting destroyers find their liberty of action impeded and are themselves compelled by the accumulation of events to split up. . . . Against the massed ships of a convoy, then, obviously the only right course is to engage them with every available U-boat simultaneously."

The realization that this was the best strategy for future U-boat campaigns at sea came at a particularly disheartening moment for Doenitz. It was the second-to-last month of the war. His submarine was supposed to have been joined in the Mediterranean by another German U-boat that wound up never appearing. When Doenitz came across a British destroyer that he knew to be an "outrider" for a convoy, he began to skulk after it. But "soon more shadows loomed up in the darkness, first more destroyers and escort vessels, and finally the great solid silhouettes of the merchantmen themselves." He tried to slip all the way through the convoy to attack the leading ship on the outside column and actually struck one of the merchant vessels with a torpedo. But a power failure on board the U-boat in the midst of a dive sent the vessel into a tailspin. His only means of recovery was to surface as quickly as he could, and when he did, Doenitz found himself in the middle of the convoy. Sirens howled around him and ships bore down from all sides with guns blasting. His submarine was soon hit and started taking on water. Doenitz gave the order to abandon ship. He and his men were left floating in their life jackets as the British convoy continued on its journey, leaving one ship, the *Snapdragon*, to pick up the German seamen left behind.

Doenitz was pulled from the ocean like a fish. Though he had no particular recollection of his saviors, there was a young lieutenant commander named William John on the *Snapdragon* who would remember him for years to come.

CHAPTER 27

Crossing

Soon after the *Contessa* took to the sea, a radio message was sent out across the ocean from Norfolk: "*Contessa* flying Honduran flag departed. 2030 October twenty-sixth unescorted. Mixed crew. Clearance for Gibraltar. Naval guard. Lieutenant Leslie in charge. Direct Route. Speed of advance 14.5 knots."

From Gibraltar a couple of days later came a curious response: "What is cargo ship mentioned? Nothing in plans indicate she is expected by British at Port given. They now inquire."

Quickly the operators in Norfolk sent a reply: "[*Contessa*] departure delayed. Cargo for task group. Ship to join en route. Lieutenant Leslie directed to change destination after departure."

Despite the clarification, it was evident that after all the attention given her by the command of the Western Task Force in Norfolk before she sailed, the *Contessa* was now on her own.

One hundred ships stretched twenty by thirty miles across the ocean leave an obvious memory of themselves. Oil slicks and floating garbage mark the trail for any vessel passing in a convoy's wake. It was a good and bad thing for the *Contessa* that her more direct course across the ocean meant that she wasn't traveling precisely in the path of the task force. Bad because she was on her own, which made her easy pickings for any U-boat that happened by. Good because the convoy was more likely to attract the attention of a pack of submarines.

When he had first been given his assignment back in Hampton Roads before the ship set sail, Lieutenant Leslie had busied himself accumulating and studying the intelligence that he would need for the mission, including sortie and communication plans. In the chaos of the departure, ,

Leslie was not fully briefed on some of the finer points of his mission, but the knowledge of these holes was yet to be discovered.

For now, however, Leslie kept the U.S. Navy orders for the ship to himself. In the meantime, he directed Captain John to set a course to a point abreast of the Azores, suggesting, as the radio messaging going back and forth between Virginia and Gibraltar indicated, that the *Contessa* was heading toward the Pillars of Hercules. Though John remained in the dark about their ultimate mission, he was enough of a military man to take his orders without question. What others on board speculated about their path is unknown.

The amount of cargo stored in the *Contessa*'s holds was calibrated to afford her a draft of seventeen feet, six inches, which was the estimated clearance that she would have entering the River Sebou. The gasoline and munitions stored below provided the *Contessa* a steadying load, and her freshly tightened rivets and welded seams revealed no leaks as she set out at a daytime clip that would average more than fifteen knots.

The weather was cloudless for the first several days of the voyage, which calmed crew jitters to a degree. During daylight hours, the ship assumed a zigzag course across the ocean, which was standard procedure in U-boat territory. Almost immediately, however, a number of false alarms, prompted by phantom submarine sightings, set sirens ringing on the *Contessa*. Nerves were still wired despite the clear skies.

Leslie set up a radio watch schedule using two operators whom he'd brought along from the armed guard unit, along with two commercial operators who were already part of the *Contessa* crew. The dozen remaining members of the guard crew were placed on rotating watches at their gun stations, while Leslie, Lieutenant Cato, and an ensign assigned to the trip took turns on the bridge in shifts of four hours on, eight hours off.

Whether or not Leslie made any indication to his unit that they should keep a special eye on the behavior of the Norfolk inmates is unrecorded. In fact, Leslie himself was as unknown to the company as they were to him. There was acquainting to do there as well.

Ambrose Schaffer, a signalman, enlisted in the U.S. Navy and got assigned to this armed guard unit when he was ordered to report to the *Contessa* for its second voyage to England in September 1942. An up-and-coming young welterweight boxer from Norwalk, Ohio, prior to the war, Schaffer was headlining a fight card in a local auditorium along with his younger brother, Herb, on a dreary April Fools' Day in 1935, when their father, Harry Schaffer, watching in the stands, keeled over from a heart attack. Ambrose, who fought under the name "Kid" Schaffer, wasn't told about the coronary until after the fight. The next day his father died in the hospital, and Kid Schaffer, who won the bout, went on with his boxing career. They were tough times; he was a tough kid. Through the rest of the decade, Schaffer established a solid 8–1 record with four knockouts, but he and Herb, who would eventually fight under the name "Marine" Schaffer, in honor of the path of service he would take in the Second World War, both found their careers put on hold by the start of the war.

Along with the man who commanded the fourteen-member guard contingent on the *Contessa,* thirty-five-year-old Lieutenant j.g. William Cato, Schaffer was the old-timer in the guard crew at the ripe old age of twenty-seven. He was also one of the few midwesterners.

There were a handful of guys from Jersey, including Patsy Lambusta of Newark and Paul Manganaro, a seventeen-year-old kid born and raised in Glassboro and nicknamed "Slick."

Wally Mason of Quincy, Massachusetts, had spent his first year out of high school working for the Civilian Conservation Corps before he signed up with the U.S. Navy in May. A good-looking, happy-go-lucky kid, Mason had to creep up on tiptoes to make the minimum height requirement for service. He was a gunner's mate.

So was Hazelton Gilchrest McLaughlin—"Hank" or "Hakie" to his friends (after the breed of fish that was so prevalent in the waters off the Maine coast). McLaughlin was born and raised not far from Bar Harbor. He had uncles who were lobstermen, and Hakie had spent some time on the sea with them. Prior to enlisting, however, he'd graduated from the North Yarmouth Academy, where he'd learned the machinist's trade.

Bill Pottiger came from a small town in Michigan; Adolph Krol was another of the Jersey guys, being from Camden; seventeen-year-old Harman Thomas, along with Lieutenant Cato, was a Virginian.

There were four teenagers in the group, four twenty-year-olds, and four more who were less than twenty-five years old. Aside from Cato and a couple of the East Coast boys, including McLaughlin, what they knew about the sea was not much. Like so many of the American naval forces heading to war that fall, they were as green as algae and offered a stark contrast to the merchant crew who had sailed with Captain William John out of New Orleans.

Like John and Leslie, the officers on board the *Contessa* were experienced hands of a similar age to the cocaptains. Chief engineer John Henry Langdon was a naturalized citizen of the United States, born in Plymouth, England. He'd worked with Standard Fruit for a number of years, serving on the *Gatun* and the *Ceiba*, as well as the *Contessa*. Like John, he was approaching his fiftieth birthday.

The second engineer was a native of Poland, Arthur Baumgart, who, like Langdon, was now a naturalized citizen of the United States and lived in New Orleans. He had sailed for Standard Fruit for more than twenty years and had served under John on the *Amapala* through the late 1930s.

The chief mate was a native of Italy, Alexander Vallerino. Like Langdon and Baumgart (and carpenter Harry Haylock and steward Mario Violini), he had acquired U.S. citizenship. Fifty-two years old that fall, he'd shipped with Standard Fruit for a number of years, but these—the first and second voyages of the *Contessa* to England in August and September and now this trip to Africa—were his first journeys with John.

Haylock and Violini, by contrast, had served with the captain for many years, on both the *Amapala* and the *Contessa*. Haylock was born in Honduras in 1894; Violini was baptized in Italy half a dozen years later. Violini had dark, hooded eyes and a prominent nose. He was just five foot four and 130 pounds when soaking wet, wore striped scoop-necked T-shirts in the style of a Mediterranean sailor, and was nicknamed "The Unsinkable" for his fervent belief that his faith would see him through any troubles that might befall any ship on which he sailed. He made his home in New York, while Haylock was based out of New Orleans.

A Norwegian sailor, Jan Norberg, was the second officer on the *Contessa*, and a Swede, Ture Jansen, was an able seaman who had been promoted to quartermaster for this voyage, as the *Contessa*'s original quartermaster, Eden Wood, was one of the seamen who had left the ship in Norfolk.

The chief radio officer was Alfred Turner, one of just a handful of native-born Americans in the crew and a former roommate of Haylock's in New Orleans.

Bill Sigsworth, John's brother-in-law, had been hired as part of the steward's department under the occupation of "writer"—a nontypical post on a merchant ship. In Sigsworth's case, it was probably akin to the position of purser—he helped with and kept track of the ship's administration for the captain. Sigsworth was one of the tallest men aboard and lanky: at six feet two inches, he carried just 150 pounds. Like his brother-in-law, he wore a dapper mustache and swept-back hair. He'd always wanted to go to sea and had done so for the first time as a seventeen-year-old in 1929, when he escorted his parents from Wales to New Orleans. There the Sigsworth family took up residence with Captain John, his wife, Bess, and their two children in a home off Charles Street. Circumstances had never allowed Bill Sigsworth his wish of getting back on the ocean. Until his voyage on the *Contessa*, he had worked in New Orleans for a lumber company, appraising and reclaiming the wood, mainly cypress, from old homes that were being torn down in the city.

He made good company for John, as did Leslie. The latter two shared many hours on the bridge with no apparent difficulties between them concerning the divided leadership. Both had spent many years at sea, both had served in the First World War, and both were accustomed to and respectful of command. John accepted that the U.S. Navy was in charge of the direction of this ship and her mission; Leslie understood that John knew the *Contessa* better than anyone else. Despite his twenty-some years in New Orleans, not only did Captain John keep his Welsh accent, but "bloody" was his most frequent adjective when he was irritated. They both liked early-morning hours. John liked his Winston cigarettes and tea. Like everyone else on this ship, they were bound together in a mission that was hardly of their own making, but one that they were now pledged to carry out.

The weather stayed fine for a full week out of Hampton Roads, and the *Contessa* made good time in her crossing, continuing to average above fifteen knots during daytime steaming and close to fifteen under the light of the moon. She was a full twenty-four hours ahead of her schedule as she neared the Azores. The submarine jitters continued, but no genuine sightings occurred. Still, tensions on the voyage began to rise as the *Contessa* neared the far side of the Atlantic. Here were the waters leading toward the Mediterranean and the coast of Africa; here they were nearing the convoy itself; and the prospects of bumping into U-boats were growing. Leslie ordered a series of test firings of the weaponry on board.

Leslie soon became concerned, too, about a piece of intelligence that had not been given to him in all of the material that he'd reviewed before climbing aboard the *Contessa*. It turned out that the ship had not been provided with an identification code, nor had he been given challenge and reply signals. It also lacked the proper radio frequencies to hear command communications. In other words, aside from its lack of physical contact with the convoy, the *Contessa* had no signal contact either. It was doubly isolated, and few commanders attached to the invasion force even knew of its existence. It also continued to fly the Honduran flag of its national registry. All of which made it an odd duck.

The boxer Kid Schaffer, along with Harman Thomas and Bill Pottiger, wore the crossed semaphore flags of signalmen in Leslie's armed guard unit. In addition to lookout duties, signalmen were responsible for transmitting, receiving, encoding, decoding, and distributing messages obtained via the visual transmission systems of flag semaphore, visual Morse code, and flag-hoist signaling. Leslie called this group together to give them their orders. If challenged, in addition to raising the Honduran flag they were to signal the ship's international call letters, as well as the position the *Contessa* had been originally assigned to (but had been unable to assume) in the convoy. They were also to signal the code "blind mice"—a prearranged message within the navy meaning, "I have been unable to complete my mission." He might have also added, "And then cross your fingers," to these instructions.

Ten days into the ship's voyage, a plane coming from the northeast emerged from the sky above and did a slow circle overhead. As it neared, watchers could tell it was a Sunderland, a large British float plane, flying, no doubt, out of Gibraltar. The Sunderlands, manufactured in the city of the same name in England, were originally used as long-distance rescue planes to aid in picking up the crews of ships that had been attacked by Nazi U-boats. As the war progressed, they were given fighting capabilities as well and armed with a pair of nose-turret guns and depth charges. In other words, the Sunderland circling above was a potentially dangerous adversary, if it had no clue what was the intention of the *Contessa*. Leslie ordered his signalmen to hang the ship's "laundry" but the Sunderland continued to circle above. For two tense hours, this pas de deux continued, until finally the plane flew off, presumably convinced the ship was harmless.

Captain John had sounded almost eager to run solo across the ocean a few days earlier, on that wild Saturday when he first learned from Colonel Wilder that he'd have to immediately return to sea. He'd doubtless grown disenchanted with the congestion and snail's pace of convoy travel that he'd experienced on the *Contessa*'s two transport trips to England that summer and fall. Now, as the ship neared its destination off the Azores and the prospect mounted of increased interest from German U-boats, as well as friendly yet dangerous craft who had no idea who they were, the confines of a destroyer escort seemed as snug as a safe harbor.

CHAPTER 28

"Je m'engage et puis je vois"

As October came to a close and the date of the invasion of North Africa neared, the Western Task Force continued its zigzagging course across the Atlantic ahead of the *Contessa*, first in a generally southeast direction, heading vaguely toward Dakar; then, after pausing midway across the sea for refueling, taking its zigs and zags in a more northeasterly course toward Gibraltar, still with the object of confusing any observers about where exactly it was heading.

Allied intelligence had estimated that about forty U-boats were hunting along the trade routes of the Atlantic Ocean as the convoy sailed, but its journey was passing with a remarkable calm given its size and the potential for violence that surrounded it. The weather was holding nicely; one hundred ships tiptoed across the ocean seemingly without disturbing anyone. Radar on the *Augusta* picked up a single unidentified aircraft flying from port to starboard on November 1, but it soon disappeared and was not heard from again. As they neared the African coast, they were now in the thick of submarine waters, but no attacks had yet occurred, nor would they.

On November 2, Admiral Hewitt called his commanders to give his instructions on the deployment of the three separate groups in the task force. The southern group would detach from the main body of the convoy on November 7—D-day minus one—and head to a point fifty-five miles off the coast of French Morocco at Safi. The central and northern groups—carrying the forces of Patton and Truscott—would remain concentrated until noon on D-day minus one and continue to head in the general direction of Gibraltar until that time, when the northern group would veer off slightly toward Port Lyautey.

On board the old World War I destroyer USS *Dallas,* preparations were under way for the special mission that awaited her. Unlike the seamen on the *Contessa,* her crew knew that she was headed up a river in Morocco and that trouble awaited her if the French put up a fight. The ship had already been shorn of her masts in order to drop weight for her journey up the shallow Sebou. The crew knew that an airport on the river was their ultimate destination and that they would soon be taking aboard a contingent of Truscott's Army Rangers, whom they were to deposit at the field. Beyond the fact that the river was shallow, they knew nothing about its other parameters or the lay of the land around it. Aside from the officers, who'd been briefed in greater detail about their mission, they knew nothing of the *Contessa,* which was to trail them up the Sebou.

The crew, like the rest of the U.S. Navy in this first action against the Axis, was a mix of veterans and men who were at sea for the first time in their lives. The *Dallas* was captained by a talented young officer, Robert Brodie Jr., and had spent the past year escorting convoys both in the North Sea and along the Eastern Seaboard. The ship itself was hardly impressive; in fact, when the old World War I four-piper had been refueled by a carrier just a couple of days earlier, sailors from the huge ship looming above the *Dallas* had teasingly tossed candy bars and oranges down to the seamen on the deck, like they were boys diving for trinkets around the ships in a foreign port.

As the *Dallas* neared its destination, tensions naturally increased. Each man on board was issued a gun—a Thompson submachine, a Browning automatic rifle, or a Springfield—and each spent his spare time learning how to clean and use it. They were told that the guns were necessary in case they had to abandon ship and go ashore in the middle of the fighting. ·

Medics on board did nothing to allay fears when they suggested that all of the beards that had been growing on crew faces through their days at sea be shaved—the sailors were told that facial hair left a greater risk of scarring in case of a wound. They were also issued a designated battle uniform: a one-piece coverall the color of grass, which was supposed to provide camouflage but would actually stand out against the sand beaches near Port Lyautey.

According to Yeoman Second Class George Doyle, letter writing increased dramatically on board the *Dallas* as she neared Morocco. So did the number of snapshots taken and the exchange of mementos. Perhaps more sobering than any of the other preparations, however, was the moment when Captain Brodie ordered the ship's depth charges tossed overboard. This was the last bow to the overriding need to lighten the ship's load for its voyage up the river; but to the crewmen on board, the charges were their only lethal protection against the deadly U-boats that they'd just navigated through in their voyage across the Atlantic. Along with the guns they'd been issued and the grass green coveralls, it was a clear signal that they were not only sailors enlisted to bring the *Dallas* safely across the ocean, but soldiers, too, drafted to fight a land war in Morocco.

The crew and passengers on board the *Susan B. Anthony* were ordered soon after the midocean refueling to don and wear their life jackets at all times. Again, the fear of German submarines near Africa was the cause for this precaution. In addition, enemy aerial surveillance from Morocco would soon be a possibility. An alarm on November 2 sent planes from task-force carriers scrambling into the skies above, but night came to René Malevergne and the others on the *Anthony* with no further distractions.

On the third and fourth, heavy seas pounded the convoy for the first time on the voyage. Colonel Toffey visited with Malevergne in the Frenchman's cabin and told him that the invasion would not begin before Sunday, the seventh. That sent Malevergne to the map, where he calculated the arrival of the fleet at Mehdia to be at 4:00 a.m. on the eighth, about two and a half hours after high tide.

Malevergne, now dressed in his newly issued U.S. Army uniform, received equipment as well: insignia of rank, a helmet, a revolver, ammunition, and a gas mask. By the end of the day on the fourth, everyone on board was ordered to wear their helmet, in addition to their life jacket. As he packed his civilian mufti into a kit to be sent to him after landing, Malevergne was momentarily stymied as to how to label the bag. Should he address it to Viktor Prechak? Malevergne? Even the Shark? Finally, he chose to cover all bets and address it to Viktor Prechak, in care of Malevergne at Mehdia.

Rumors spread on board that the Spanish were on the verge of intervening in the affairs of French Morocco, which raised the question of how the French would respond if they did so. It was also reported that Radio Berlin had announced that a large American convoy was sailing to Gibraltar, but the rumor came and went and, at least from the perspective of life at sea, nothing came of it.

On the *Augusta,* George Patton was privy to all the radio news, including the Radio Berlin story, the story about the Spanish intervention, and a strong rumor that the French general Henri Giraud was "on the fence" about defending Morocco and that Robert Murphy was encouraging Allied command to delay the invasion until matters were settled.

Patton's response was typical: "As if 100,000 men, all at sea, can wait," he wrote scornfully in his diary on the fourth. Since radio communication from the convoy was blacked out, all of the reports were one-sided: received but not responded to. Command at Gibraltar, London, and D.C. were spared what surely would have been a profane retort from Patton to this bit of news.

Like Malevergne and everyone else in the convoy, he had experienced the storm for the past couple of days, but Patton took it as a sign that things "are bound to get better." When winds hit forty miles per hour, he did "some extra praying" to ensure that was the case.

The Western Task Force commander, as always, kept one eye on destiny—his and his army's—and one eye on the day-to-day activities around him. "Every once in a while the tremendous responsibility of this job lands on me like a ton of bricks, but mostly I am not in the least worried," he wrote in an expansive moment a few days before the eighth. "I can't decide logically if I am a man of destiny or a lucky fool, but I think I am destined. . . . I really do very little, and have done very little, about this show. I feel that my claim to greatness hangs on an ability to lead and inspire. Perhaps when Napoleon said, 'Je m'engage et puis je vois' [I start the fight and then I see], he was right. It is the only thing I can do in this case as I see it. I have no personal fear of death or failure. This may sound like junk, or prophecy, within a week."

Back to earth, he added: "We had a CPX [command post exercise] this morning which was very dull. I can't see how people can be so dull and lacking imagination. Compared to them I am a genius." For good measure, he added, "I think I am."

On November 4, Dwight David Eisenhower took off from London in the same bad weather that afflicted the convoy. His destination was Gibraltar, from where he intended to monitor the two-pronged invasion of Africa. The convoy from Great Britain, steaming largely under British sail to the Mediterranean from several ports in England and Scotland, was already well on its way, as was the Western Task Force under Patton and Hewitt. Like George Patton on the *Augusta*, there was little Eisenhower could do now to change what was about to happen. The steam was already driving the fleet toward its destiny, and now all there was to do was to await the outcome.

The Mediterranean Task Forces, divided into central and eastern groups, carried 23,000 British and 60,000 U.S. troops, all mounted from the United Kingdom. The Eastern Task Force, sailing with the Royal Navy under the command of Major General C. W. Ryder of the U.S. Army, was to capture Algiers. The Central Naval Task Force, another Royal Navy operation, carried 39,000 U.S. ground troops under the command of Major General Lloyd R. Fredenhall. Its object was to capture Oran, Algeria. Militarily, these were larger operations than the Western Naval Task Force and were more likely to face opposition from the Luftwaffe. They were less likely, however, to meet strong resistance from the French navy in North Africa, whose power was centered on the battleship *Jean Bart* in Casablanca.

Eisenhower flew in a group of six B-17 Flying Fortress planes, which turned out to be pummeled by the weather and an attack from a German fighter plane. He was piloted by Major Paul Tibbets, the man who would one day fly the first atomic bomb mission in the *Enola Gay*. Despite the bad weather and the German plane, Eisenhower and his entourage landed safely on the Rock and were soon sped to the underground headquarters there, where, it turned out, there wasn't much to do but wait. As mentioned, radio communication between Eisenhower and the two great convoys sailing to Africa was blacked out, so Ike, Mark Clark, and Captain Harry Butcher essentially sat in the offices, biding their time without information about the status of the fleets on their way to North Africa.

Clark had recently returned from a secret mission to Algeria, arranged by American diplomat and spymaster Robert Murphy. For weeks, Murphy had been meeting with officers in the French army in North Africa to assess how they would respond to an Allied invasion. His hope was to convince them to cooperate and join forces with the Americans and the British and thus avoid bloodshed in North Africa altogether; but before any agreements were made, the French wanted to meet directly with representatives of the Allied Forces headquarters. So in late October, Clark and a handful of officers took a remarkably hazardous and risky journey from Gibraltar to the shores of North Africa, where they met secretly with General Emmanuel Mast of the French army.

Mast was a protégé of General Henri Giraud, a great hero of the French and a man unsullied by association with the Vichy government. He had been the commander of the French Seventh Army at the start of World War II. Mast suggested to Clark that the Allies bring Giraud, who had recently escaped from German custody and was hiding in the south of France, to North Africa. There Giraud would galvanize French resistance and draw three hundred thousand Vichy soldiers to the Allied cause. If the Allies would wait until the following spring, they could also invade southern France with the aid and under the command of Giraud.

Clark was sworn to keep from the French the fact that the Allied invasion of North Africa was just weeks away. There was also simply no way that the Allies were going to give Giraud or anyone else in the French army the command of Allied forces, particularly since it was apparent that Giraud, hiding out in France, currently commanded no French troops. It was apparent that there was no certainty beyond their own impassioned sensibility that either Mast or Giraud could guarantee that any forces in the French army would join the Allied side in the coming invasion.

For all their hopes that the French army would drop arms and ally itself against Germany and its own Vichy government when the invading force appeared on the shores of North Africa, Allied headquarters had had no contact with the French army in North Africa until Clark made his bold trip to Algiers. While Murphy, who had fostered the hope that the French army would not resist, continued to do so even at this late hour, no one in London, or now in Gibraltar, could be certain of anything regarding the French army's response to attack. It could, however, be almost guaranteed that the French navy, controlled by Admiral Darlan, would fight.

Little wonder, then, that Eisenhower, now ensconced on Gibraltar and waiting for the invasion to begin, remained no less edgy about the outcome of Operation Torch than he'd been through the months of September and October when it was in its planning stages. In fact, he'd recently sent a note to Marshall in which he confessed with regard to the upcoming assault, "If a man permitted himself to do so, he could get absolutely frantic about questions of weather, politics, personalities in France and Morocco, and so on." The risks of what the Allies were doing, given their level of unpreparedness and uncertain knowledge of what was about to happen, were remarkable. Still, he felt that "a certain amount of good fortune will bless us when the critical day arrives."

CHAPTER 29

Rendezvous

As the *Contessa* came abreast of the Azores, Lieutenant Leslie finally informed Captain John of the ship's ultimate destination. They were heading to a port on the coast of French Morocco, northeast of Casablanca. Mehdia was the village they would first encounter at the entrance to the Sebou River, and then twelve miles farther up river, they would deposit their load at an airfield at Port Lyautey. The *Contessa* would follow on the heels of a destroyer. The airfield would be secured by the time the banana boat arrived; the *Contessa* was to simply unload its cargo and await further orders.

The fact that the cargo was a highly volatile cocktail of explosives; that the river was narrow, winding, and twelve miles from sea to port; that the Atlantic coast at Morocco would make entry into the river a serious hazard; and that the river itself had a depth of just seventeen and a half feet were all nail-biting circumstances. But given the uncertainties of their current situation—looking for their convoy and in the midst of an area known to be prime U-boat hunting grounds—their ultimate mission seemed less an imminent danger than simply an end to the hazards that currently engulfed them.

Presently, the *Contessa* had no idea where the convoy that she was to join was located; in fact, she still had not seen another ship at sea. The gale that afflicted all the other vessels crossing the ocean that early November struck the *Contessa* too, rocking her wickedly off the coast of the Azores and causing Leslie and John to spend the most disconcerting evening of the trip on the sixth. In spite of the storm whipping the ocean around them, they knew they must maintain a fast clip on their way to catching up with the convoy—maintaining their average speed of fifteen knots—because as they neared Africa, they were once again in the thick of German U-boat waters. Given their lack of identifying signals, however, they worried deeply about running headlong into the convoy, which, because of their proximity to Morocco, they knew couldn't be far off. There was also no moon above to illuminate either them or the convoy, thus increasing the possibility for blind trouble.

Daylight broke with glad tidings on the seventh, D-day minus one. Dead ahead of the *Contessa,* about five miles distant, the convoy emerged out of the early-morning light. To John, the sight of the fleet was a satisfying thrill. As ready as he'd been to travel singly across the ocean, he was now more than happy to hook up with the rest of the invasion fleet.

To the USS *Philadelphia,* the flagship of the southern group of the Western Task Force, the sight of the *Contessa,* sailing at the ship's stern at seven forty-five that morning, was simply "strange." No one knew who she was or could be, so the destroyer *Cowie* was sent to investigate. Once again, the *Contessa* had a difficult time explaining her identity precisely. Her signalmen, Schaffer, Thomas, and Pottiger, wig-wagged their flags. When she finally made the *Cowie* understand that she was a lagging part of the convoy and the *Cowie* had that information confirmed through the *Philadelphia,* it turned out she was still several hours from where she was supposed to be. The southern group of the task force was headed for Safi; she needed to be off of Mehdia. The *Cowie* was dispatched to escort the *Contessa* to her proper group and the pair of ships steamed north.

The storm had moved off to the east, and the weather was decent on the morning of November 7, though a light breeze put a little chop in the water. On board the *Susan B. Anthony,* René Malevergne attended Mass and, afterward, watched as rations were distributed and troops lined up to fill cartridge belts from the cases of just-opened ammunition boxes. He bade his good-byes to the four young Americans, Georges, Tommy, Jacques, and Jimmy, with whom he'd spent hours chatting in French on the journey over; he also said good-bye to Colonel Toffey, whom Malevergne learned would be leading the assault on the north side of the River Sebou. His battalion would aim for the bridge that crossed the river north of Port Lyautey, at the height of the Sebou's bend, above the airfield. Malevergne promised to offer Toffey the support of the guns of the destroyer he would be guiding up the river.

At about three in the afternoon, the convoy had been broken up into its separate components, with Malevergne, on the *Susan B. Anthony,* heading north toward Mehdia; General Patton's large contingent heading east toward Fedala, just north of Casablanca; and the southern wing of the three-pronged attack already heading south toward Safi.

On board the transport *Henry T. Allen,* Lucian Truscott was contemplating the fact that the invasion the next day would come on the heels of speeches from the president and General Eisenhower in which the French would be implored and invited to lay down their arms and join forces with the Allied cause against Germany. The messages would emphasize that Americans were coming to Morocco as friends and that no offensive action would be taken if the French army decided to capitulate.

Uncertainty about what was going to happen the next day had trailed American forces all the way across the ocean to this moment just off the coast of Morocco on the evening before D-day. As ready as they were for action, there were still those on the ships gathered off the shore who doubted that much would come in the way of fighting tomorrow. While Truscott was a professional soldier and knew he must be prepared for any eventuality, he also was loath to precipitate a bloodbath if it could be avoided. He worried that because his sub–task force Goalpost was aimed at a less populated area of Morocco than the two southern forces, that the messages coming from the president and Eisenhower might not be heard, or that the French commanders in the vicinity of Port Lyautey might not have the authority to act quickly or independently on the suggestion that they lay down their arms. He decided to prepare a personal note to the French commander at Port Lyautey that "might reinforce these radio appeals."

He called his French-speaking aide, Ted Conway, to his cabin and dictated a letter that Conway translated *en français.* To give the document a more ceremonial feel, they found someone familiar with calligraphy to create ornate Old English lettering and then rolled the paper into a scroll, bound it with a wax seal, and tied it in a ribbon.

To deliver the letter, Truscott chose his other close aide, Major Pierpont Hamilton, whose charm, diplomatic skills, and command of the French language made him a natural for the errand. He hesitated before deciding to send Colonel Nick Craw as well. Craw, the Army Air Force liaison to Truscott's group, would have command of the airfield once it was taken; and this diplomatic mission seemed, on D-day minus one, a particularly dangerous assignment. But for all the reasons that he'd already contemplated in writing the document, Truscott decided it was worthwhile to send Craw as well. From his prewar days working as an observer throughout Europe, Craw was familiar with a number of French officers and, like Hamilton, knew the language. Besides, he had asked Truscott if he could go.

It was a Saturday evening. The ships of the northern group were blacked out as they cruised through the soft chop of the sea along the coast of Morocco. On the decks of the transports, destroyers, cruisers, and the battleship *Texas* an eerie quiet prevailed, while below, the men of the First, Second, Third Battalions of the Sixtieth Infantry tried to get some rest while imagining what might lie ahead for them come morning. In their minds, they climbed smoothly over the sides of their transports and down the rope ladders into the waiting landing craft; and the landing craft swiftly and easily took them to a place they knew would be very different from the beach they'd practiced on at Solomons Island back in Hampton Roads, but not so different they couldn't make their way safely to shore, couldn't find a good cover to protect them as they made their way inland. Sand was sand, wasn't it? Beaches were beaches. And there seemed to be no pounding surf—the potential trouble that had worried the navy and everyone else familiar with the Moroccan coast since the plans for the North African invasion had first been formulated.

Through the course of the voyage from Hampton Roads, the troops and their commanders in sub–task force Goalpost had been going over again and again the outline of their plans and what to expect once they hit the beaches. Mehdia was an ancient village of about three hundred founded centuries earlier by the Carthaginians. Today, it existed as a resort community about a thousand yards inland from the Atlantic Ocean, just at the mouth of the Sebou River. Landmarks in the village included a casino, a cannery, and a nearby lighthouse.

To the south of Mehdia, parallel to the coastline, ran a narrow lagoon two or three miles long. Between the lagoon and Port Lyautey was a bare high ground marked by rolling hills that ran up to the airfield to the northeast. Less than a mile upriver from Mehdia was a sixteenth-century fortress built by the Portuguese in the heyday of their African trade routes and known locally as the Kasbah. It was perched on a bluff above the river and spread out over several acres of highland and contained coastal batteries aimed seaward and toward the mouth of the river.

The Port Lyautey airfield—the prize of this expedition—was well guarded by antiaircraft defenses and native Moroccan troops, who were called Goumiers—a French corruption of the Mahgreb Arabic word "goum," which meant "people." The designation was used as a generic term that circumvented the need to refer to the natives by tribal distinction. They were widely regarded as solid fighting men and had proven themselves more than capable in the war of the Rif. They were officered by Frenchmen and, despite the generic nickname, they were usually organized in units of Berbers of the same village. Their uniforms were topped with gray burnooses with vertical brown stripes that served as good camouflage in the dry landscapes they typically fought in.

Aside from the Goumiers at the airfield, U.S. forces knew that another detachment guarded the bridge north of Lyautey (the one that Colonel Jack Toffey's battalion was assigned to take). High ground in the river loop between the Kasbah and the airfield was honeycombed with trenches occupied by French troops.

In all, the defense at Port Lyautey consisted of a regiment of infantry consisting of three battalions of Tirailleurs with twelve 25 mm guns. These soldiers were joined by several 75 mm batteries manned by

Foreign Legionnaires stationed at the Kasbah; a group of engineers; and a transport company. Reinforcements were available to Lyautey from Meknes, about fifty miles to the east, where parts of the French Foreign Legion were stationed. Of greater concern to Truscott were forty-five tanks stationed in Rabat, which could quickly arrive on the battlefield via the Rabat road. He was hoping for little opposition from the French air force based at the Port Lyautey field, where intelligence suggested that only a few dated planes were hangared.

The assignments given to the three battalions of the Sixtieth Infantry that would be leading the assault on the region were pretty straightforward. The Second Battalion was to land at the most central of five landing locations, designated Green Beach, right at the doorstep of Mehdia. Their goal was to head for and capture the Kasbah, hopefully by 0600, before first light.

A demolition party was assigned to cut the boom that crossed the Sebou. Immediately afterward, the destroyer *Dallas,* piloted by René Malevergne, was to enter the river carrying its raider detachment, composed of Sixtieth Infantry troops specially trained as Rangers. The *Dallas* would steam upstream to the airfield and drop her commandos at the runways, where the attack would proceed.

North of the river, the Third Battalion, under Colonel Jack Toffey, was to land at Red Beaches 1 and 2 and traverse the ground above the Sebou until it reached the high ground directly opposite the airfield. One unit was to be dispatched to seize the bridge north of Port Lyautey; another was to cross the river in rubber boats and assist in the capture of the airfield.

To the south of Mehdia on Blue Beach, Major DeWitt McCarley was to move inland and reconnoiter to the south with the First Battalion. This combat team would move around the southern edge of the lagoon, establish roadblocks, set up machine guns and antitank weaponry, and generally protect the invasion from attack by those French tanks coming up the road from Rabat.

Lieutenant Colonel Harry Semmes, with an armored battalion combat team from the Second Division that would eventually include fifty-four light tanks, was to land in the wave immediately after the assault battalions on Blue Beach and Green Beach. His battalion would likewise reconnoiter to the south and face any threat that appeared along the Rabat road.

Colonel Frederick de Rohan, commander of the Sixtieth Infantry, was to coordinate activities of the various combat teams and would be headquartered at Green Beach.

Soon, as the northern convoy steamed toward its position opposite Mehdia, the ship's loudspeaker system would begin repeating these assignments to the troops as they prepared to depart on the landing craft, drilling into each soldier what his battalion was expected to accomplish, so that it would become so deeply engrained in each mind that there would be no thought of any other purpose to the mission. *First Battalion will gather south of the lagoon and reconnoiter along the Rabat road. . . . Second Battalion will move on Mehdia. . . . Third Battalion will land on Red Beaches 1 and 2 and head inland toward the high ground opposite the airfield.*

Whoever determined the password and its response for U.S. troops once they'd landed was likewise thinking that he didn't want his soldiers doing any excess searching of their minds. The choice was a name front and center in the consciousness of the Western Task Force. "George" was the call; "Patton" was the response.

Weather reports coming from Washington and from the admiralty in London had predicted pounding seas for D-day, with surf up to fifteen feet hammering the coast of Morocco; but on the seventh the moderate swells encouraged Admiral Hewitt to make the decision to go forward with the invasion. Patton, of course, applauded the go-ahead. By the time the convoy reached North Africa, his growing estimation of Hewitt's ability had come close to eliciting an indirect apology from Patton for his earlier behavior. "I should like to call your attention to the fact that the relations between the Army and Navy in this convoy could not possibly be more satisfactory," he wrote to Marshall. "Admiral Hewitt and his chief of staff, Admiral Hall, have shown the utmost cooperation and the finest spirit. I desire to bring this to your attention because prior to leaving I had some doubts. These doubts have been removed."

During the course of the day on November 7, Patton noted the breaking off of the components of the task force. The Safi contingent headed south at 0600; the Mehdia group, heading north, didn't steam off until 1500.

Patton's own central attack group, aimed at Fedala, steamed directly toward the village beaches on the evening of November 7 with the largest of the three attack commands. Twelve transports, three cargo ships, almost twenty thousand officers and enlisted men, 1,700 vehicles, and fifteen thousand tons of supplies awaited the word to hit the shores of Morocco. An additional seventeen thousand naval personnel were there to escort and protect them as they made their way onto the beaches.

Aboard the *Augusta,* George Patton issued a letter to his troops:

```
Soldiers: We are to be congratulated
because we have been chosen as the units
of the United States Army best trained
to take part in this great American
effort. . . .
    It is not known whether the French
Africa army, composed of both white and
colored troops, will contest our landing.
It is regrettable to contemplate the
necessity of fighting the gallant French
who are at heart sympathetic toward us,
but all resistance by whomever offered
must be destroyed. However, when any of
the French soldiers seek to surrender, you
will accept it and treat them with the
```

respect due a brave opponent and future
ally. Remember the French are not Nazis
or Japs. . . .

   When the great day of battle comes,
remember your training, and remember above
all that speed and vigor of attack are
the sure roads to success and you must
succeed—for to retreat is as cowardly as
it is fatal. Indeed, once landed, retreat
is impossible. Americans do not surrender.

   During the first few days and
nights after you get ashore, you work
unceasingly, regardless of sleep,
regardless of food. A pint of sweat will
save a gallon of blood.

   The eyes of the world are watching us;
the heart of America beats for us; God
is with us. On our victory depends the
freedom or slavery of the human race. We
shall surely win.

Patton spent the evening before the invasion trying to relax in his cabin. He read a detective story called "The Cairo Garter Murders" by Van Wyck Mason and tried to get a little sleep. At 2120—9:20 that night—the *Augusta*'s radar detected land dead ahead. They had reached Morocco.

To the north, at about that same hour, the Goalpost sub-task force was sailing stealthily past Rabat. The city lights were brightly visible from the sea, while the blackout conditions on board the convoy gave the ships a ghostly, whooshing presence as they steamed by.

   René Malevergne had been called to the bridge of the *Susan B.*

Anthony, where he stood now, indicating the landmarks to the captain as they passed. The group of lights to the right was Rabat; on the left was the city of Salé. The black trench between was the Bou Regreg, a river that empties into the sea south of the Sebou.

Suddenly, the lights of Mehdia twinkled beneath the dark African sky and a confusing wave of emotions swept over the Frenchman. Soon he would be home amid a liberating force of Americans; Morocco would be free from the taint of Vichy governance and the heel of les Boches. But it was also impossible for Malevergne not to consider that Germaine and the boys might be sleeping at this very moment in their little white cottage near the Kasbah. He tried not to think of the awful things that might happen in the morning, but sailing within this awesome force it was unavoidable to consider: When the guns opened fire and the shells began to fly, where would his family be?

CHAPTER 30

"Viva la France eternelle"

The landing on the shores of Morocco was to take place at 0400 hours on November 8. Precision was needed so that combat teams could hit the beaches before sunrise, which was expected at 0600. The three sub–task forces were supposed to be in position for loading at 2300 hours the night before.

The navy had worried about the timing of operations for weeks. The army was asking this convoy to cross the second-largest ocean in the world and set its forces down on a particular series of beaches on a notoriously volatile coastline essentially without pausing to regroup and reorganize in order to synchronize movements. With zigzagging and evasive maneuvers added to the length of the journey, the pitometer logs on most of the ships in the convoy were reading in the area of 4,500 miles—this was the distance they'd traveled from Hampton Roads. Remarkably, the navy managed to deliver each of the three landing groups to its destination within an hour of that 2300 time slot: the Safi group was ready at 2345; Patton's Fedala force at 2353; and Truscott's north assault wing at 2340.

About half an hour after midnight, the landing craft of sub–task force Goalpost began to be lowered into the water and then steered toward their designated transport ships with the intention of loading troops beginning at 0130. The swarming sound of dozens of boats could be heard in the darkness, and problems arose immediately in the traffic. Because the ships continued to be blacked out, there turned out to be an obvious difficulty in finding the correct ship on the darkened sea. In addition, the ships maintained radio silence, which inhibited the ability to sort out the confusion. Landing craft simply couldn't find the transports housing the troops they were supposed to take to shore. Megaphones from the

craft could be heard in the area calling up to the transport ships questions like "Is this the *Allen*?"

There were troubles with winches, cables, and davits, which added to
confusion, delays, and difficulties both before and after the landing craft
were lowered. Loading areas were suddenly switched from starboard to
port on some of the transports for no apparent reason; different nets
were employed, as well. Other ships that weren't involved in the initial assault, including the *Dallas,* were confused about their positioning,
leading them to drift into the transport area and adding to the mess.

The lack of training of everyone involved was immediately evident,
but one army witness was willing to discreetly point the finger of blame
at the other service involved in the operation: "I believe that navy personnel were cooperative and wanted to do their best, but inexperience in
such operations was a great handicap."

On Truscott's transport, the *Henry T. Allen,* landing craft were to be
lowered beginning at 0030, with troops disembarking forty-five minutes
later. Seeing the chaos evolving around him and thinking that, because of
the radio blackout, he could provide more help from the water, Truscott
clambered down the nets and into a landing craft, which he ordered to
cruise around the staging area. He soon encountered yet another problem: "We found ships everywhere but each one was reluctant to identify
itself for they were suspicious of this unexpected visit." When these ships
were finally willing to identify themselves and let the sub–task force commander come aboard, Truscott found that none of the ships could point
to where other ships were located in the area.

After an hour and a half of cruising around the transport area, hoping to sort matters out, Truscott returned to the *Allen* only to be faced
with yet another unexpected difficulty. Immediately after he climbed
aboard, he was pulled to the ship's communication room, where he was
astonished to hear General Eisenhower's message to the French people
being broadcast over the radio. Eisenhower's address had come on the
heels of President Roosevelt's, and, in fact, Truscott was listening to a
rebroadcast, which meant that both speeches had been aired twice now,

beginning at 0300, when, apparently, Allied forces on the Mediterranean side of the invasion had landed. The only problem here in Morocco, of course, was that no one had yet landed! FDR's stirring invitation to French forces to lay down their arms and join the Allied cause ended with the cry "Viva la France eternelle!" But from Truscott's perspective, this was simply an alert to the forces on shore that his army was coming. "My heart sank," he would later write. "Our people in the Mediterranean had landed an hour before our scheduled time. If the French were not now alert and waiting at their guns we would indeed be lucky!"

Just before the broadcasts began, René Malevergne climbed down the hull of the *Susan B. Anthony* and into a waiting craft. The boat made the short trip over to the *Dallas,* where Malevergne climbed aboard and was immediately taken to the bridge, where he shook hands with the commanding officer, Lieutenant Commander Robert Brodie Jr.

"I am Viktor Prechak," said Malevergne.

Brodie shook his hand and handed the Frenchman a pair of field glasses. "Good weather," the captain said.

"There is better, but more importantly there is worse," replied Malevergne.

Shortly after his arrival, an alarm sounded on the *Dallas* bridge, and in the distance Malevergne and Brodie could make out the emerging lights of at least five vessels heading directly toward the convoy. They were French merchant ships, and Truscott saw them as well from the *Allen.* The vessels began to flash signals to the American ships: "Be forewarned," was the message. "Alert on shore for 0500."

Whether by the radio broadcast or some other factor, French forces on shore had obviously become aware of the pending assault. From Truscott's point of view, it hardly mattered anymore. The landing craft were in the water and loaded with troops, ready to hit the beaches. Though they were already past their 0400 landing time, there was no turning back.

Headaches continued in getting the landing craft organized. Each battalion sailing for its designated beach had been assigned a control ship upon which it was to congregate and prepare to head in synchronized fashion to shore. Toffey's Third Battalion, aimed for Red Beaches north of the River Sebou, was to be organized around the minesweeper *Osprey*, but it took a good hour after loading the troops for all the landing craft to find her. It would ultimately be daylight by the time they reached the Moroccan shore—0630—and as it turned out, they were five miles north of their designated landing area.

To the south, the Second Battalion combat team became the first section of the northern invasion force to hit the Moroccan beaches; units landed at Green Beach at 0540. Soon after, the first two waves of the First Battalion were also ashore. Aiming for Blue and Yellow Beaches, they drifted farther south to land on Blue and Green Beaches.

As the first waves hit the beach, the shore batteries opened fire and U.S. destroyers responded, sending red and green tracer shells arcing across the sky toward the guns on shore. From his post on the bridge of the *Dallas*, Malevergne could hear the "dry clacking of machine guns and automatic weapons from both sides." Everyone on the ship was at his combat station, and the commandos grouped along the deck, as loudspeakers ceaselessly transmitted orders to each unit. A pale sun, "sad and without brilliance," arrived at dawn; it was quickly veiled by gray, dirty clouds and a light rain.

Earlier that morning on the *Texas*, UP reporter Walter Cronkite had been summoned to the bridge by Admiral Monroe Kelly. Like Patton, Kelly had wanted to transmit a message to the men on board as the battle approached. He was looking for an appropriately inspiring conclusion to his speech but was having trouble coming up with the right language. "You're a writer, Mr. Cronkite," he said to the journalist. "Perhaps you could come up with something."

Cronkite was stumped. He did, however, witness the opening salvo from the battleship's gigantic fourteen-inch guns, and its awesome display loosened his writing ability. "The great belch of yellow flame threatens to engulf the ship itself, and the blast of heat sears the freshman war correspondent on the bridge. The gun blows its own great smoke ring and the shell can actually be seen disappearing toward the horizon in the middle of the donut. Whatever has been loose on deck is sent skyward, sucked into the vacuum the explosion has left behind."

Seconds after witnessing the initial blast from the guns, Cronkite, standing with his hand on a rail on the bridge, was amazed to find a deck of cards floating in the air around him, sucked skyward by the whoosh of the explosion. A single card, the ace of spades, rocked back and forth on the current in front of his eyes, before it fell gently on the back of his hand.

Cronkite's cabinmates, the team operating Radio Maroc, were also affected by the blast. Working with U.S. Army communications engineers, they had spent hours through the course of the voyage setting up their equipment in order to broadcast the speeches of the president and General Eisenhower. Having successfully sent those messages over the air to French Morocco, they were beginning general transmission of Allied news of the invasion shoreward when the *Texas* opened her guns. In the process, their equipment was bounced around the communications room, and Radio Maroc fell silent.

"If they had asked, we could have told them how to prevent that," a navy communications officer subsequently told Cronkite with a shrug.

From the *Allen,* Truscott saw the shore batteries open up to the south of Mehdia and watched the U.S. Navy batteries respond from the sea. As he described it later: "Great chains of red balls streaked through the darkness toward shore." He had just bade adieu to Pierpont Hamilton and Nick Craw as they climbed down into a waiting LCM. They were clad in their best uniforms—starched shirts and caps, brass and leather gleaming, rows of ribbons and pilots' wings festooning their chests and

sleeves—and carried Truscott's beribboned message to the French commander at Port Lyautey. They arrived on shore just before the sunlight
at 0600.

The pair ran into immediate trouble as they neared their landing
site. Craw sent a message back to Truscott. "At mouth of river," he
radioed. "Being shelled by enemy and our own Navy. Going to land at
Green Beach." A little later, after they'd found safe harbor and a jeep,
Craw sent an update. "On Green Beach. Bantam stuck. Looking for [a
new jeep]. Troops landed and moving inland. Proceeding on mission."

Meanwhile, five miles north of Red Beach on the other side of the
Sebou, Toffey's Third Battalion found itself facing an extremely steep
escarpment and the same soft, white sand that René Malevergne had
feared would impede their progress inland. Toffey knew instantly that
the landscape would make a trial not only of unloading the landing craft
but of transporting supplies off the beach. Adding to his miseries was
the sudden appearance of the French air force, in the form of four planes
swooping in from the nearby Port Lyautey airfield. They began to strafe
the beaches and the landing craft, both those ashore and those that had
made it off the sand and were heading back to the convoy to pick up the
second wave of troops and cargo.

The Third wasn't the only combat team having a difficult time exiting
the beach. The sand dunes to the south of the River Sebou were just as
difficult to traverse as the escarpments to the north. In fact, only at Blue
Beach was a simple route inland found. Compounding these difficulties
was the fact that there were delays in getting bulldozers and engineers
on shore. The appearance of the French planes and the shore batteries
prompted the transport and cargo ships waiting offshore to move further
out to sea to safeguard troops climbing into the boats. That meant longer
trips to and from shore for the landing craft, thus slowing debarkation
to a crawl.

Still, the French defense of the beaches themselves was not fierce.
And when Toffey's group was able to unload two .30-caliber machine

guns and a trio of .50 caliber guns to take aim at the French planes buzz-
ing overhead, it soon became even less daunting.

The guns knocked down two of the four aircraft. One, which turned
out to be piloted by Captain Mathon, commandant of Port Lyautey
airport, was sent in swirling flames to the sea two hundred yards off Red
Beach.

Aside from being bombarded by their own navy (the *Texas* would
later be pinpointed as the culprit), Craw and Hamilton had also been
strafed by the same French planes that had attacked the Third Battalion.
But once they got their Bantam jeep off the beach and pointed in the direction of Port Lyautey, the way seemed clear. Along with driver, Private
First Class Orris Correy, they started off through the highland between
Mehdia and the port with a prominent white flag attached to the back of
their jeep and smaller American and French flags hooked on the radiator
in front.

They approached a French outpost near the Kasbah and asked the
soldiers stationed there if an escort could be made available for their trip
for safety purposes. They were told either that one was not available or
that it was unnecessary. Correy drove on with Craw beside him in front
and Hamilton behind Craw.

Near the edge of the city of Port Lyautey, they rounded a blind curve
on the corner of a hillside and ran headlong into a machine-gun nest,
from which immediately spluttered a burst of machine gunfire. Nick
Craw fell heavily against Correy, who brought the jeep to a halt. It was
quickly surrounded by the Moroccan soldiers who had fired upon it.
Their rifles were now aimed at Hamilton and Correy.

Naturally shocked and frightened, Hamilton had enough bold
adrenalin to "exhaust all the French profanity that I'd learned in eight
years in Paris" on the French lieutenant who was in charge of the group.
How dare they fire on a white flag! How dare they inhibit this opportunity for peace between their two great nations! Hamilton also insisted
that he be taken to Port Lyautey to present his neatly bound document

to the commander of French forces there. In fact, with Craw slumped in the front seat and Hamilton defenseless in the back, he was hardly in a position to dictate what would happen next. The great-great-grandson of Alexander Hamilton, along with Private Correy, was subsequently taken to Port Lyautey, where Hamilton was able to present Truscott's letter. Unfortunately, the commander was in no position to negotiate with the Americans. Only General Mathenet had that power, Hamilton was told, and he was not in the city.

Major Hamilton and Correy were taken into custody. The last opportunity to avoid a full-scale battle over Port Lyautey had passed, but its first American victim had a name. Nick Craw was dead.

*   *   *

The violence of the invasion was general now, both at sea and on shore. The First Battalion, which had landed between Blue and Green, had gotten off the beach and moved inland, south of the lagoon. Its members organized there at 1045, setting up roadblocks toward the direction of Rabat, from where the French Renault tanks were expected to come. They didn't have to wait long for that eventuality.

Two platoons were arranged on either side of the highway. One antitank group was armed with one of the newfangled bazookas, and one had a machine gun. Early in the afternoon, the French tanks appeared and came within fifty yards of the trench holding the soldiers armed with the bazooka. The Americans fired their weapon and missed the tank; but a thick eucalyptus tree, about ten yards off the road behind the French, was mowed down like a weed. The blast of the launcher alerted one of the French tanks to the existence of the Americans. It pivoted its gun in their direction and fired, knocking out the gunner and killing his loader. The second American unit was soon destroyed as well.

Afterward, as the French paused to take their prisoner and inspect the launcher that he'd been holding, they refused to believe that a hand-carried weapon could simply slice through a foot-thick eucalyptus tree, decapitating it in one vicious swipe. The consensus among the French was that some artillery must be in the area as well. The tank column from Rabat proceeded to waste precious time reconnoitering for a non-existent battery.

Closer to Mehdia and the Kasbah, the Second Battalion was having a hard time organizing. After its landing at Green Beach early in the morning, two assault teams advanced toward the Kasbah but were stopped by U.S. Navy gunfire. They crossed the northern tip of the lagoon and occupied high ground above the lighthouse. From there, through misunderstanding of an order, the Second began to advance toward the airport, rather than focusing on the Kasbah. As it headed in that direction, French infantry and tanks drove it back, and the teams wound up between the Kasbah and Mehdia, back near the lighthouse. Here they stayed for the afternoon, pinned down by the French infantry and the continuing fire from the U.S. Navy.

Toffey's Third Battalion was the most advanced of the three attack teams, but it, too, had its stumbles and fumbles. From its landing north of Red Beach, the battalion moved rapidly inland and by noon had occupied a hill overlooking the airport from the north side of the Sebou—a move of about five or six miles. But the lack of exits through the sandy escarpments prevented the battalion from getting artillery or any other heavy equipment to their position until 2230 on the night of the eighth. It wouldn't be until D-day plus one that the big guns would arrive at their position; and the rubber boats, which had been critical to their orders to cross the river and aid in the assault on the airport, were left in half-tracks at the beach. They, too, would not be arriving at the Third Battalion position until the next day.

From their post on the bare hills to the north of the Sebou, Toffey and company had perhaps the best view of the river and the action taking place along it between the Kasbah and the airport. They could see the full extent of the Sebou's horseshoe shape as it veered northeast from Mehdia and the Kasbah for four or five miles, then took a turn to the east for about two miles opposite the airport, and then took another hard turn to the south, almost bending back on itself, toward Port Lyautey four or five miles upriver. A deep blue green, the river was about a quarter of a mile wide at its most expansive but considerably narrower at its turns.

Anticipating this view and its advantages, the navy had sent along a radio operator and spotters, who set up a transmitter in the caves above Red Beach and then ran wire up to the high ground. There the spotters began locating French artillery fire for the ships out at sea. From their post opposite the airfield, the battalion could see "large numbers of French troops . . . running as a result of the fire."

The battalion itself had not yet been discovered by the French; it drew no fire all that first day. Toffey sent out foot patrols to the north and east toward Port Lyautey—the battalion's second destination after the airport. Late in the afternoon, the unit spied a French steamer, heading downriver from Port Lyautey toward the sea, slowing near the bend directly north of the city. They watched as it was run intentionally into the north bank of the Sebou. Two men were seen leaving the ship, which began to slowly keel over onto its side. Toffey ordered a patrol to check on them and the vessel, but to no avail: the two French sailors had obviously scuttled the ship at the most difficult bend in the river to bollix any and all American ship traffic to come. Worse, in the morning, there would be a second steamer scuttled on the south bank of the river at the same bend. René Malevergne's job had just become much more difficult.

Out on the ocean, positioned just beyond the transport group, the *Contessa* awaited word of when she would make her run up the river. Like everyone else involved in the action near Mehdia, Captain John and Lieutenant Leslie were aware that the invasion had been pushed off schedule; and since their ship's moment in the drama was predicated on the ascent upriver of the *Dallas* and the taking of the airfield, they could do nothing but await further events and orders. They waited further.

Meanwhile, on the *Dallas* itself, those events actually seemed to be progressing. An announcement came over the ship's loudspeaker that the Kasbah had been taken, and almost simultaneously, a dimming of fire came from the French 75 mm battery just beyond Mehdia.

But the ship had received no definitive word about the boom crossing the entrance to the Sebou. A specially trained navy squad was supposed to have gone in and cut this cable early in the morning of the invasion. If they were successful, a red star was to have been fired over the mouth of the river and a radio code—"Steve Brodie"—was supposed to have been transmitted.

The *Dallas* had seen a red star shoot out over the Sebou earlier in the morning but had not yet received the "Steve Brodie" message. Yet to the surprise and dismay of René Malevergne, they soon heard over the ship's radio an order for the *Dallas* to prepare to storm the estuary. Captain Brodie looked to the river pilot for a response. Malevergne was frank: "I answered that it was possible three hours earlier, but now with low tide, it was no longer possible." He told Brodie, very simply, that the ship would run aground if it made the attempt; nonetheless, he would follow orders and take the ship up the river if asked.

At noon, the *Dallas* headed toward Mehdia. To test whether the battery near the Kasbah was or was not active, Brodie and Malevergne decided to run the ship through its field of fire "before indicating our intention to cross the bar." They took the *Dallas* forward in a sweeping semicircle, coming from the south and running on a line parallel to the bar. Malevergne's intention was to turn abruptly forty-five degrees to port and enter the estuary at full speed. Splashes of gunfire could be seen landing to the south of the ship, but not directly at it. So the *Dallas* arced toward the jetties.

In preparation for its assault, the communication officer on board the *Dallas* packed up all confidential documents on board the ship and tossed them overboard in a weighted sack to prevent them from falling into enemy hands. Just as they neared the jetties, however, word arrived on board that the Kasbah was not taken. Almost simultaneously, the batteries near the fort opened fire directly at the *Dallas*. Nor, it would turn out, had the boom been cut.

The *Dallas* quickly turned and left the scene at flank speed and in the haze of a smoke screen. She opened her own three-inch batteries as she went back to the deep waters of the ocean. There would be no ascending the Sebou on this day for either her or the *Contessa*.

Lucian Truscott had taken off for Blue Beach from the *Allen* at about 1230 with Conway and others and spent most of the afternoon sorting through a series of confusing reports about the progress and status of his three battalions. Chaos reigned on the beaches around him. The sand was much softer than anyone had anticipated, meaning that scores of vehicles were stuck there, unable to get off the beach. Cargo that was supposed to be moved inland began to pile up on the beaches. Wire netting and burlap roadways were proving an inadequate means for getting traffic moving. A number of landing craft were likewise stuck in the sand, and their crews wandered aimlessly about or, as Truscott later reported, "tinkered ineffectively with stranded craft." There was such a mess at the landing sites that Harry Semmes, who arrived on shore at roughly the same time as Truscott, was able to get only seven of his fifty-four tanks onto Green Beach.

Communication was extremely difficult as well. The shells coming from shore batteries that had prompted the transports to head farther out into the ocean forced them outside the range of radios on shore. Messages were being sent by hand via the landing craft, but of course many of the landing craft were still stuck on shore.

A single radio at Blue Beach headquarters tried to sort through information coming from inland, but Truscott had heard nothing from Toffey's Third Battalion, and what he'd heard from the First and Second was contradictory and confused. There were rumors that the Kasbah had been taken when it hadn't. They could hear heavy gunfire coming from the hills to the north but didn't know who was involved. Truscott heard of the fighting along the Rabat road earlier in the day but didn't know its extent and worried about what was to come. He had heard nothing from Craw and Hamilton, either.

Truscott headed out from the beach in a half-track looking for elements of the First Battalion. He found a company along the south side of the eastern edge of the lagoon and then headed north. Naval gunfire cracked over his head, and there was machine-gun fire ahead on the east side of the lagoon, where a skirmish was obviously in progress. Artillery shells were falling in the cork oak forest beyond. Finally, Truscott located Colonel McCarley of the First Battalion and ordered him to hook up with the Second Battalion in the morning to jointly attack the Kasbah.

As dark settled around the region, there were concrete reports that more French infantry, tanks, and armored vehicles were moving up the Rabat road and that French forces in Lyautey had been reinforced by Legionnaires from Meknes. The fight was going to get no less difficult in the morning.

Truscott headed back to headquarters at Blue Beach, but even there he was stymied. The half-track he was traveling in got stuck in the sand, and so the Goalpost commander finished his trip back on foot, arriving exhausted, as everyone else on the beach appeared to be. He sent Conway off in the hope of finding Semmes. He wanted his tank commander in position on the Rabat road first thing in the morning. But finding Semmes in the chaos would be no easy task.

Scores of men wandered aimlessly around the beach, either looking for their units or stranded from the landing craft. The password call and response, "George" and "Patton," echoed in the darkness.

Truscott was chilled and in desperate need of a cigarette. He knew lighting up, the flare and glow of a smoke near enemy fire, was strictly forbidden by his own command. But as he looked out on the ocean and saw the signal lamps of the ships in the convoy, he rationalized that smoking a cigarette could be no more dangerous than those signal lights blinking in the distance. He snapped a smoke out of his pack and lit it. Soon other cigarettes began to glow on the beach. *Small comfort for these boys,* Truscott thought. He wondered what they would think if they knew it was their commander who'd first violated the blackout?

General George Patton woke up on D-day at 0200, dressed, and immediately made his way to the deck of the *Augusta,* where he saw the lights of Fedala to the north and Casablanca to the south. The sea was calm with no swell, and he thought, *God is with us.*

As with Goalpost at Mehdia, the central sub–task force was set to jump off at 0400; and likewise it was delayed, not once but twice, by the same sort of confusion. Finding and loading landing craft in the transport area in the dark turned out to be a task too difficult for the inexperienced hands of both army and navy.

At 0530, a searchlight appeared in the skies of Fedala, shining straight into the heavens. Since a sentence in Eisenhower's address to the military of North Africa earlier that morning had suggested that defenders who wanted to lay down their arms without a hopeless battle indicate their willingness to do so by pointing their searchlights to the vertical, there was a temporary excitement on the *Augusta.* The French would not fight! That notion was quickly squashed, however. The same searchlight quickly angled down and began sweeping the two-mile-long beach that fronted the city and was even now receiving the first wave of landing craft from the American transports out at sea. Immediately, Hewitt's destroyers opened up with whistling red tracers aimed directly at the searchlight. It was extinguished ten minutes later.

As the landings progressed at Fedala, Patton received word from Truscott shortly after 0700 that fighting had begun and was continuing at Mehdia. No word on whether or not the airport was under assault, but Patton assumed he would have been told if it were. There was far better news from General Ernest Harmon in Safi: The southern group had achieved complete surprise and had essentially taken that port already. Troops were under some sniper fire on the beach, but Harmon would soon receive the surrender of the commander of a battalion of Foreign Legion there.

Meanwhile, on his own front, Patton was witnessing a tough little naval battle. Six enemy destroyers had been sent from Casablanca at about the same time that Truscott's message arrived. They were greeted with withering fire from the assorted U.S. Navy vessels in the central group, including the *Augusta, Brooklyn,* and *Mississippi,* and soon retreated.

Patton decided to head for shore himself at 0800. His landing craft had been loaded with supplies and was on davits outside the ship, when again from Casablanca came a group of ships. This time the French sent more firepower, in the form of a light cruiser and a pair of large destroyers. The *Augusta* once again joined in the welcoming barrage, but now, when it opened fire, a blast from a rear turret shattered the very landing craft that Patton was planning to take to shore. The only items saved from the vessel were Patton's own ivory-handled revolvers.

Soon after the appearance of the destroyers, the French sent a group of bombers out over the ocean to attack the transports. The *Augusta* turned to protect them but was soon engaged again by the French ships from Casablanca. A destroyer in the American group, the *Ludlow,* was hit and set on fire, and the *Brooklyn* was hit as well. Shells fell so near to the *Augusta* that Patton was splashed by a close hit. The salvos of the bigger guns came from nine cannons firing jointly at the rate of twice a minute. They were so painfully loud that everyone, including Patton, wore cotton in their ears. For three hours the battle continued, until finally the French again retreated to the harbor in Casablanca, where the battleship *Mississippi* continued to bombard them and, for good measure, the French battleship *Jean Bart,* which hadn't yet ventured out into the melee.

Meanwhile, Patton took lunch, remarking later to this diary that "naval war is nice and comfortable." Afterward, he left for shore, arriving there at 1320. Patton found a beach in disarray similar to what Truscott encountered at Mehdia—there was serious overcrowding; units were having trouble organizing; many landing craft were beached, and their personnel wandered aimlessly about—but here French resistance was at a minimum. In fact, as Patton toured the town after landing, he received salutes and smiles from a number of French soldiers whom he encountered. Only the French marines were diffident. To further boost his spirits, he learned that eight members of the German Armistice Commission had been captured.

That night, as Truscott huddled with his cigarette on the beach, Patton took a room in Fedala's beachfront Hotel Miramar. It had been hit several times, knocking out its electricity and water pipes; nonetheless Patton was able to cadge a meal of fish and cheese, washed down with champagne.

It appeared at the end of D-day that the tough fighting remained around Port Lyautey and Casablanca, but all in all, as the general noted in his diary, "God was very good to me today."

CHAPTER 31

"Crack it open quickly"

The beach outside Patton's hotel was no more ordered on the morning of the ninth than it had been the day before. He went there after sunrise and immediately got involved in trying to organize matters, ordering a launch to go out and steer incoming lighters toward the harbor, rather than continuing to clog the beaches for unloading.

A French plane swooped in, strafing and dropping bombs on the scene. Patton was unfazed by the assault and so enraged by the reaction of the troops on the beach that when he found a soldier cowering in a fetal position, he booted him "with all [his] might" in the ass. "[The man] jump[ed] right up and went to work."

Perhaps obviously, Patton was disappointed in the way his soldiers responded to the circumstances. Later that day he would write, "The men were poor, the officers worse; no drive. It is very sad. I saw one lieutenant let his men hesitate to jump into the water. I gave him hell. I hit another man who was too lazy to push a boat. We also kicked a lot of Arabs."

Of the nearly twenty thousand troops in Patton's central force, roughly eight thousand had landed on the first day. Unfortunately, the percentage of supplies available to them was significantly less—in fact, it was about 10 percent of what they needed. Sorting through the mess on the beach would take much of the day. More than half of the landing craft and lighters used to bring troops, vehicles, and supplies to the Fedala beach were either sunk or stranded, and many lay scattered on the beach like wreckage.

Simply unloading what was there turned out to be complex as well. The priority of the inexperienced army troops was to defend themselves against the French forces they encountered as they came on shore; the priority of the inexperienced navy personnel was to get to the beach and get out as quickly as possible. Few volunteered for the hazardous grunt work. While packing at Norfolk was supposed to have been done in combat-ready fashion, a number of the landing craft were loaded haphazardly, leaving vital supplies needed immediately, like medicine and radio equipment, buried at the bottom of loads. And as was the case at Mehdia, a shortage of vehicles arriving on the first day made transporting matériel from the beaches that much more difficult.

Unfortunately, the weather on the ninth was not as cooperative as it had been on D-day, either. The surf, which had been so kind the day before, was now at six feet and growing. Rain began to fall as well. The Moroccan shore was finally showing its feistiness.

Eyeing the weather in the wee hours of the morning, Harry Semmes quickly realized that he would have no more than the seven tanks that had come ashore on the eighth to hold the Rabat–Port Lyautey road from the anticipated assault by the French. There was simply no way the tank lighters could bring any more of his vehicles ashore that morning.

At the order of Lucian Truscott the night before, Semmes had taken his armored battalion and headed to the south edge of the lagoon. There he waited in the predawn hours to hear the creak of the French tanks signaling their advance. Semmes's crews were experiencing their first night in Morocco, their first night in enemy territory, and the sheer foreignness of the experience was striking. Accustomed to training in the field in the southern United States, Semmes would later recall that he and his troops were used to the sweet and pungent smells of piney woods. But here "the ground near this pestilential lagoon had a sour, acrid, penetrating smell entirely unfamiliar and foreign." It was an aroma "compounded of 5,000 years of sheep and nomads living on the land." Adding to the general sense of alienation was a "sepulchral croaking" noise that filled the midnight air around the lagoon and reminded Semmes of Edgar Allen Poe's squawking raven. In fact, it turned out to be the mating call of the great African tree toad.

Semmes had other concerns aside from the eeriness of the setting. Not only did he have just seven tanks on hand against however many Renaults the French might throw toward Mehdia, but he was uncertain about the effectiveness of his vehicles. There had been no opportunity on the voyage to Morocco to sight them, which meant their fire could be wildly inaccurate. In addition, because of the communications blackout in the convoy, the tank radios hadn't been tested. It turned out that they were completely inoperative, which meant that his crews would have no communication with one another.

Nonetheless, come dawn, Semmes's Third Armored Landing Team moved away from the lagoon and into position. Led by crew members on foot because of the lack of radio communication, two tanks were guided to the east side of the Rabat road; the remaining five set up to the west. They came to a halt within a hundred yards of a farmhouse occupied by French infantry. No sooner had they arrived at their position than the French Renault tanks appeared as well. In all, there were fourteen of them, accompanied by a couple of battalions of Moroccan Tirailleurs. A moment of contemplation passed quickly. At that distance of a hundred yards, the combatants opened fire.

The two American tanks to the east side of the road cut a devastating swath through the French infantry by the farmhouse; but in general, and probably due to the fact that they hadn't been sighted, the U.S. armored vehicles weren't hitting their marks. The cold November rain was wreaking havoc with the breech mechanisms of the American guns, as well. Shells were not ejecting properly, and by the end of the day, all of the tank loaders would be missing fingernails from digging empty cartridges from their barrels. The American light tanks were also proving vulnerable to roundhouse punches from the French; the sides of the U.S. tanks were less heavily armored than their fronts. To compensate, Semmes ordered his crews to move their vehicles forward and backward, so that they always faced in the direction of their attackers. This stiff but effective two-step allowed the vehicles to present only their thicker fronts to the French and prevented the armor-piercing shells employed by the Vichy from doing as much damage as they otherwise might have.

Despite all of this, the U.S. armored team held their own and more, actually knocking out four of the French tanks by 0830. The tanks of the Third Armored remained outmanned, however, and Semmes felt his situation was growing desperate, when suddenly, over the landscape on the French side of the battlefield, shells began pouring in from the U.S. Navy. A spotter plane had pinpointed the location of the French tanks for the cruiser *Savannah,* and her eight-inch shells were suddenly raining down with terrifying accuracy on the Vichy, gouging tank-size craters in the countryside.

By 0900, the French had withdrawn to the south toward Rabat. Though they would re-form and attack later in the day, once again the *Savannah* would help send them scurrying. "We will always have a warm spot in our hearts for the *Savannah* and her crew," Semmes would later write.

To Semmes's rear, the First Battalion moved inland over the high ground to the south of the airport in preparation for assault on the field. There, at midmorning, they got hung up by a combination of stiff French infantry resistance and bombardment of two sorts: the U.S. Navy, aiming at the batteries surrounding the airport and Port Lyautey, joined with French planes, focused on bombing and strafing the American positions to make advance on the field a hazardous proposition. The First dug in and remained trenchbound for the day.

At the same time, the Second Battalion faced a strongly reinforced Kasbah. French Legionnaires from Meknes had arrived in the night to fortify the fort. At the same time, the American battalion remained badly disorganized from its chaotic arrival and advance the day before, with each company able to account for only thirty to fifty of its men. Several ineffective attempts were made at taking the Kasbah, but each was rebuffed. The French counterattacked, trying to push the Second back toward the beaches, but they too were unsuccessful. U.S. forces were able to clear the trenches to the south of the Kasbah, but the thick-walled old Portuguese bastion remained in French hands through the course of the day.

To the north of the Sebou, Toffey's Third Battalion began the day on its hill overlooking the airport. It was still waiting for the rubber boats that would provide it transportation across the Sebou, but these didn't arrive at its position until 1400. Even then, it was no easy thing to get them inflated and operational. A single hand pump was employed in the task, and the process caught the attention of the French, who sprayed fire in the direction of the battalion. The Third remained relatively safe in foxholes that they'd previously dug after drawing some accurate French battery fire from near a barn southwest of the airport.

Toffey sent a patrol to the strongly defended bridge north of Port Lyautey. Nonetheless, the Third's efforts were dictated by two basic assignments: get across the Sebou to aid in the assault of the airfield; and take that bridge. After meeting with company commanders at 1430, Toffey ordered that both should happen by the end of the day.

Just after dark, at 1900, the Third Battalion's I Company baptized its rubber boats in the Sebou, near the bend in the river where the French had scuttled the two steamers. Once again, a lack of preparation confounded the exercise. The rubber boats turned out to be barely navigable, and it wound up taking seven trips to get the whole company across. Once they were on the airport side of the river, the members of I Company found themselves wallowing in a muddy bottom. The weight of equipment on their own backs made any movement a plodding chore. They also managed to mire themselves deeper in the muck by heading south, parallel to the river, toward the heart of the swamp. Finally, they turned west, but they now were moving parallel to the airport, rather than toward it. They also were discovered, and got hit by enemy artillery coming at their backs from the east. It was then that they decided to retrace their steps to the point at which they'd originally crossed. Here, they dug in as best they could and awaited the sunrise.

The attack on the bridge was similarly slowed by heavy equipment. But on the north side of the Sebou, it was that weight carried in sandy terrain that bogged the movements of K and M Companies. Both vehicles and infantry found negotiating the dunes a laborious task. It took four hours to get the two companies in position for attack. Toffey, who was leading the assault, ordered his C Battery to open fire on the west side of the bridge at 1830. Out at sea, a destroyer leveled supporting fire on the airport.

As K Company came within 1,200 yards of the bridge, it was hit with machine-gun fire from solid positions in ditches on either side of the road. Two infantrymen were killed in the initial blast. Toffey sent out a patrol to knock out the enemy nests, but grenades couldn't dislodge them. Several mortar rounds were more successful and wiped out one of the machine guns. A second gun, however, wreaked more havoc on the Americans until a patrol from M Company, using a combination of bazooka, grenades, and machine guns, was finally able to chase it off.

M Company moved within four hundred yards of the bridge, but the process of trying to move up some artillery to help take the bridge alerted French batteries to its position. Enemy artillery zeroed in on Toffey's troops, inflicting more casualties. He left portions of M Company at their post near the bridge but pulled the rest of his forces back to the hill where the Third Battalion had started the day.

Down at the Hotel Miramar in Fedala, George Patton was reviewing a day that had not gone quite to his liking. While a portion of his force, the Third Infantry Division, had headed south toward Casablanca and was poised to attack the city the next day, the rough surf and mess on the beach had slowed reinforcements. He was considering pursuing the assault with just the Third, in conjunction with a naval bombardment.

To the south at Safi, Harmon had taken a small airport and was beginning to organize his tanks for their advance on Casablanca; but to Patton news of his movements had dried up by the end of the day.

The task force commander knew that Truscott was in a tough fight at Port Lyautey—word had arrived of Semmes's tank battle on the Rabat road—but here, too, further information had ceased. Patton did, however, know that the airport had not yet been taken. He also knew from Truscott's last message of the ninth that he could use some help. But Patton, who was planning to assault Casablanca with limited force, had none to spare.

Adding to his pressures in the early morning on the tenth was a telegram from Eisenhower reporting on the progress of the Mediterranean task force. "Algiers has been ours for two days," it read. "Oran defense crumbling rapidly. . . . The only tough nut is in your hands. Crack it open quickly ask for what you want."

By evening on the ninth, Truscott was feeling an intense pressure to take the Kasbah and the airfield as quickly as possible. The surf that day had effectively eliminated any landings on the Mehdia beaches by midafternoon. He also knew that he would have no reinforcements from Patton. His orders to Colonel de Rohan, commander of the Sixtieth Infantry, were straightforward: de Rohan was to personally lead the assault of the Second Battalion on the Kasbah at daybreak the next day. As he did so, the First Battalion from the southwest and the Third Battalion from the north were to attack the airfield in conjunction with the commandos on board the *Dallas*, which was likewise supposed to enter the Sebou at dawn and make its way upriver as quickly as possible. This battle needed to be over by the close of day on the tenth. Period.

In the night, detachments were sent out to eliminate the heavy French sniper activity between Mehdia and the Kasbah. The naval demolition team was sent off to blow up the cable that barred river traffic just past the jetties. And out at sea, both the *Dallas* and the *Contessa* were given word that they were about to enter the fray.

CHAPTER 32

The *Dallas* Goes First

On the night of November 9, René Malevergne and Captain Robert Brodie shared the bridge of the *Dallas* as well as the exhaustion of two long days waiting for the moment when they would finally steam up the River Sebou. Malevergne sat at the map table, trying to stay awake; but when he put his head down, he gave in to sleep. The captain woke him and told him to go get a decent rest in Brodie's own cabin. He would wake the Frenchman when the time came. That wasn't long. It seemed just moments later that Brodie shook his shoulder: "The admiral wants you to tell him if we can enter the river at dawn," he said.

Malevergne did the calculations: It was 0130. High tide was at 0300. At low tide, 2.4 meters (approximately 8 feet) of water covered the bar at the mouth of the river. High tide increased that level by about 2.7 meters (approximately 9 feet)—combined that raised the total a little above 17 feet of water. The *Dallas*'s draft was about 3.3 meters (nearly 11 feet). But dawn would come at 0600 on the tenth, which meant that he and the ship would be entering the Sebou on an ebb tide, with water fast dropping and pouring out in the direction of the sea. The question was, would there still be enough depth to allow the *Dallas* over the bar and into the river? In plain fact, Malevergne couldn't answer that question with certainty. What if there were delays in getting to the jetties? What if they didn't arrive until 0630 or 0700? What if they smashed into the bar? At this point in the invasion, however, everyone involved understood that risks had to be taken. "It's okay," Malevergne said to Brodie. "Tell the admiral we can enter at dawn."

The *Contessa* was pondering similar equations as she cruised around the transport area, awaiting her own run up the river. Late on the ninth, the ship's officers had been ordered to report to Captain Gray on Truscott's transport, the *Allen*. There they had been told to stand by and be prepared to follow the *Dallas* upriver as soon as the destroyer silenced the batteries and took the airport. Lieutenant Leslie and Captain John made arrangements with Gray to send a pair of LCM-3s upriver after the *Contessa* to help with the unloading. Afterward, they began a quest among the transports for cargo nets. In their haste to get out of Norfolk, the ship had neglected gear and, naturally, they would want to unload their cargo as quickly as possible. The more cargo nets, the more hatches they could use simultaneously. The more hatches they could use, the quicker they would be out of the airfield. They managed to cadge twelve nets by begging from the various transports.

The *Contessa* had other concerns. Like the *Dallas,* its most immediate problem was getting through the jetties and over the bar at the mouth of the river. For the banana boat, however, this obstacle was even more acute. Her draft, at seventeen feet, was not as shallow as that of the *Dallas* and—according to Malevergne's calculations—could only make it over the bar at precisely high tide. Because at 0300 on the morning of the tenth, the *Dallas* had not even begun to sail for the river, Leslie and John understood that they would not be heading up the Sebou until the next high tide, in the afternoon. Otherwise, it would be simply impossible to navigate the entrance to the river. In other words, they could not sail in the immediate wake of the destroyer but would be running alone at around 1400—that is, if all went well.

The *Contessa* also lacked a river pilot. Whether or not John and Leslie knew of René Malevergne's role with the *Dallas* early that morning is unknown, but they were surely worried about their entry into the river without a guide, especially after witnessing the pounding surf on the Moroccan shore. While the weather report was favorable on the morning of the tenth, that didn't mean that it couldn't turn ugly quickly; or that, given the circumstances of navigating the bar with the volatile load they carried, even in moderate swells, matters couldn't turn dicey in an instant.

It was also to say nothing of their ignorance of the river beyond the bar. Beyond the fact that it was shallow and winding, Leslie and John knew next to nothing of the Sebou's treacheries. But they and the crew of the *Contessa* were resolved to get their load up the river, just as the *Dallas* was resolved to lead the way.

At 0500, the destroyer set out from thirteen miles' distance from the jetties. The sky was overcast and the wind came from the northwest. It was still dark outside, but Brodie, at the wheel, and Malevergne beside him, ordered the ship forward at a speed of thirteen knots, timed to reach the bar at daybreak. At 0545, as they neared the jetties, the waves were breaking on the ship's stern, pushing her too rapidly toward the narrow channel. Brodie ordered her speed cut to ten knots.

Some light was evident on the horizon in front of them, and the water beneath began to appear yellowish, indicating deposits of sand marking the mouth of the river. It was still too hazy to see the jetties, which jutted several hundred yards out from the shoreline. All hands on deck were ordered to ignore threats from French artillery, and keep a lookout for signs of land.

The channel inland hugged the south jetty, and that is where Malevergne wanted to take the ship, but he still couldn't be certain about where exactly he was. He asked Brodie if he could take the wheel, and the captain gave it to him. Malevergne ordered the engines cut until he got his bearings. The sudden end of the pounding pistons from the engine room below caused a deep and eerie stillness to sweep over the *Dallas*. Deckhands at the rail stared intently into the murk, just as Brodie and Malevergne did from the bridge. Malevergne listened to the sound of the surf, waiting to hear "a familiar growl," the sound of the bar.

Malevergne steered slightly toward port, and the *Dallas* approached the bar slowly. Backlit by the rising sun he could make out the pile of rocks marking the south side of the jetty in the morning haze. Malevergne brought the *Dallas* around toward starboard at forty-five degrees and could see ahead of him waves breaking on the rocks. To the south, the village of Mehdia appeared in the half light with American troops and equipment cluttering the edge of its beach. (General Lucian Truscott was there, eyeing the progress of the destroyer with interest and fingers crossed.) Despite Malevergne's preoccupation, it was impossible for him not to look briefly for his own cottage among the many white houses that were scattered through the town.

The ship yawed as Malevergne pointed it toward the channel, which ran tight to the south side of the jetty. It first veered toward the rocks on the right and then wobbled to the north side of the river's entrance, near the shoal side of the jetties. As the *Dallas* approached the bar, the swells got heavier. As she pointed between the jetties, a shell landed thirty yards ahead, splashing in the river. Moments later, a second shell whistled over their heads. In the background, from the direction of the Kasbah, they could hear rifle and machine-gun fire, but none of it was reaching the *Dallas*.

At three minutes past six, she approached and then hit the bar. All the wobbles and rocking of the ship now became intensified and concentrated. The *Dallas* vibrated like a tuning fork as the pounding force of swells in the stern, river current in the bow, and land scraping her keel below made the destroyer a tiny vessel caught between forces far more powerful than she. The ship hung quivering on the bar for several seconds but then churned forward. She was over and in the river. Malevergne ordered full speed ahead.

From down in the engine room the call came up to the bridge that the *Dallas* had reached her maximum speed, a full twenty-five knots. The action report of the ship would later tell the true story: "A glance over the side showed . . . that we were making less than five."

Behind the ship, a cloud of river muck dug up by the bottom of the hull indicated where the difference lay. She was scraping her way upriver.

The *Dallas* maintained her line in the channel and slowly picked up speed. As she neared the Kasbah, however, another obstacle loomed. It turned out that the boom crossing the river had been only partially cut. The cable still stretched over the channel from the south bank to a point about halfway over the channel, and the point where it had been exploded by the navy team in the night was shoal. Not only that, beyond the cable to the north side of the jetty, where the river broadened, Malevergne knew the Vichyists had set mines. When he saw where the obstruction had been cut, he said, "Captain, there is no depth there."

A machine gun opened fire at that moment from near the Kasbah, again short of its target, but near enough now to spur them forward. Malevergne and Brodie decided to run right through what was left of the cable, and Malevergne ordered full speed ahead.

The boom was strung across the river through a series of anchored floats. The cable remained intact through the first two of these but was down at the third—the one that rested over the shoal. Malevergne pointed the *Dallas*'s bow directly between floats one and two and felt the ship pick up speed to a full eighteen knots. He closed his eyes when he heard the hull grind against the chain, but the destroyer was able to part the boom without a tremor. She rushed deeper into the river.

Up the northeastern angle of the river and through the first bend she sailed, occasionally scraping, occasionally racing ahead. Now the airport loomed. All hands were ordered to take cover and watch for sniping, and, indeed, several machine guns opened fire from the hills above the field. The distance was too far. The rounds sent up puffs of water and sludge from the swamp on the south bank of the river, two hundred yards from the ship.

Next came a series of artillery blasts—three-inch shells now, which once again spluttered in the mud, short of the *Dallas*. For the first time on her voyage, the *Dallas* opened her own three-inch guns and fired in the direction of the barrage. The French gun was quickly silenced. As 0700 neared, the ship approached the bend in the river where the Vichyists had sunk the pair of steamers two nights before as Toffey and company watched. The *Batavia* and the *Saint Emile* lay junked in the river, obstructing passage up the Sebou except for a narrow path between the two ships.

Above, two planes from the *Sangamon* started to fly cover for the old four-piper. From the shore, the men on board the destroyer could see the column from Toffey's Third Battalion, who'd spent the night on the edge of the swamp. They waved at one another, like friends surprised at the sight of each other, and for a moment it felt to Malevergne that the fighting had stopped around them.

The space between the *Batavia* and the *Saint Emile* was just large enough for the *Dallas* to squeeze through; but here, too, the channel of the Sebou was shallow, and to make the bend she would have to run headlong into a strong current rushing out to sea or risk getting hung up in the shallows. If she carefully picked her way through the wrecks, the *Dallas* would face the possibility of running aground as she slowed. If she rushed through the French ships too quickly, she wouldn't be able to make the bend and would run straight into the riverbank directly behind the wrecks.

Malevergne again ordered full speed ahead. The men at their battle stations watched in silence as the destroyer aimed for the gap between the scuttled steamers. Eyeing the narrow passage between the ships, guiding her against the current, Malevergne felt the *Dallas* roll first to starboard and then to port; but not only did she right herself, but she was able to navigate the corner and get her bow pointed upstream, directly toward her destination. Ahead they could see the airport. The *Dallas* and the commandos she carried with her were now the lead column of the American invasion of Port Lyautey.

At half ebb, the *Dallas* continued to slog her way forward. Again her engines were working at an exaggerated speed. They cycled at twenty knots, while the ship strolled at ten. Just after 0730, she came to a halt in the middle of the river and sat there, stuck in the mud.

Trapped "like a Dutch canal boat" midstream, the *Dallas* quickly became a target, tempting the same batteries that had stymied the Third Battalion at the Port Lyautey bridge the night before. They began to lob shells that hit her port side and then began to whistle through the *Dallas*'s halyards as the commandos prepared to disembark in rubber boats to starboard. The destroyer once again opened her three-inch guns, and at the same time, one of the escort planes above located the battery

and dropped a depth charge on top of it. The guns fell silent and the commandos were able to finish their disembarkation and reach shore without
a casualty.

Once there, they linked up with the company from the Third Battalion, with whom they'd just shared friendly waves. From the southwest
side of the airport, elements of the First Battalion, which had moved onto
high ground there in the night, formed the other claw in the pincer. The
commandos, with the First and Third Battalions, moved immediately
on the field, and the French forces there soon high-tailed it toward Port
Lyautey. By 1030, the airport was in American hands.

Reconnoitering on the ridge above the Port Lyautey bridge, Colonel Jack
Toffey and a company from the First Battalion spied French artillery setting up to the northeast on the Tangier highway—the same road that had
carried René Malevergne out of Morocco nearly two months earlier. The
U.S. Navy spotters with him called in strikes from the *Texas,* the *Eberle,*
and the *Kearny.* The batteries were silenced but evidenced that there was
still some fight in the French.

From the ancient crenellated walls of the Kasbah, soldiers of the
French Foreign Legion fired down at Colonel de Rohan's Second Battalion below in a setting that seemed, except for the modern weaponry,
like a tableau from an earlier century. The Americans had thrown all of
their available troops at the attack, including reserve forces of engineers
and the "cooks and clerks" organized in the aviation companies by Nick
Craw in transit across the ocean. They had cleared all entrenchments
and machine-gun nests outside the wall of the structure but were pinned
down by heavy machine-gun and mortar fire from within. Soon a call
came to Truscott's command center. Would it be possible to get some air
support? And if so, how long would it take for it to get to the Kasbah?

As it happened, eight naval dive bombers were nearby, about to fly
missions further inland to Meknes. Truscott's command was able to locate a U.S. Navy spotter, who raced forward from the beach in a Bantam

jeep. Now stationed near the cannery in the shadow of the fort, Truscott watched as the planes circled above the site and then began their descent upon the target. The bombs whistled down on the fort and landed, rocking the ground all the way back to Truscott, who saw "great clouds of smoke and dust rolling upwards" from within the bastion. "It was a beautiful sight for an old soldier's eyes," he would write later.

Major Dilley of the Second Battalion moved a company forward with bazookas, and they took aim at point-blank range at the Kasbah's gate. An opening was blasted into the fort, and infantry rushed forward with bayonets at the ready. Soon a steady stream of French soldiers was coming out with hands up, prisoners of the Sixtieth Infantry.

Late in the morning of the tenth, Army Air Force pilot Daniel Rathbun was looking down from his P-40 at the Port Lyautey airfield, wondering where he was supposed to land. Launched a few minutes earlier from the *Chenango,* his plane was the first of some seventy-five P-40s that were coming into the airport, but what he saw on the strips below was more than a little daunting. Bomb craters pockmarked the concrete runways from one end to the other. Grass fields on both sides of the strip had been flooded. Also littering the ground were seven French Dewoitine D.520s that had been caught refueling and put to rest by Navy Wildcats on the first day of action.

To avoid the most hazardous crater at the start of the runway, Rathbun decided to begin his touchdown just past it; however, the strip was not very long to begin with—about 1,800 to 2,000 feet, he guessed—and landing at the spot he'd chosen would leave him just 1,000 feet in which to come down. He cut his speed so he wouldn't come in so hot he'd run right off the runway, but as he did so, Rathbun's engine stalled and his plane dropped down on the very crater he had tried to avoid. He skidded and turned and wound up in one of the watery grass strips beside the runway, but he was alive and uninjured.

The next P-40 to land, coming in on Rathbun's tail, saw what had happened to the first flier and decided to land in the swampy grass. He, too, landed in one piece, but his wheels were mired in mud, and the nose of his plane wound up pointing upward with a damaged propeller.

Rathbun immediately decided that he had to warn the other P-40s coming in that the airfield was in no condition to receive them. He saw a destroyer stuck in the river to the east of the Port Lyautey field and raced in her direction. Rathbun hollered to the *Dallas* to please send a message to the *Chenango* to halt further launches until the runways could be repaired. Whether the message was sent and ignored or never sent Rathbun never knew. Forty-five minutes later, more planes began to arrive, and the airport remained in no shape to receive them.

CHAPTER 33

Twelve Desperate Miles

Great, billowing clouds of dark smoke blossomed above the city of Port Lyautey and rose skyward early in the afternoon of the tenth. The canopy of smoke and flame was coming from oil storage tanks located near the port, hit by U.S. Navy gunfire. Evidence of continuing battle could be heard and seen to the southeast of the airport as well, toward Meknes; and to the north, the French had blown several arches on the bridge above Lyautey, which drooped down toward the river. P-40's were still trying to land at the airport, but the damaged field continued to take its toll. Planes avoiding the potholes that Daniel Rathbun had tried to warn them about were ditching into the swampy water on either side of the east/west runway. Before the day was through, at least twenty P-40s had been made inoperable by the landings.

Meanwhile, the *Dallas* stayed trapped in its mire, waiting for high tide to come and push it free. René Malevergne sat feeling the uneasy mix of tension and exhaustion that had been his ongoing condition for days now. Rumor in the officers' wardroom had it that the Kasbah was taken, and its capture, along with the taking of the airport, meant that the battle was winding down. He assumed he would soon be able to see Germaine and the children, but as much as anything else it was this nearness to the finish line that was driving his tension. He was so close to home now that he could feel the warmth of reunion, but he still must do his duty for the Americans.

A *Dallas* officer asked Malevergne if he could come to the bridge. Three citizens of Port Lyautey, who'd been found wandering between the lines, were on board for questioning, but they spoke little or no English. Could he translate? So apparently Malevergne, the man who had had trouble making himself understood to Al Gruenther a month earlier, was now an interpreter for the Americans, as well as a river guide. He got up to help and found himself greeting a trio of French Moroccans who turned out to be acquaintances of his. They had gone out toward the bridge out of simple curiosity; and now, looking at Malevergne, they were astonished to find their neighbor on this American ship, serving as translator of their explanation.

Malevergne asked immediately about his family. Unfortunately, no one in the group had any news for him. He was asked by the Americans to quiz them about French troop strength in the city, but they were hesitant to supply information. Despite the obvious evidence that a new regime was here, they still were concerned about the Vichyists. *What if the police commissioner finds out?*

"You are going to be released," Malevergne said to them, with obvious satisfaction, "and you can tell the police commissioner that Malevergne, who has been forbidden to live in Port Lyautey, bids him good day."

It was not the last American request of the river pilot. Early that afternoon a radio message arrived on the bridge. A cargo ship carrying materials—"indispensable for the commandos" is how it was presented to Malevergne—was waiting out in the transport area to make a run up the river. It needed to catch the next high tide at 1400. A launch would soon be pulling up to the *Dallas* to take him out to the ship. Would he be willing to guide it to the airport, just as he'd done with the *Dallas*?

P-40s had already achieved fame in the war in Asia, fighting the Japanese under the air group nickname "The Flying Tigers." They were single-engine fighter planes capable of carrying 1,500 pounds of bombs that could be attached in three fixed locations, two on the wings and one directly beneath the cockpit. The munitions came in three sizes: 250-, 500-, and 1,000-pound bombs. All types were carried in the holds of the *Contessa,* but the majority were of the 250-pound variety. It's not known exactly how many shells the *Contessa* carried but at a minimum—filled only with thousand-pound bombs in a nine-hundred-ton load—it would have held 1,800 projectiles. At a maximum—carrying only 250-pound bombs—the number would have been 7,200. No doubt the *Contessa*'s munitions load was somewhere on the high end between these numbers.

Paired with the bombs were two thousand four-hundred-pound drums of high-octane airplane fuel (four hundred tons) stowed in separate holds. In all, the load constituted about a quarter of the tonnage that the *Contessa* could typically carry, if she were hauling bananas in Honduras and not trying to navigate a river whose depth at high tide barely matched her draft. More pertinent to the crew of the ship than tonnage numbers, however, was the simple fact that if that mix of bombs and gasoline was pierced and exploded, they and their vessel would be an instant memory.

Exactly when Captain John and Lieutenant Leslie learned that they would have the use of the Port Lyautey river pilot is uncertain, but they were surely glad at the news. It had become obvious to them since the day they arrived off the shores of Mehdia that the deepest hazards of the final leg of their journey would be found in navigating the *Contessa*'s load against the pounding shores of Morocco and up the River Sebou, not among the French defenses.

Captain John and Lieutenant Leslie also knew that the tide at Mehdia was shifting. Its height along the Moroccan shoreline would diminish each day after the tenth of November, until later in the month. The *Contessa*'s draft was not going to shrink with it. If she did not go up this day, she would not be able to enter the River Sebou for days to come. George Patton, on the brink of assaulting Casablanca to the south and still expecting help from those P-40s, would not countenance further delay.

Neither, it turned out, would Lieutenant Leslie (or "Leslay," as René Malevergne pronounced and wrote the name). When the Frenchman came aboard the *Dallas* from a launch at nearly 1500, Leslie insisted, in Malevergne's words "that the impossible be done." That they head immediately up the river.

For his part, Malevergne still didn't know exactly what sort of load he was piloting up the Sebou. He saw a ship of about six thousand tons, flying the flag of Honduras (Malevergne thought it was Panamanian), and continued in his belief that the *Contessa* was carrying a load essential to the commandos at the airport. That and that alone.

He learned from Captain John that the ship drew only seventeen feet of water or five meters fifteen, but that she could move at a solid speed of fourteen or fifteen knots. He also knew, as the high tide had already passed, that there was not a minute to lose in getting the ship to the bar.

The weather for the voyage was fine, and visibility now, at midafternoon, made entry into the jetties not nearly the problem it had been that morning with the *Dallas*. Far more troubling—and dangerously so—was the combination of the diminishing tide, the depth of the bar, and the load the *Contessa* carried.

They were no big guns pounding from the *Texas* or any of the destroyers or cruisers behind them. There was no rat-a-tat of machine guns or reports of rifles coming from near the beach at Mehdia; but ongoing efforts at clearing the area of supplies made the village a busy scene. A number of landing craft were still inoperable; and others continued to arrive from the transport area as the *Contessa* headed for the bar. Her merchant marine deckhands—the Brazilians, the Arabs, the Danes, the Italians, and all the others—now lined the rail, watching for land in the waters below and getting their first close-up views of the beaches of Morocco. They saw the same yellowish water that the *Dallas* crew had viewed that morning, the same surf pounding against the rocky quay.

Gun crews from the armed guard, manning stations on a deck where tourists like William Bendix, Leo Carroll, and Miss New Orleans had first seen the harbors of tropical seaports in the Caribbean, were now looking at a blue African sky. Beyond the entrance to the river, they could see the Sebou pouring down from the interior. To the north of the river were high sand cliffs and dunes beyond them. To the south stood the stucco-colored village of Mehdia and just beyond it, the old Portuguese bastion, the Kasbah, which they knew had been taken just a few hours earlier. Despite the dominant presence of the American army near the shore, they knew they were not pulling into Havana, Ceiba, Norfolk, or Brooklyn. All aboard assumed—or prayed, in the case of the steward, Mario Violini—that the army and the destroyer *Dallas* had made the way safe for them, but who could be certain? Gunner Hakie McLaughlin would remember for years to come a feeling of isolation and a sense of being "a sitting duck" as the ship neared the mouth of the jetties.

They entered one hour after high-water slack. The timing could have been better, but currents were not yet strong. Malevergne guided them in at half speed, looking for the channel near the south jetty, as he had done with other ships a thousand times before. The *Contessa* was carrying enough weight to make a fairly steady course into the channel. The pilot hoped there might be enough water in the ebb tide and beneath her keel to give her a boost over the bar, but the ship scraped heavily on the sand and took a sharp sheer toward the south jetty.

Malevergne immediately rang for full speed ahead in the hope of correcting her, but the *Contessa* didn't respond quickly enough against the yaw. She shuddered violently going over the bar, but instead of veering away from the rocks at Malevergne's turn of the wheel, she skidded more sharply toward them, like a car caught in a skid. Everyone on deck, all the armed guard members at their stations, all the crewmen from their various nations, all the recent inmates of the Norfolk County Jail, and all the officers on the bridge, took deep breaths and waited as the *Contessa* slammed headlong into the rocks on her port bow.

It is safe to say that the only person on the vessel who didn't think their time had come at that moment was the man at the wheel. Malevergne, of course, was the only one who didn't know precisely what the ship was carrying in her holds. The crash of the *Contessa* was violent enough to send her foremast twanging forward so heavily that Leslie felt certain it would come snapping out of the deck. From top to bottom of the ship, crew members went flying. The number one hold was staved in, and water instantly began gushing in the bowels of the vessel. In the midst of the crash, all the way through its reverberating conclusion, everyone on board but Malevergne paused and waited for one of those cans of fuel to slosh open and pour toward a spark; or waited for a rack of those cradled bombs down below to bust free; waited for the explosion that would blow them all to kingdom come.

It didn't happen. Water poured so heavily into the hold that it reached thirteen feet in a matter of two minutes. Captain John sent his old shipmate, carpenter Harry Haylock, to assess damages, but there was little that could be done except try to get as much water as possible out of the hold as quickly as possible. The utility crew, heavily staffed by Norfolk inmates, got the pumps going, and the water level was soon maintained. Most important, the ship did not blow.

Luckily, too, it did not get hung up on the rocks. The impact of the *Contessa* against the jetty actually created its own rebound. She heaved back against the crash, aided by the river current and the ebb tide. Malevergne guided her away from further damage in the channel and ordered the engines up. Like a fullback heading once more toward the goal line, she put her head down and plowed forward. Over the bar she went "churning up mud and sand . . . with all the grace of a hog going over a mudbank."

On the other side, she was floating again, but barely. With her draft six feet deeper than the *Dallas*'s, and now with thirteen feet of water in her front hold adding to her weight, she became less a vessel than a plow. She had no momentum and moved strictly on the strength of her engines and their ability to propel her keel through the bottom of the river.

Down among the catwalks and stifling air of the engine room, the pounding of cylinders was deafening. John rang for as much steam as she could safely muster, and chief engineer John Langdon and his crew responded. The firemen monitored the boiler gauges; the oilers raced around the machinery, checking bearings, pistons, and valve stems for overheating and lubrication. The possibilities for disaster were a long list: a neglected water gauge could shut down the boiler; a burned-out bearing could stop the engine; an order implemented too slowly could cause the propeller to grind to a jerking halt. In the tight confines of the walkways in and out and around the engines, wipers, engineers, and fire-men pirouetted and plied, oilcans and wrenches at the ready, in time with the ungodly din of the engines. And still she inched forward at a rate no quicker than a fast walk.

On deck, the members of the armed guard continued to man their stations, eyeing the hills to the right and left of them as the *Contessa* inched past the Kasbah—sightlines strained upward at the crenellated walls—and then headed northeast toward the top of the first bend in the river, where elements of Toffey's Third Battalion were tucked in and secure. Occasionally a landing craft or two would whiz by, now able to bring supplies inland from the beach to one battalion or another in the interior. But having a little company on the river turned out to be no comfort. There was still sniping going on from the hills between the Kasbah and the airport. Shots pinged around the banana boat and her highly explosive load as the navy gunners looked out from their sta-tions, trying without success to find something to shoot at. The *Contessa* inched along so slowly that she couldn't help but draw attention to her-self. In contrast to the landing craft that were zipping by, she was in a slow-motion war. Time had never ticked by with such difficulty for the men on board as she climbed up the river.

The men on deck could plainly see American troops moving along the hillsides; they could see half-tracks and jeeps rushing over open ground. There was a clear sense that the battle had been won, yet it was impossible not to consider how exposed they remained to some uncoor-dinated attack from the enemy. The sensation intensified as the *Contessa* inched her way through the northeastern bend of the river and traveled by the swamp that had mired the Third Battalion the evening before. A single strafing run from a French Dewoitine rushing in from the air-port at Meknes would place them in dire circumstances. A lost French battery zeroing in on the *Contessa* could blow them to kingdom come. One of the mines in the river nudging past the recently baked degaussing coils and against her hull could precipitate the biggest explosion wit-nessed at Port Lyautey in those three days of action. And still there was

no way to speed the mission of this polyglot contingent of merchant
seamen.

From entry into the river to the second bend in the Sebou, where
the *Batavia* and *Saint Emile* lay scuttled in the river, it took more than
four hours. The *Contessa* could see those sunken steamers coming from
miles away, in late afternoon sunshine and in dusk. There they sat like
a part of the landscape, unavoidable and immovable. While navigating
the *Dallas,* Malevergne had been able to ring for full speed at the bend,
using the ship's mobility and momentum to bite into the corner as he
took the destroyer through. He had been able to swing her stern around
the ships quickly, to keep her moving forward and pointed toward the
airport. Now, with the *Contessa,* he had no momentum for the same maneuver, though once again Malevergne rang for full speed. The banana
boat could only respond with a moderate surge that pushed her between
the scuttled ships, and she simply wasn't able to swing around into the
bend and head to the south. Instead, the tired ship kept plowing forward
with a resigned inevitability into the far bank of the river. Though she
was trapped and finding soft ground on the shore, the *Contessa*'s engine
continued to force its way into the muddy soil of Morocco to a distance
of fifty feet. Unlike at the hard rocks at the river's entrance, she came to
a cushioned halt in the slop. If she wasn't going to explode at the rocks
on the jetty, she wasn't going to explode here. Nonetheless, it was 1830
and she was hard aground.

As the airfield at Port Lyautey continued to be repaired, a column of
French trucks carrying reinforcements headed toward the region from
Meknes. Spotter planes saw them coming and sent a range to the battleship *Texas,* which opened fire with her main battery at about seventeen
thousand yards. Soon gaping holes from the fourteen-inch high-explosive
shells began appearing in the highway, and the trucks turned around.

Through the day and into the night, the beaches continued to be
cleared of wreckage and cargo. More and more launches began speeding

up the river to deliver supplies to companies that had progressed toward Port Lyautey. Disorganized units of French infantry drifted back in the same direction through the course of the day. Occasional sniper fire continued, which the French military would later blame on native troops.

As night came to Port Lyautey, the First Battalion entered the city and captured the French commander and most of his remaining troops. The French colonel asked to arrange an armistice with Truscott, who replied that he would do nothing until Major Pierpont Hamilton was released. It was well after dark when the French took Hamilton to the airfield, where, by a tank radio, he was able to contact Colonel Semmes at another tank radio down at the beaches. Semmes relayed Hamilton's message to Truscott: General Mathenet had arrived in Port Lyautey and wanted to *parlez* the next morning at the Kasbah. Hamilton sent a similar message to the *Dallas*, which radioed Admiral Kelly about the next day's meeting.

On the *Contessa*, there was nothing to do but wait for the next tide to come in and raise the level of the river and the ship with it. The pumps continued to do their job on the number one hold, draining the water that had accumulated there since she was holed at the south jetty; but the engines were shut down. The exhausted engine department could finally get some rest, and on deck it was possible to hear a stillness in the Moroccan night.

There was plenty of uneasiness on board in the night. Rumors of enemy troops moving twenty miles north and east of Port Lyautey surfaced. George Patton was still poised with his central task force at the edge of Casablanca, fully intending to attack the city in the morning. French forces remained in Meknes and Marrakech. Truscott had ordered Semmes to prepare to move the next day on Rabat with his tanks; and who could say with certainty what lay out there in the quiet hillsides above the *Contessa*? But it would be another day before the P-40s would be receiving any of the gasoline or munitions she carried.

★   ★   ★

For René Malevergne, still lingering on the *Contessa* after its run was over, the fight was out of him. He wanted to go home and see Germaine and the boys. Leslie had the *Dallas* radioed, and a launch from that ship arrived midevening. Malevergne first went back to the destroyer, where he asked Captain Brodie if it would be possible for him to go home that night. Brodie gave him a handwritten pass and the operative passwords—"Georges," as Malevergne recorded it, and "Patton"—that would enable him to travel safely to Mehdia and back to his cottage.

For all the while it had taken him to travel up the river that day in both the *Dallas* and the *Contessa*, his trip downriver in the launch felt almost as long. Up through the bend in the Sebou above Port Lyautey; downriver in the northern loop; the dip down toward the Kasbah; and then the darkened profile of Mehdia, its lights blacked out to protect it from stray bombing runs. Malevergne was deposited at a dock just above the village, where he was able to bum a ride on a jeep to the beach. It was 2200 hours, 10:00 p.m., when the guards at the entrance to his home-town examined his pass from Captain Brodie and allowed him entry into Mehdia.

He could see no lights on at his home as he approached the stucco wall that surrounded the property. Malevergne shared the call, "Georges," and response, "Patton," with a sentry posted outside the gate and was allowed inside his own courtyard. Some sort of shell had obviously wounded the veranda. Tiles were smashed, and a tree had fallen. The nearness of the explosion to his home suddenly stopped Malevergne as he considered the possibility that his wife and children might have been right here when the bomb came. But sandbags covering the approach to the cellar door reassured him, and he hurried in that direction, where he saw a light filtering outward from the door.

"Georges," he called outside the door.

"Patton," came the response from inside.

There were a group of American soldiers and Mehdian villagers sharing the protection of his darkened cellar. Its only illumination was two flickering candles. As his eyes adjusted to the dim light, Malevergne could see astonishment in the faces of his neighbors as he entered the room. *Where had he been? Why was he here now with the Americans?* Malevergne suddenly felt a pair of arms grab his legs at the knees.

"Papa! Papa!" cried his son Claude, who recognized his father in spite of his strange uniform and the many weeks it had been since he'd seen him last. René and Germaine were there to hold him too. They clung together in the candlelight. His long journey finally over, René Malevergne was home at last.

CHAPTER 34

Armistice Day

It was 0130 on November 11 when the tide began to sweep up the River Sebou and boost the *Contessa* out of her riverbank. Captain William John had the wheel of his ship once again that morning and was faced with an immediate difficulty. As the tide came in, it lifted the first part of the *Contessa* that it touched, her stern, and swept it south toward the airport, rather than downriver toward the sea. With the two scuttled French steamers directly behind her, Captain John simply didn't have enough room to turn his ship back upriver and point his bow toward Port Lyautey. He made a quick but dangerous determination: he would back the *Contessa* upriver to the airport, leading with her stern. With engines full speed to the rear, John eased his ship off the mudbank and into the stream. In the darkness of that early morning, the *Contessa* was now being led up this shallow river by her propeller.

The maneuver was precarious, to say the least. Not only would John have to feel his way upriver, trying to sense a navigable channel through the shifting sands at the river's bottom, and without a pilot to aid him, but the propeller shaft, which is one of the most vulnerable parts of any ship, needed to be protected. The *Contessa*'s was connected directly to the engine through a bearing tube that, in her case, was made of a Caribbean hardwood called lignum vitae. Lignum vitae is so densely tough that it is heavier than water. The wood also carries within it a supply of its own oil, which makes it a self-lubricating bearing. Lignum vitae had been popular among seamen for many years. Ernest Shackleton, for instance, used it to frame the *Endurance* on his famous Antarctic voyage. Its strength and ability to protect the propeller shaft from seawater made it a popular bearing-tube material on steamships too. It was an expensive shipbuilding item but one that Captain John was happy to have in the *Contessa*.

As she had the day before, the banana boat churned her way up the

270

Sebou, raking the bottom as she trembled backward toward the airport. Her load made her heavier in the front end, which helped keep the propeller up and away from obstacles, but steaming blind on a river that he'd never seen before left John and everyone aboard uneasy about what lay ahead. He felt his way along the slow-motion journey, waiting to hear the thud and abrupt conk of his propeller running into the sand and his engines coming to a grinding halt.

The end came, however, as it had the night before: less a violent stop than a sigh of utter exhaustion, as the *Contessa*'s keel eased slowly and deeply into the river bottom. There was no going backward, no going forward. She was hard aground once again, and her trip was over. The *Contessa* had made it as far as she needed, however; the airport rested just eight hundred yards off her starboard side.

Lieutenant Leslie ordered the cargo gear rigged and the hatches opened, but no landing craft appeared from the *Allen* to aid in her unloading, as had been promised before the *Contessa*'s run. Leslie wound up commandeering several local barges, as well as a pair of fishing boats, for the job. He had to enlist army troops as longshoremen, had to go three miles upriver to the docks at Port Lyautey to find cranes capable of unloading the *Contessa*'s cargo from the lighters, and, once in the port, had to arrange the opening of a rail line back to the airport in order to deliver the munitions and ga s to the P-40s. "Working twenty-four hours a day was able to finish discharging in three days, although it may have been four—for the passage of time at this point was beyond recall," Leslie wrote in his final report on the trip.

"It should not be omitted to say that, although there were twenty-six nationalities comprising the crew of the vessel, no trouble was had with them at any point," Leslie added, regarding the entirety of the voyage. "Action of the Navy crew was exemplary; also Captain John, an ex–Lieutenant Commander in the British Navy, . . . showed himself more than willing to handle his ship into whatever dangers may have been a part of the operation." Without John's presence, Leslie continued, "it is doubtful if the show could have been carried off. He is, in my opinion, most deserving of official recognition of his contribution to the opening of shore based air operations at this point."

Despite numerous requests, Leslie was never able to get help from the *Allen*; and in fact he found out later that, because of the dangers of the load, transports were purposely being diverted from the *Contessa*.

Though the *Dallas* and the *Contessa* were crucial instruments in the rush to open and supply the Port Lyautey airfield in support of George Patton's assault on Casablanca, none of the munitions or gasoline that the *Contessa* carried up the Sebou were used in Operation Torch. Not a single P-40 got into the air before hostilities in French Morocco came to a conclusion.

At 0800 on November 11, just as Lieutenant Leslie was scrambling to find help in unloading the *Contessa*, forces were gathering at the Kasbah. General Lucian Truscott, in the company of Harry Semmes's tanks "to lend something of a military display to the event," approached French general Mathenet in the shadow of the high walls of the Kasbah. He also brought his aide Ted Conway along to translate. Mathenet was in full dress uniform, complete with a blue cape, lined in scarlet, tossed over his shoulder. Elsewhere "a brightly colored pageant of varied French and colonial uniforms, Arab costumes, and flags" greeted the Americans. Truscott felt "battle-stained" in contrast.

Truscott and Mathenet saluted each other, and the French general said that he was authorized by Admiral Darlan to terminate all hostilities in the Port Lyautey area. Truscott told Mathenet that his troops would be allowed to keep their weapons if they promised to remain in the barracks until the final cessation of fighting in Morocco. In addition to giving up the immediate area, Mathenet agreed to the surrender of the airport in Salé, near Rabat, which obviated Truscott's plans to march on that city.

The battle for Port Lyautey was over. Eighty-four American soldiers had given their lives in the fight, beginning with Nick Craw. Another 11 members of the U.S. Navy were dead, and more than 250 soldiers and seamen were wounded. Soon ground would be broken on a cemetery. It was decided that a corner of the Kasbah would be an appropriate site, and Nick Craw was the first person interred there.

Early in the morning on the eleventh, a car holding a pair of French officers coming from Rabat approached an American outpost north of Fedala with a bugle blaring and white flags affixed to its bumpers. It carried papers from General Lascroux in Rabat to General Esre in Casablanca ordering the French army to immediately suspend hostilities against the Americans. The car was directed to George Patton (at the Hotel Miramar in downtown Fedala), who authorized their continued trip to General Esre in Casablanca. Patton warned the envoys that they must hurry: he had ordered an attack at dawn, and it would be too late to prevent it if they could not return with an agreement from Casablanca before then. As a precaution against needless bloodshed, however, Patton radioed Admiral Hewitt after the French officers left, to let the navy know that a cease-fire was pending.

Not only was this Armistice Day, but November 11 was George Patton's fifty-seventh birthday as well. He'd spent the night at the hotel, sleeping in the bed previously occupied by the chief of the German Armistice Commission—a symbolism that Patton relished. He'd gone to sleep with a great deal of confidence about what the morrow would bring. His army forces, under the command of General Jonathan Anderson, ringed 180 degrees of the city of Casablanca; "only the Sherman tanks from Safi were wanting for a complete investiture." The day before, Truscott had taken the airfield and Kasbah at Port Lyautey, and Harmon's tanks, after successfully thwarting an effort by the French in Marrakech to reinforce Casablanca, were speeding north from Safi. Furthermore, in Casablanca harbor, the *Jean Bart,* which had been silent since being hit on the first day of the invasion, had suddenly opened up on the *Augusta.* This last-gasp attack prompted a nine-plane assault from navy bombers from the carrier *Ranger.* Two hits from a couple of thousand-pound bombs put gaping holes in the side of the French battleship's hull. She did not open her guns again.

Essentially, Casablanca was surrounded from the sea and land. Attacks on the city proper had been incidental and damage light, but should the French continue to resist, the peace in Casablanca would be gone. At 0600, as Patton waited in Fedala to hear back from the officers who'd sped away to the city, Anderson sat poised to enter; the warships of the navy, including the *Augusta,* the *New York,* the *Cleveland,* and several destroyers, ringed the harbor of Casablanca, ready to finish off the *Jean Bart* and support the army's advance; and planes from the *Ranger* were set to begin the first of many bombing runs on the city. The attack was scheduled for 0715. At 0655, the French officers returned under a flag of truce. General Noguès, commander of the French army in Morocco, and Admiral Michelier of the French navy had received word from Admiral Darlan, who had been recognized by Eisenhower as the chief military authority in French Morocco, to suspend hostilities.

The Western Task Force of Operation Torch had achieved its goal: French Morocco was in American hands, and now the Allies could turn their attention to the Germans. The French had fought, but not so fiercely as to truly test American forces. Many, especially the British, would continue to question the strategic need for the invasion of Morocco, but it had brought almost 35,000 troops to Northwest Africa with a relatively light amount of damage and many lessons learned about amphibious assault in the process.

For Patton, it was now time to begin the process of reestablishing ties with the United States' ancient allies, the French. An Armistice Day celebration was in order.

"General Noguès and Admiral Michelier came [to the Miramar Hotel] to discuss terms at 1400," Patton told his diary that night. "I had a guard of honor for them. No use kicking a man when he is down."

At 1400, surrounded by that guard, Patton and Hewitt received Noguès and Michelier at the Hotel Miramar. Hewitt apologized to Michelier, regretting that he had been forced to fire upon French ships.

"I had my orders and did my duty," the French admiral said. "You had yours and did your duty; now that is over, we are ready to cooperate." Patton complimented the French military commanders on the effectiveness of their defenses and read a draft of the armistice statement.

Like Truscott's regional proposal delivered at the Kasbah, it was generous and informal. Prisoners would be exchanged; French troops would be confined to their barracks but not disarmed; and Americans would control and occupy the region. They would await word of more lasting terms from the Joint Allied Command meeting then in Algiers.

This business taken care of, champagne and lunch were brought to the table. Patton rose to deliver the first of many toasts made with many glasses of champagne: "To the liberation of France," he said, "by the joint defeat of a common enemy."

It had been a good birthday, indeed.

EPILOGUE

"The little *Contessa* did the trick"

On that same Armistice Day, Warner Brothers sales executives in New York sent an excited suggestion to Jack Warner in Hollywood: To take further advantage of the studio's unbelievable good luck in having a soon-to-be-released picture with a title that matched the exact location now at the center of the war effort, let's shoot an additional scene that will reference the invasion. The idea was to add a coda to the film. Put Claude Rains's Renault and Humphrey Bogart's Rick Blaine on the deck of a freighter on its way to a landing at Casablanca. Surround them with about fifty extras dressed as French freedom fighters. Have them listening to FDR's stirring speech from early morning on the eighth as they approach the shore. Shoot it in a sound studio at Warner. Put it all on a foggy night.

Fortunately for the movie, cooler heads prevailed in Hollywood, and ultimately the sales reps in New York were vetoed. Jack Warner himself put the kibosh on the idea: "It's impossible to change this picture and make sense with story we told originally," he wrote. "Story we want to tell of landing and everything would have to be complete new picture and would not fit in the present film. It's such a great picture as it is, would be a misrepresentation if we were to come in now with a small tag scene about American troops landing etcetera, which as I have already said is a complete new story in itself. . . . Entire industry envies us with picture having title 'Casablanca' ready to release, and feel we should take advantage of this great scoop. Naturally the longer we wait to release it the less important title will be."

The movie was originally scheduled to be released in early 1943. To take advantage of the timing of the invasion of French Morocco, Warner Brothers pushed up *Casablanca*'s New York premiere to Thanksgiving Day 1942. It was an instant success. In a ten-week run at the Hollywood Theater in Manhattan, box-office receipts reached almost a quarter of a million dollars—the proceeds from one theater covering nearly a quarter of the cost of making the movie. The movie was given another boost when it opened across the nation in January. That release happened to coincide with FDR's visit with Winston Churchill in Casablanca, centering worldwide interest once again on Morocco. As author Aljean Harmetz put it in *Round Up the Usual Suspects,* "*Casablanca* had sold the need for engagement on the side of the Allies in a war against fascism. Now the war sold the movie."

On the morning of the thirteenth, two days after the armistice, UP reporter Walter Cronkite was allowed to go to Port Lyautey in the company of a *Texas* gunnery officer who wanted to assess the accuracy of the ship's firing during the campaign. It was the first time he'd set foot in Morocco; Cronkite had filed a number of stories from the *Texas* via radio to British communications offices in Gibraltar, but he hadn't yet been allowed on the battlefield itself by Navy authorities. As Cronkite and the *Texas*'s officer approached the center of Port Lyautey, an army colonel, spying the Navy man, came speeding toward them in a jeep. It turned out that there was an unexploded shell from the *Texas* just blocks ahead of them. What, the colonel wanted to know, was the navy going to do about it?

"We've got an old rule in the Navy," the lieutenant said in response. "Once the shell leaves the muzzle of the gun, it doesn't belong to the Navy any longer."

As far as the accuracy of the *Texas*'s fire was concerned, Cronkite offered an assessment in another anecdote from the same tour: Much of the *Texas* artillery over the past few days had been aimed at the Port Lyautey arsenal. When he and the gunnery officer approached this site, they came across a moonscape of shell holes on the roads and surrounding acreage, but the arsenal still stood. An old French soldier, a World War I artilleryman, approached them. He wanted to congratulate the Americans on the precision of their shooting. "You cut every road leading to the arsenal and not one shell inside to do damage," the old soldier said. "You have left it intact for yourselves."

Cronkite, attached to the *Texas,* was forced to return with the ship to Norfolk a week after the armistice. He was hoping that he could be the first war correspondent back to the United States from Morocco, but he learned en route that another correspondent from the INS news agency had already left for Boston on the battleship *Massachusetts*. A navy pilot came to his rescue. He offered to fly Cronkite to Norfolk from the sea, once the ship was within safe flying distance of the shore. It would save a couple of days of ocean travel.

Cronkite jumped at the offer. The plane was catapulted off the *Texas,* literally fired off the ship by way of one of the *Texas*'s fourteen-inch cannons. He and the pilot made it to Norfolk, and Cronkite immediately caught a plane for New York. When he entered the UP offices there, he was greeted like he had been lost at sea since October. It turned out that he might as well have been. None of the stories he'd filed from Morocco had been forwarded by the British at Gibraltar. "I later learned that this had happened to several of the American correspondents in North Africa," Cronkite later explained, "as the British military favored the dispatches from their own newspapers and press agencies."

Cronkite did have the satisfaction of beating the INS reporter back to the States and soon filed the first of his many stories as a war correspondent.

The *Contessa* remained trapped in the Sebou for a full week after the end of hostilities, waiting for the monthly shift in the tide to raise the water high enough for her to navigate back down the river to the sea. In the meantime, a team of repair specialists from the *Texas* came aboard to patch the hole in her bow, but the fix was only intended to get her to Gibraltar, where major repairs could be done. She left Morocco on the nineteenth and spent the next twenty-one days at anchorage in the British port while a more lasting repair made her fit to travel back across the ocean. U-boat activity around the coast of Africa had grown thick in the wake of the American invasion, so two destroyers accompanied the *Contessa* back to Casablanca. There she hooked up with convoy GUF 2A for a return voyage to the States. Once again the *Contessa* lost her group on the trip across the Atlantic, but she made it singly to New York at last, on Christmas Day 1942.

Accolades for the ship had already begun to arrive. In a November 22 letter to SOS commander Brehon Somervell, George Patton heaped praise on Somervell for his and his staff's hard and good work in supplying the Western Task Force. He also made special note of the banana boat. "Please tell [General] Gross that the little Contessa, which he secured for us at the last moment, did the trick," Patton wrote. "She crossed the Atlantic alone and delivered the ammunition and gas at the airport. I have recommended the civilian captain of this vessel for a Legion of Merit Medal."

Captain William John never got that medal. He did, however, receive commendations from Patton, Admiral Hewitt, and Secretary of the Navy James Forrestal. "By his outstanding professional ability and courage, Captain John of the Merchant Marine set an example worthy of the traditions of American seamanship," read Patton's tribute. "Alone and without naval escort of any kind, Captain John, with a dangerous cargo, successfully took his ship from an American port to . . . the French Moroccan coast, delivering essential war matériel to the combat troops, in time for operations of November 8–11, 1942. The waters through which Captain John passed were infested with enemy submarines and the nature of the cargo was such that complete annihilation of the ship and crew would have resulted from enemy torpedo action."

Lieutenant Albert Leslie of the naval armed guard was similarly honored. Admiral Monroe Kelly recommended Leslie for the Silver Star, and he was promoted to lieutenant commander. His first assignment was at Port Lyautey, where he was appointed port commander in the wake of the fighting.

John, Leslie, and the crew of the *Contessa* wound up achieving a measure of fame back in the States. In August 1943, the *Saturday Evening Post* published an account of the ship's voyage to Morocco and up the Sebou by writer Bertram Fowler. Called "Twelve Desperate Miles," the article offers an exciting version of the *Contessa*'s trip but neglects the role of the *Dallas* and René Malevergne in the operation. The story was picked up by the popular CBS radio program *Cavalcade of America* later that fall. Under the same title, it was produced as a half-hour drama starring Edward Arnold.

The *Contessa*'s star power was limited—at least as far as the ship was concerned. After she returned to New York in December 1942, her war service continued for more than three years. By February 1943, she was back making the New York–to–England transport run, with Captain John once again at the wheel and much of the same crew still on board. By the end of the year, the *Contessa* had shipped out to the Pacific, where she continued to serve as a merchant ship through the end of 1945. The hard-used vessel was finally sailed back to New Orleans in early 1946, where it went into dry dock for some much-needed repair work and refurbishing.

Captain John did not sail with it to the Pacific. He'd seen enough service. In the fall of 1943, he took a job as port captain of the Standard Fruit Company in New Orleans. The minor celebrity that washed over his former ship splashed a little bit on him, too, back in his hometown. The *New Orleans Times-Picayune* did a story on his adventure, and the *New York Times* called him about his past association with Admiral Doenitz of U-Boat fame.

Aside from his new position at Standard Fruit, John had other things on his mind. The fact that he had been master of a ship registered in a foreign country for all these years had precluded his ability to become a citizen of the United States. Now that he was retired from the *Contessa*,

Captain John could join his wife and daughters as an American citizen. He was naturalized by a U.S. district judge in New Orleans in
September 1943.

In February 1943, Major Pierpont Hamilton was awarded the Medal
of Honor by Franklin Delano Roosevelt. A month later, the widow and
ten-year-old son of Colonel Demas T. Craw received a similar honor at
the White House. Along with Colonel William Wilbur, who served with
Patton at Casablanca, they became the first recipients of the Medal of
Honor in the European theater.

   Two months earlier, Brigadier General Lucian Truscott had recommended that the French river pilot of Port Lyautey, René Malevergne,
be awarded a Silver Star for gallantry in action. The citation read in
part:

> M. Malevergne volunteered his services
> to troops on the USS Susan B. Anthony
> and was invaluable in rendering G-2
> [intelligence] information on the
> subject of French Morocco, vicinity of
> Mehdia, and Port Lyautey. He constantly
> assisted in the dissemination of French
> information, assisted in the instruction
> in the French language, and customs of
> North Africa. . . . On the morning of
> 10 November 1942 he piloted the USS
> Dallas into the Oued Sebou and safely
> up the tortuous channel of the river he
> had not followed for ten months. With
> utter disregard for his personal safety
> and with constant attention to detail
> that he showed throughout the voyage, he

```
made possible the landing of the Raiding
Detachment at the Airport. It is to be
noted that the hazards under which M.
Malevergne worked were enhanced by his
wearing of the American uniform, which
would have undoubtedly resulted in his
treatment as a spy, should he have been
taken into enemy hands.
```

Malevergne became the first Frenchman in World War II to be awarded an American Silver Star. He also became the first Frenchman to be awarded the Navy Cross, "For extraordinary heroism as pilot of the USS DALLAS during the assault upon and occupation of the Port Lyautey Airfield." Malevergne received the navy medal at the very same airfield, along with Captain Brodie of the *Dallas,* who was similarly honored. General Truscott himself pinned the Silver Star on Malevergne's chest in a ceremony in a grove near the Kasbah in the spring of 1943.

Malevergne was already back in Mehdia, readjusting to life in his old village. In the months immediately after the invasion, he worked as a translator and unofficial cultural liaison with the Americans at Port Lyautey, which became (and would remain for many years) an important military base for the United States in northwest Africa.

Eventually, Malevergne opened a little waterfront café in Mehdia called Jack's Bar, which continued to support Germaine and the boys after his death in the mid-1950s. A few years prior to his passing, Malevergne sent his war diary to William Eddy, his old OSS boss in Tangier. An ironic choice, perhaps; if Eddy had known Malevergne was keeping a diary of his activities leading up to the invasion, Malevergne surely would have been removed from any further work with the OSS.

Correspondence between the two, however, shows their enormous respect for each other. Eddy tried and failed to find a publisher for the work. Unfortunately, the manuscript itself was lost or misplaced in the process. After a long and circuitous journey, it was rediscovered and wound up in the hands of a scholar, Leon Borden Blair, who had served in the U.S. Navy at Port Lyautey in the 1950s and had known René Malevergne. Blair, now teaching French colonial history at the University of Texas–Arlington, got permission from Germaine to translate his story into English.

Blair, too, was unable to publish the manuscript. He died in 1990, passing his work on to an old friend from Morocco, Ben Dixon, the president of the American Friends of Morocco Society. The copy of the manuscript of *The Exfiltration of René Malevergne*, which has been so vital to this book, was found in the library of that organization in Washington, D.C.

★   ★   ★

Spiffed up and restored to prewar condition and better, complete with mahogany furniture, her swimming pool, and newly added air-conditioning, the *Contessa* returned to duty in the Caribbean after the war. It wasn't long before Captain William John returned to take the wheel of her too.

She sailed for Standard Fruit to all the old ports and began a new regular run up to New York as well. She had some good years and some bad until a fire in 1956 gutted her forward holds—including the one that had been smashed in by the Sebou. In weighing the costs of repairing and keeping her against giving her up, Standard Fruit chose the latter. The fact of the matter was that *Contessa* was getting old, and the sort of combination ship that she was—part passenger, part cargo—was being supplanted on both ends of the equation by more luxurious tourist ships and larger, more efficient cargo carriers. Standard Fruit sold her to a Dutch firm, which renamed her the *Leeuwarden*.

Captain John retired in 1957. After fifty years at sea, more than thirty-six of them with Standard Fruit in New Orleans, he had had enough of sailing—but not enough of the sea. He and Bessie moved to a home on the Gulf of Mexico in Bay Saint Louis, Mississippi. As a memento of his years with the company and on the *Contessa,* Captain John was presented with the wheel of the ship upon his retirement.

In August 1969, Hurricane Camille was in the Gulf of Mexico and bearing down on Bay Saint Louis. William John had been through countless storms, including hurricanes, during his years at sea and had ridden them all out. He was in his late seventies and had cataracts. He didn't want to leave, and neither did Bessie. They decided to ride this one out together.

When the storm came in, followed by the rising water, it is assumed they climbed to the highest reaches of their retirement cottage, but the structure was swept completely away. When their bodies were found near each other after the water had returned to the Gulf, Captain John and Bess were found clutching photographs of themselves to their chests, presumably so that their identities would be known to those who found them.

The *Contessa* came back to the Gulf in the early 1960s, purchased by Tropicana. She never did much work for this new fruit company owner, however, and by the end of the decade wound up rusting at a dock in Tampa, where it was reported that "a band of 'hippies'" had occupied and were now squatting on her decks. At about the same time that Hurricane Camille struck the Gulf, she was purchased by an Italian company, which towed her on a final trip across the Atlantic, where the *Contessa* wound up in a ship "boneyard," her history complete.

NOTES

PROLOGUE

A Good Citizen of Mehdia

  1 **The authorities in Port Lyautey:** Details of René Malevergne's arrest and life before 1940 are from Malevergne's unpublished diary (René Malevergne, *The Exfiltration of René Malevergne*). The English adaptation, completed in 1999, also unpublished, is by Leon Borden Blair with assistance from Ben F. Dixon. Quotes used in the book are from the adaptation.

      "Kenitra" is the current and historical name of the city of Port Lyautey in northwest Morocco. During the war and the latter days of French colonialism in North Africa, it was referred to as "Port Lyautey." Both Malevergne and the Allies used "Port Lyautey." I've chosen to use that name too.

  1 **By October 1940:** Leon B. Blair, "René Malevergne and His Role in Operation Torch," *Proceedings of the French Colonial Historical Society,* April 1978, p. 207.

  2 **"Are you a Gaullist":** Malevergne, *Exfiltration of René Malevergne,* p. 16.

  2 **"Even if de Gaulle":** Ibid., p. 18.

  3 **"clandestine organizations":** Ibid., p. 20.

  4 **"a grim hatred":** Ibid., p. 20.

  5 **"deep down the French authorities":** Ibid., p. 21.

  6 *But what about Brunin:* Ibid., p. 22.

CHAPTER 1

New York, June 1942

  11 **"docks, piers, and wharves":** Joseph F. Meany Jr., "Port in a Storm: The Port of New York in World War II," New York State Museum, http://www .nysm.nysed.gov/research_collections/research/history/hisportofnewyork .html.

  11 **up to 575 employed:** Ibid.

  11 **Brand-new PT boats:** Robert Donovan, *PT-109: John F. Kennedy in World War II* (New York: McGraw-Hill, 1961), p. 31.

  12 **Upward of a thousand warehouses:** Meany, "Port in a Storm."

13 "spiritual defeatism": "Defeatism held unjustified now," *New York Times,*
   June 22, 1942.

13 "The best things": Ibid. *New York Times,* June 22, 1942.

14 "Happy Time": Karl Doenitz, "The Conduct of the War at Sea," U.S. Navy
   Division of Naval Intelligence, January 15, 1946, p. 17 (available at http://
   www.karl-doenitz.com/doenitzconductofwar.pdf).

15 "We might as well": Bruce Felknor, *The U.S. Merchant Marine at War,
   1776–1945* (Annapolis, MD: U.S. Naval Institute, 1999), p. 217.

15 "All the vacationers": Ibid., p. 206.

16 Coastal lighting restrictions: Ibid., pp. 217–18.

16 The hardest nut to crack: Ibid., p. 219.

17 "the losses by submarines": Ibid., p. 222.

17 "Has every conceivable": Ibid.

17 "defense work": War Shipping Administration to Standard Fruit, May 8,
   1942, National Archives, RG 178, entry P1, box 4702, file 901-6571.

18 Named after the Italian village: Mark H. Goldberg, *Going Bananas* (Kings
   Point, NY: American Merchant Marine Museum Foundation, 1993),
   p. 193.

18 "large enough for every element": Standard Fruit Company, "Through the
   Storied Caribbean to Unspoiled Tropic Beauty," in the collection of Bjorn
   Larsson and available at http://www.timetableimages.com/maritime/images
   /sta30i1.htm.

19 His first ship: Standard Fruit Company, "The True Adventures of Captain
   John," *Standard Fruit Company News,* May 1957, available in the Standard Fruit Company collection at the Tulane University Archives.

   For a few of Captain John's many voyages, see, for instance, National
   Archives Microfilm Publication serial: "Passenger and Crew Lists of Vessels
   Arriving at New York, New York, 1897–1957," T715_8892, T715_3559,
   et al. Records of the Immigration and Naturalization Service, National
   Archives, Washington, D.C.

20 even members of his own family: Tim Koerner, interview by the author,
   March 4, 2010.

21 including munitions so dangerous: "Curran asks mayor to get facts straight
   before criticizing pier smoking cases," *New York Times,* May 13, 1942.

23 When John asked how things were: Standard Fruit Company, "The True
   Adventures of Captain John," *Standard Fruit Company News,* May 1957.

23 Quite frankly, Captain John: "1918 rescuer of Doenitz sorry he didn't kill him," *New York Times,* May 5, 1945.

CHAPTER 2

Airborne to London

24 In fact, Marshall had recently sent him: Stanley Hirshson, *General Patton: A Soldier's Life* (New York: HarperCollins, 2002), p. 265.

25 curtained sleeping compartments: Robert Henriques, *From a Biography of Myself,* (London: Secker & Warburg, 1969), p. 55.

25 "all talk was of fishing": Martin Blumenson, ed., *The Patton Papers* (New York: Da Capo Press, 1996–1998), p. 81.

26 "I sometimes wondered": Hirshson, *General Patton,* p. 254.

26 "Get those goddamn tanks": Blumenson, ed., *Patton Papers,* p. 80.

26 led them on their jogs: Harry Semmes, *Portrait of Patton* (New York: Appleton-Century-Crofts, 1955), p. 82.

27 "Here's to the wives": Ibid., p. 81

27 His soldiers called him "The Green Hornet": James Wellard, *General George S. Patton, Jr.* (New York: Dodd & Mead, 1946), p. 52.

27 Patton's father came from Virginia: Semmes, *Portrait of Patton,* p. 4.

28 His education was unique: Ibid., p. 7.

29 "select the weapon": Ibid., p. 37.

30 He also liked to see a salute: Ibid., p. 42.

30 "the manly virtues": Ibid., p. 62.

30 "As the car approached": Ibid., p. 38.

31 Wasn't their theater of action: Ibid., pp. 38–39.

31 The two would spend: H. Paul Jeffers, *Command of Honor* (New York: NAL Caliber, 2008), p. 37.

33 And the British were more than a little: William B. Breuer, *Operation Torch* (New York: St. Martin's Press, 1985), p. 3.

35 "just fantastic": Ibid., p. 6.

35 Marshall felt that Brooke: Ibid.

35 "there was a lively danger": "Eisenhower's Report on Operation Torch," declassified June 21, 1965; available at http://www.american-divisions.com /doc.asp?documentid=138&pagenumber=1, p. 3.

36 "a thousand miles south of London": Stephen E. Ambrose, *Eisenhower,* vol. 1,

Soldier, General of the Army, President-Elect, 1890–1952 (New York: Simon and Schuster, 1983–1984), p. 181.

37 "Darkly depressed": Ibid., p. 181.

38 "the blackest day": Ibid., p. 181.

38 To Marshall and Eisenhower: Ambrose, *Eisenhower,* p. 183.

CHAPTER 3

Incorrigible

39 "a doubtful liquid": René Malevergne, *The Exfiltration of René Malevergne* (unpublished diary), p. 23.

39 "Such an operation would be idiotic": Ibid., p. 28.

40 "If she burned the money": Ibid., p. 28. In fact, Germaine, who watched their finances very closely, would later scoff at the idea that she would burn money. "I hid it in a sack of beans," she said.

40 "probably ten million Frenchmen": Ibid., p. 26.

41 "in a sort of cage": Ibid., p. 44.

41 "Do you think that the Légion": Ibid., p. 49.

42 left a message for his family: Ibid., p. 53.

42 "compromised in the affairs of the Resistance": Ibid., p. 59.

42 "A lady of light morals": Ibid. p., 59.

44 "I was unstrung": Ibid., p. 68.

44 "That, being a French citizen": Ibid., p. 65.

44 "I ask you to stop": Ibid., p. 71.

CHAPTER 4

Claridge's

46 "half alive with very few people": Martin Blumenson, ed., *The Patton Papers* (New York: Da Capo Press, 1996–1998), p. 81.

47 "Dammit, Lucian": Lucian Truscott, *Command Mission, a Personal Story* (New York: Dutton, 1954), p. 59.

47 As a child wandering around: H. Paul Jeffers, *Command of Honor* (New York: NAL Caliber, 2008), p. 9.

49 a little "dim": Robert Henriques, *From a Biography of Myself* (London: Secker & Warburg, 1969), pp. 84–85.

50 "officers who feel they have": Captain Harry C. Butcher, *My Three Years with Eisenhower* (New York: Simon & Schuster, 1946), p. 47.

50 "Patton is a good fellow": Ibid., p. 47.

50 "Had supper with Ike": Blumenson, ed., *Patton Papers*, p. 82.

50 "There were no taxies": Ibid., p. 82.

51 "was certainly not on their toes." Ibid., p. 82.

51 "if I have to go alone": Butcher, *My Three Years*, p. 50.

52 "It is very noticeable": Blumenson, ed., *Patton Papers*, p. 82.

52 "damn fine fighting men": Truscott, *Command Mission*, p. 59.

52 "typical member of the English aristocracy": Ibid., p. 60.

52 "With gleaming boots": Ibid., p. 60.

52 "A dowager of sixty-five": Ibid.

53 "I think this is fortunate for me": Blumenson, ed., *Patton Papers*, p. 82.

54 "I feel that we should fight": Ibid., p. 83.

54 "No wonder Ike's so pleased": Butcher, *My Three Years*, p. 63.

CHAPTER 5

Halifax to Belfast

55 rub elbows with: Tim Koerner and Louis Koerner, interviews with the author, New Orleans, Louisiana, and Pass Christian, Mississippi, March 3 and 4, 2010. Louis Koerner has a photo of Captain John and William Bendix at Bendix's home on Long Island.

55 An article in the *New Orleans Times-Picayune*: "Veteran skipper plays Cupid in disguise as daughter weds," clipping from the papers of Peggy Koerner, held by Louis Koerner. Date unknown.

56 probably conceived on the cruise: Louis Koerner, interview with the author, March 3, 2010.

56 The holds were partitioned: Bill Kimble, interview with the author, Pass Christian, Mississippi, March 4, 2010.

56 The smell of fruit would waft: Details of the *Contessa*'s dimensions and costs come from Mark H. Goldberg, *Going Bananas* (Kings Point, NY: American Merchant Marine Museum Foundation, 1993), pp. 193–202.

57 Stripped of its swimming pool: Kimble, interview.

57 HX 201 was composed: www.warsailors.com/convoys/hx201.html. Exact counts of convoys are sometimes hard to come by.

58 Collisions would turn out to be: Bruce Felknor, *The U.S. Merchant Marine at War, 1776–1945* (Annapolis, MD: U.S. Naval Institute, 1999) p. 240.

59 the numbers of German submarines: www.usmm.org/ww2.html.

59 These ties sent up: www.warsailors.com/convoys/hx201.html; The recollections of convoy HX 201 from Arthur Searby (of the *Santa Isabel*) sent to Warsailors, a clearinghouse for information on WWII convoys. See also Felknor, *U.S. Merchant Marine,* p. 240.

60 Even at this pace: Ibid.; convoy HX 201.html. Notes from the log of the commodore of convoy HX 201, W. de M. Egerton.

60 The destroyer also blasted "Hail Britannia": Ibid.; Searby, recollection.

61 Her April sinking: Deposition of Harold Christiansen, May 21, 1942, *Amapala* file of the Standard Fruit Company Papers, Special Collections, Louisiana Research Collection, Howard-Tilton Memorial Library, Tulane University.

61 linked to an incident: Thomas Karnes, *Tropical Enterprise: The Standard Fruit Company in Latin America* (Baton Rouge: Louisiana State University Press, 1978), pp. 217–18.

62 German planes had pulverized: Louis Chirillo, *I Knew a Lad,* "Swansea," internet self-published reminiscence (http://lou.chirillo.com/?page_id=7), p. 26.

62 "all the men and women": John family history, "Cpt. John" file, Louis Koerner papers, New Orleans.

CHAPTER 6
Walking the Tightrope

65 "the Legion seems to have adopted": René Malevergne, *The Exfiltration of René Malevergne* (unpublished diary), p. 113.

66 "Born of the idea": Ibid., p. 113.

66 "There was nothing for them to do": Ibid., p. 114.

66 "arrange your time as you like": Ibid., p. 117.

67 "he had followed my odyssey": Ibid., p. 119.

68 Malevergne began to assist the Americans: Leon B. Blair, "René Malevergne and His Role in Operation Torch," *Proceedings of the French Colonial Historical Society,* April 1978, p. 210.

68 Then, toward the end of the summer: Malevergne, *Exfiltration of René Malevergne,* p. 136.

CHAPTER 7

D.C.

69 **"I feel like the lady"**: Stephen E. Ambrose, *Eisenhower,* vol. 1, *Soldier, General of the Army, President-Elect, 1890–1952,* (New York: Simon & Schuster, 1983–1984), p. 191.

70 **three hundred thousand women**: "Army will double women workers," *New York Times,* September 4, 1942.

70 **lines to buy newspapers**: Robert Henriques, *From a Biography of Myself* (London: Secker & Warburg, 1969), p. 62.

70 **Hewitt had served in the navy**: Rick Atkinson, *An Army at Dawn: The War in North Africa* (New York: Henry Holt, 2003), p. 21.

71 **"I am not among"**: Lucian Truscott, *Command Mission, a Personal Story* (New York: Dutton, 1954), p. 72.

72 **"it was an essential though costly lesson"**: Ibid., p. 72.

73 **"quite desperate nature"**: Captain Harry C. Butcher, *My Three Years with Eisenhower* (New York: Simon & Schuster, 1946), p. 84.

73 **"If we can take into North Africa"**: Ibid., p. 84.

73 **Marshall, too, had begun to worry**: Ibid., p. 84.

CHAPTER 8

The Apostles

78 **The consuls were a highly educated group**: Details on the backgrounds of the "apostles" come from Hal Vaughan, *FDR's 12 Apostles* (Guilford, CT: Lyons Press, 2006), p. 46–78.

79 **"The city was neat, white"**: Kenneth Pendar, *Adventure in Diplomacy* (New York: Dodd, Mead, 1945), p. 12.

80 **no shortage of refugees**: Vaughan, *FDR's 12 Apostles,* p. 62.

80 **Eddy passed along an order**: Anthony Cave Brown, ed., *Secret War Report of the OSS* (New York: Berkley Publishing, 1976), p. 136.

81 **"represent a perfect picture"**: Pendar, *Adventure in Diplomacy,* p. 17.

82 **He flew to Washington**: William L. Langer, *Our Vichy Gamble* (New York: Alfred A. Knopf, 1947), pp. 305–11.

82 **"Stretching of the facts"**: Ibid., p. 308.

82 **"The sonofabitch has been shot at enough"**: Maj. Thomas W. Durrell Jr., *The Role of the Office of Strategic Services in Operation Torch,* a master's

thesis presented to the faculty of the U.S. Army Command and General Staff College, Leavenworth, Kansas, 2008, p. 67.

82 **Eddy advised that British forces:** Langer, *Our Vichy Gamble*, p. 309.

83 **"We can count on":** Ibid., p. 310.

83 **"knows every rock":** Ibid.

CHAPTER 9

The Hazards of Port Lyautey

84 **One of the thornier issues:** Lucian Truscott, *Command Mission, a Personal Story* (New York: Dutton, 1954), p. 75.

85 **To Truscott's mind:** Ibid., pp. 76–77.

86 **a sub–task force named Goalpost:** John J. Toffey IV, *Jack Toffey's War* (New York: Fordham University Press, 2008), p. 238.

86 **snapshots and film footage:** Samuel Eliot Morison, *History of United States Naval Operations in World War II*, vol. 2, *Operations in North African Waters October 1942–June 1943* (Boston: Atlantic Little, Brown, 1954), p. 25.

86 **"extremely reluctant to undertake":** Truscott, *Command Mission*, p. 77.

86 **the basic objectives of Goalpost:** "Estimates for Plan of Attack," North Africa; operational plan for Operation Goalpost, Northern sub-task force (designated "Z") of Torch's Western Task Force, General Lucian Truscott commanding, p. 1). Records of Headquarters Army Ground Forces, 1916–1954, Record Group (RG) 337, 55:799–803 B.799: AF381 National Archives Building, College Park, MD.

88 **A small unit of:** Truscott, *Command Mission*, p. 78.

CHAPTER 10

"I should like to embrace you"

90 **The idea of extricating René Malevergne:** Dave King, report, July 19, 1944, p. 6, Torch anthology, Records of the Office of Strategic Services (O.S.S.), 1919–1946, Record Group 226 99:49:197 National Archives Building, College Park, MD.

90 **transporting Malevergne in the Chevy:** Ibid., p. 2.

91 **go ahead, Eddy told him:** What Eddy meant by this was that Malevergne should be concealed under baggage rather than smuggled out through

the use of false papers. Unfortunately, neither King nor Holcomb nor Browne quite understood the meaning, which would shortly be a source of confusion.

91 "face was weathered": Ibid., p. 138.

91 King was the sort: Ibid., p. 138.

91 "I ask only for that": Ibid., p. 138.

92 "Old friend, this time": Ibid., p. 139.

92 "Count two months": Ibid., p. 139.

CHAPTER 11

Snatching the Shark

94 **To Gordon Browne:** Details of the Malevergne extrication come from the King report, July 19, 1944, Torch anthology, Records of the O.S.S., 1919–1946, RG 22699:49:197; and a report from Gordon Browne in the same anthology, (RG 226:99:49:198), National Archives Building, College Park, MD. Details are also drawn from René Malevergne's diary, *The Exfiltration of René Malevergne*. It should be noted that René Malevergne's name was misspelled by virtually every OSS officer involved in his extrication. King spelled it "Malverne"; Browne spelled it "Malvern"; others spelled it "Malavergne."

95 **"Then what's the argument?":** King Report, Torch anthology, O.S.S. Records, 1919–1946, RG226 99:49:197, p. 6.

96 **"this miniscule box":** Malevergne, *Exfiltration of René Malevergne*, p. 148.

96 **The road between Casablanca and Tangier:** Robert Murphy described the road to Eisenhower and said that he had made the drive to Casablanca on this road all the way from Oran in sixteen hours. Captain Harry C. Butcher, *My Three Years with Eisenhower* (New York: Simon & Schuster, 1946), p. 111.

99 **"Tout va bien":** Browne report, Torch anthology, O.S.S. Records, 1919–1946, RG 226 99:49:198, p. 2.

100 **The word from King:** Ibid., p. 2.

101 **had exhausted the supply:** A footnote in Malevergne's diary (p. 149) says that Holcomb told Professor Blair that they had stopped south of the border—the place where they ate their ham—to replenish their gasoline from a previously hidden stash, but unfortunately someone had swiped the gas.

101 It was Coon's idea: Carleton Stevens Coon, *A North Africa Story: The Anthropologist as O.S.S. Agent, 1941–1943* (Boston: Gambit, 1980), p. 31.

103 The old dog was poised: Browne report, Torch anthology, Records of the O.S.S., 1919–1946, RG 226 99:49:198, p. 2.

104 "We passed all the controls": Ibid., p. 2.

CHAPTER 12

Romping

105 stretched out to a distance: Report of Commodore M. Lennon Goldsmith on Convoy HX 208, Sept. 17, 1942 (New York) to October 2, 1942 (Liverpool), Warsailors.com/HX208.html.

105 "filthy load of coal": Ibid.

106 "The result," Goldsmith reported: Ibid.

106 "All Masters of merchant ships": Ibid.

106 "I lost none of the Leaders": Ibid.

106 "at least two Signalmen": Records of the Office of the Chief of Naval Operations, 1875–1989, Record Group 38, Armed Guard Reports:145:*Contessa*, Lt. William Cato commanding, October 23, 1942, National Archives Building, College Park, MD.

107 "resentful of the gold braid": Ibid., p. 299.

107 "These lads had": Samuel Eliot Morison, *History of United States Naval Operations in World War II*, vol. 1, *The Battle of the Atlantic* (Boston: Atlantic Little, Brown, 1954), p. 297.

108 Hard-won union fights: Bruce Felknor, *The U.S. Merchant Marine at War, 1776–1945* (Annapolis, MD: U.S. Naval Institute, 1999), p. 172.

109 All had emerged: Ibid., p. 174.

109 "Any ship in which": Morison, *History of United States Naval Operations*, vol. 1, pp. 299–300.

109 "abolishing the color line": Ibid., p. 298.

110 "emphatic opinion that if and when": Ibid., p. 300.

111 Sailing at that rate: Mark H. Goldberg, *Going Bananas* (Kings Point, NY: American Merchant Marine Museum Foundation, 1993), p. 194.

112 "That wasn't no fun": Smithsonian National Museum of American History, "On the Water," http://americanhistory.si.edu/onthewater/exhibition /6_3.html; audio recollection of Sam Casarez.

113 "Attention is called": RG38 Armed Guard Reports: 145:*Contessa*, Lt. William Cato commanding, October 23, 1942.

CHAPTER 13

Hollywood

118 He ordered the rights purchased: Hal Wallis and Charles Higham, *Starmaker: The Autobiography of Hal Wallis* (New York: MacMillan, 1980), p. 83.

119 "were brought in on time": Aljean Harmetz, *Round Up the Usual Suspects* (New York: Hyperion, 1992), p. 63.

119 **Wallis never seriously considered:** Ibid., p. 88.

119 **Ingrid Bergman, in contrast:** Ibid., p. 90.

121 **verbal messages cause misunderstandings:** Ibid., p. 29.

121 "a good punchline": Wallis, *Starmaker,* p. 91.

121 **a clear-cut moral:** Harmetz, *Round Up the Usual Suspects,* p. 234.

122 **To give the scene:** Ibid., p. 237.

123 **But on August 7:** Ibid., p. 263.

CHAPTER 14

Tangier to Gibraltar to England

124 **Uncoiled from what he called:** René Malevergne, *The Exfiltration of René Malevergne* (unpublished diary), pp. 151–57. In his diary, Malevergne describes his brief stay in Tangier and journey to Gibraltar.

124 "rude French": Ibid., p. 153.

124 "comforting sensibility": Ibid., p. 151.

125 "the intelligence section": Ibid., p. 153.

127 "The boat is very small": Ibid., p. 156.

128 "a prisoner once again": Ibid., p. 159.

128 "I do not like this": Ibid., p. 160.

129 "very tall, dry and rigid": Ibid., p. 161.

CHAPTER 15

Needs and Wants

130 "It is reported here": George Marshall to Dwight D. Eisenhower, incoming cables AGWAR, vol. 12, October 2, 1942, Records of the Mediterranean Theater of Operations, United States Army, 1942–1947, Record Group 492 85:1387:311.23 National Archives Building, College Park, MD.

131 The problem, thought Eisenhower's aide: Captain Harry C. Butcher, *My Three Years with Eisenhower* (New York: Simon & Schuster 1946), p. 128.

131 were less than impressed: General Alfred M. Gruenther, Oral History 113, p. 14, Dwight D. Eisenhower Presidential Library, Abilene, Kansas.

131 Soon after he arrived: William L. Langer, *Our Vichy Gamble* (New York: Alfred A. Knopf, 1947), p. 310.

132 The officer's body: Gruenther, p. 15.

132 London soon traced the order: Butcher, *My Three Years,* p. 128; Butcher makes the direct connection with Patton.

133 the last time it had sailed: H. Paul Jeffers, *Command of Honor* (New York: NAL Caliber, 2008), p. 88.

134 The task force from Great Britain: Richard M. Leighton and Robert W. Coakley, *Global Logistics and Strategy* (Washington, D.C.: U.S. Army Center of Military History, 1995), p. 429.

135 "It would have been desirable": Samuel Eliot Morison, *History of United States Naval Operations in World War II,* vol. 2, *Operations in North African Waters October 1942–June 1943* (Boston: Atlantic Little, Brown, 1954), p. 28.

135 In a progress report: Wesley Frank Craven and James Lea Cate, *The Army Air Forces in World War II,* Office of Air Force History, Washington, D.C., 1983, p. 59.

136 The pilots were so inexperienced: Morison, *History of United States Naval Operations,* vol. 2, p. 32.

136 For instance, twelve ships: Joseph Byfosky and Harold Larson, *The Transportation Corps: Operations Overseas* (Washington, D.C.: U.S. Army Center of Military History, 2003), p. 145.

137 In the third week: Butcher, *My Three Years,* p. 113.

137 The fact that the OSS: Ibid., p. 128.

137 While there, he witnessed: Lucian Truscott, *Command Mission, a Personal Story* (New York: Dutton, 1954), p. 78.

137 "resembled a football team": Morison, *History of United States Naval Operations,* vol. 2, p. 33.

138 "Rest assured that when we start": Martin Blumenson, ed., *The Patton Papers* (New York: Da Capo Press, 1996–1998), p. 86.

138 "Germany will never conquer Russia": "Nazis on defensive," *New York Times,* October 14, 1942, p. 1.

138 The *Times of London*: "British anticipate revived Nazi blitz," *New York Times,* September 28, 1942.

CHAPTER 16

Meeting Gruenther

139 "adjutant of the official": René Malevergne, *The Exfiltration of René Malevergne* (unpublished diary), p. 162.

139 "Colonel Eddy wrote a letter": Ibid., p. 162.

140 "Monsieur Malevergne," he said: Ibid.

140 "profoundly discouraged": Ibid.

140 "I was sincere": Ibid., p. 163.

CHAPTER 17

SOS

141 "infantry, artillery, armor": Lucian Truscott, *Command Mission, a Personal Story* (New York: Dutton, 1954), p. 79.

141 By the beginning of their second week: Ibid.

142 Conway was "another Truscott": Robert Henriques, *From a Biography of Myself* (London: Secker & Warburg, 1969), p. 86.

143 "was not unqualified fun": Ibid., p. 60.

143 " 'Again' was the savage adverb": Ibid., p. 61.

143 "a bad, mad gamble": Ibid., p. 66.

144 "that the French did not like the British": Ibid.

145 "every available ship": Ibid., p. 87.

145 She was docked in Philadelphia: Ibid., p. 90. Henriques's autobiography is not entirely reliable on the matter. Writing a number of years after the fact, he sometimes confuses the "destroyer" (the *Dallas*) enlisted in Truscott's assault with the "transport" (the *Contessa*).

145 **But rid of her masts:** Samuel Eliot Morison, *History of United States Naval Operations in World War II,* vol. 2, *Operations in North African Waters October 1942–June 1943* (Boston: Atlantic Little, Brown), p. 129.

145 **And she had some firepower:** See the section on the USS *Dallas* at http://destroyerhistory.org/flushdeck/index.asp?r=210&pid=19900.

146 **he made a political enemy:** John Kennedy Ohl, *Supplying the Troops: General Somervell and American Logistics in WWII* (DeKalb, IL: Northern Illinois Press, 1994), p. 47.

147 **"changing horse in mid-stream":** Ibid., p. 190.

148 **And the simple swamp of matériel:** William Reginald Wheeler, *The Road to Victory: A History of Hampton Roads Port of Embarkation,* vol. 1 (New Haven: Yale University Press, 1946), p. 67.

148 **if General Patton endorsed the request:** Ohl, *Supplying the Troops,* p. 191.

CHAPTER 18
Amphibians

149 **"attempt[ing] to issue orders":** Martin Blumenson, ed., *The Patton Papers* (New York: Da Capo Press, 1996–1998), p. 88.

150 **"I have now reached the situation":** Ibid., p. 89.

150 **in a couple of instances:** William Reginald Wheeler, *The Road to Victory: A History of Hampton Roads Port of Embarkation,* vol. 1 (New Haven: Yale University Press, 1946), p. 69.

150 **Combat vehicles needed to be prepared:** Ibid.

151 **but it was discovered only later:** Harry Semmes, *Portrait of Patton* (New York: Appleton-Century-Crofts, 1955), p. 86.

152 **Craw was a no-nonsense tough guy:** Background on Craw comes from "Craw grave no. 1 at Port Lyautey," *New York Times,* March 25, 1943.

153 **"navy authorities would have no difficulty":** Lucian Truscott, *Command Mission, a Personal Story* (New York: Dutton, 1954), p. 86.

CHAPTER 19
Monsieur Prechak

154 **"English methods are not pleasing to me":** René Malevergne, *The Exfiltration of René Malevergne* (unpublished diary), p. 165.

155 "his handshake on parting": Ibid.

155 "no difficulty should befall M. Prechak": Ibid., p. 166.

CHAPTER 20

Looking for a Ship

156 So it wasn't surprising: "The Voyage of the Steamship 'Contessa' from American to African Shores," p. 2; Historical Records, 1942–1944, Folder 2, November 1–December 31, 1942; Records of the Office of the Chief of Transportation, 1917–1966, Record Group 336 51-1.5, National Archives Building, Philadelphia, PA.

"The Voyage of the Steamship 'Contessa' from American to African Shores" is a narrative created from reports collected from officers involved in the *Contessa*'s loading and voyage, including phone logs of Colonel C. J. Wilder and a special action report from Lieutenant Albert Leslie.

158 As later documents indicate: George Patton to Brehon Somervell, November 22, 1942, NARA Records of the War Department General and Special Staffs, 1860–1952, Record Group 165:418:1291: Doc 109, National Archives building, College Park, MD.

159 "where the ranking strategists": Bertram B. Fowler, "Twelve Desperate Miles," *Saturday Evening Post,* August 28, 1943.

159 A day and a half later: "Voyage of the Steamship 'Contessa,' " p. 2. It may have been Vissering who first identified the *Contessa* as the best vessel for the operation, when word arrived in England that a ship of her make was needed in Norfolk.

160 There would be no way: Ibid., p. 1.

CHAPTER 21

The Pieces in Place

162 "a veritable garden": René Malevergne, *The Exfiltration of René Malevergne* (unpublished diary), p. 170.

162 Word came to the *Contessa*: "The Voyage of the Steamship 'Contessa' from American to African Shores," p. 2; Historical Records, 1942–1944, Folder 2, November 1–December 31, 1942; Records of the Office of the Chief of Transportation, 1917–1966, Record Group 336 51-1.5, National Archives Building, Philadelphia, PA.

163 Back in April 1931: "Ship lands refugees who fled Nicaragua," *New York Times,* April 19, 1931.

164 "All my life I have wanted": Martin Blumenson, ed., *The Patton Papers* (New York: Da Capo Press, 1996–1998), p. 92.

164 He visited Marshall: Ibid., p. 93.

165 "I can always pick a fighting man": Ibid., p. 93.

165 "Come in, Skipper": Ibid.

165 "The Admiral and I": Ibid., p. 94.

165 On the morning of Friday, October 23: Rick Atkinson, *An Army at Dawn: The War in North Africa* (New York: Henry Holt, 2003), p. 37.

166 "If you have any doubts": Ibid., p. 37.

166 "This is my last night in America": Blumenson, ed., *The Patton Papers,* p. 95.

166 "Darling Bea": Harry Semmes, *Portrait of Patton* (New York: Appleton-Century-Crofts, 1955), p. 91.

CHAPTER 22

Dry Dock

173 Admiral Kent Hewitt ordered: "The Voyage of the Steamship 'Contessa' from American to African Shores," p. 2; Historical Records, 1942–1944, Folder 2, November 1–December 31, 1942; Records of the Office of the Chief of Transportation, 1917–1966, Record Group 336 51-1.5, National Archives Building, Philadelphia, PA.

173 Leslie had had a diverse career: Ibid., p. 2.

174 "'If you have the will'": Ibid., p. 3.

174 In his notes from that wild day: Ibid.

176 Many years later: William Sigsworth Jr. (son of Bill Sigsworth), interview with the author, New Orleans, March 10, 2010.

176 Wilder had something crucial to learn: "Voyage of the Steamship," p. 4.

CHAPTER 23

"Our Worst War Town"

179 Despite their experiences: Phyllis A. Hall, "Crisis at Hampton Roads: The Problems of Wartime Congestion, 1942–1944," *Virginia Magazine of History and Biography* 101, no. 3 (July 1992): p. 407.

179 **"Demand is far beyond supply"**: J. Blan Van Urk, "Norfolk: Our Worst War Town," *American Mercury*, February 1943, p. 145.

180 **"a poor man's Gypsy Rose Lee"**: Ibid., p. 407.

180 **denied a last fling**: Rick Atkinson, *An Army at Dawn: The War in North Africa* (New York: Henry Holt, 2003), p. 39.

181 **"Our Worst War Town"**: Van Urk, "Norfolk," p. 146.

181 **"dances, movies, sports"**: Hall, "Crisis at Hampton Roads," p. 408.

182 **Meanwhile, that Sunday morning**: "The Voyage of the Steamship 'Contessa' from American to African Shores," Historical Records, 1942–1944, Folder 2, November 1–December 31, 1942, pp. 4–5; Records of the Office of the Chief of Transportation, 1917–1966, Record Group 336 51-1.5, National Archives Building, Philadelphia, PA.

CHAPTER 24

Off to Sea

184 **"frank and cordial"**: René Malevergne, *The Exfiltration of René Malevergne* (unpublished diary), p. 173.

185 **wanted to "cry out"**: Ibid., p. 173.

186 **"fancy civilian pajamas"**: Walter Cronkite, *A Reporter's Life* (New York: Ballantine Books, 1996), p. 83.

186 **"was as unprepared for handling"**: Ibid., p. 81.

186 **"The officers in the wardroom"**: Ibid.

187 **"halfway across the wardroom"**: Ibid., p. 84.

188 **"impresses me better"**: Martin Blumenson, ed., *The Patton Papers* (New York: Da Capo Press, 1996–1998), p. 96.

188 **two silver blimps**: Samuel Eliot Morison, *History of United States Naval Operations in World War II*, vol. 2, *Operations in North African Waters October 1942–June 1943* (Boston: Atlantic Little, Brown, 1954), p. 43.

CHAPTER 25

Uncle Sam Wants You

189 **Another hand arrived**: "The Voyage of the Steamship 'Contessa' from American to African Shores," Historical Records, 1942–1944, Folder 2, November 1–December 31, 1942, p. 5; Records of the Office of the Chief

of Transportation, 1917–1966, Record Group 336 51-1.5, National Archives Building, Philadelphia, PA.

189 **had always wanted to work:** William Sigsworth Jr. (son of Bill Sigsworth), interview with the author, New Orleans, March 10, 2010.

190 **In his notes, Wilder:** "Voyage of the Steamship," p. 6.

190 **The county sheriff and a judge:** Mark H. Goldberg, *Going Bananas* (Kings Point, NY: American Merchant Marine Museum Foundation, 1993), p. 208.

191 **"bedraggled crew [who] you'd think":** *Pittsburgh Press,* November 28, 1942, quoted in "Voyage of the Steamship," pp. 6–7.

191 **"were good seamen":** "Voyage of the steamship," p. 6.

191 **"because most of them had":** Bertram Fowler, "Twelve Desperate Miles," *Saturday Evening Post,* August 28, 1942.

191 **Among those who joined:** Microfilm Serial T715; Microfilm Roll 6672; line: 1; page 199. Passenger Lists of Vessels Arriving at New York, New York, 1820–1897; Records of the U.S. Customs Service, Record Group 36; National Archives, Washington, D.C. Particular members of the crew who joined from the Norfolk jail were identified by examining these lists to find crew members who signed on to the *Contessa* on October 26, the day the ship sailed for North Africa, as opposed to October 24 and 25, when all other members of the *Contessa* crew registered on the ship's list. The author could find no document that listed the specific seamen who were released from incarceration to sail with the *Contessa.*

192 **"whatever the attitude":** "Voyage of the steamship," p. 6.

CHAPTER 26

Convoy

194 **In all, the convoy stretched:** Samuel Eliot Morison, *History of United States Naval Operations in World War II,* vol. 2, *Operations in North African Waters October 1942–June 1943* (Boston: Atlantic Little, Brown, 1954), p. 44.

194 **On two ships mentioned:** Ibid., p. 45.

195 **"floating school[s] of amphibious operations":** Ibid., p. 48.

195 **"devoted to an intensive training":** Lucian Truscott, *Command Mission, a Personal Story* (New York: Dutton, 1954), p. 90.

195 **"space is the soldier's medium":** Ibid., p. 90.

195 After finally marrying the launchers: Harry Semmes, *Portrait of Patton* (New York: Appleton-Century-Crofts, 1955), p. 87.

196 delighted Malevergne: René Malevergne, *The Exfiltration of René Malevergne* (unpublished diary), p. 178.

196 "shall do everything possible": Ibid., p. 179.

196 "G-2 information was invaluable": John J. Toffey IV, *Jack Toffey's War* (New York: Fordham University Press, 2008), p. 65.

197 "My civilian clothing": Malevergne, *Exfiltration of René Malevergne,* p. 180.

197 It was Toffey: Toffey, *Jack Toffey's War,* p. 65

197 "that I should be doing something": Martin Blumenson, ed., *The Patton Papers* (New York: Da Capo Press, 1996–1998), p. 97.

198 "for it would sort of pull the cork": Ibid., p. 97.

198 "Only the *'Texas'* does not budge": Malevergne, *Exfiltration of René Malevergne,* p. 177.

198 "A great convoy": Truscott, *Command Mission,* p. 90.

199 "grim possibility": Ibid., pp. 90–91.

199 Doenitz had actually devised: Karl Doenitz, "The Conduct of the War at Sea," U.S. Navy Division of Naval Intelligence, January 15, 1946, p. 4 (available at http://www.karl-doenitz.com/doenitzconductofwar.pdf).

CHAPTER 27
Crossing

202 "*Contessa* flying Honduran flag": "The Voyage of the Steamship 'Contessa' from American to African Shores," p. 6; Historical Records, 1942–1944, Folder 2, November 1–December 31, 1942; Records of the Office of the Chief of Transportation, 1917–1966, Record Group 336 51-1. National Archives Building, Philadelphia, PA.

204 Ambrose Schaffer: All ships whose crews included non-American citizens were required to present port authorities with complete rosters of crews upon entry into American ports. Lists of armed guard members were found in Records of the Office of the Chief of Naval Operations, 1875–1989, Record Group 38, Armed Guard Reports:145:*Contessa,* Lt. William Cato commanding, October 23, 1942, National Archives Building, College Park, MD. Follow-up information was obtained through author interviews with descendants, spouses, and relatives, including Clara Schaffer,

Ralph Mason, Rose Mangaro, and Betty McLaughlin. The author could find no living members of the *Contessa* crew, the armed guard, or the merchant crew.

204 **An up-and-coming young:** "Ex-Pro boxer Ambrose Schaffer dies," *Newark, (OH) Reflector,* April 4, 1973.

206 **nicknamed "The Unsinkable":** Bertram Fowler, "Twelve Desperate Miles," *Saturday Evening Post,* August 28, 1943.

206 **Bill Sigsworth, John's brother-in-law:** William Sigsworth Jr. (son of Bill Sigsworth), interview with the author, September 2, 2010.

207 **Despite his twenty-some years:** Tim Koerner, interview with the author, March 4, 2010.

207 **Leslie soon became concerned:** "Voyage of the Steamship," p. 9.

CHAPTER 28

"Je m'engage et puis je vois"

210 **about forty U-boats were hunting:** "General Eisenhower's Report on Operation Torch," declassified, June 21, 1965; available at http://www.american -divisions.com/doc.asp?documentid=138&pagenumber=1, p. 12.

211 **tossed candy bars:** George Coyle (yeoman second class), "Beyond the Usual Call," an unpublished account of the *Dallas* journey sent to the author by a shipmate of Coyle, Ralph Jennings, p. 3.

211 **sailors were told that facial hair:** Ibid., p. 5.

212 **letter writing increased dramatically:** Ibid.

213 **"As if 100,000 men":** Martin Blumenson, ed., *The Patton Papers* (New York: Da Capo Press 1996–1998), p. 98.

213 **"are bound to get better":** Ibid., p. 99.

213 **"Every once in a while":** Ibid., pp. 97–98.

214 **On November 4, Dwight David Eisenhower:** Details of Eisenhower's trip to Gibraltar are from Rick Atkinson, *An Army at Dawn: The War in North Africa* (New York: Henry Holt, 2003), p. 46.

216 **"If a man permitted himself":** Stephen E. Ambrose, *Eisenhower,* vol. 1, *Soldier, General of the Army, President-Elect, 1890–1952,* (New York: Simon & Schuster, 1983–1984), p. 200.

CHAPTER 29

Rendezvous

217 **most disconcerting evening of the trip:** "The Voyage of the Steamship 'Contessa' from American to African Shores," p. 9; Historical Records, 1942–1944, Folder 2, November 1–December 31, 1942; Records of the Office of the Chief of Transportation, 1917–1966, Record Group 336 51-1.5, National Archives Building, Philadelphia, PA.

218 **a satisfying thrill:** "The fleet—a 'Great thrill' ": *New Orleans Times-Picayune,* January 19, 1943.

218 **was simply "strange":** U.S.S. *Cowie* war diary, Records of the Office of the Chief of Naval Transportation, 1875–1989, Record Group 38:765:war diaries, U.S.S. *Cowie.* National Archives building, College Park, MD.

219 **"might reinforce these radio appeals":** Lucian Truscott, *Command Mission, a Personal Story* (New York: Dutton, 1954), p. 93.

221 **Mehdia was an ancient village:** Harry Semmes, *Portrait of Patton* (New York: Appleton-Century-Crofts, 1955), p. 118. Mehdia is also spelled "Mehedia" and called "Mehdia" or "Mehedia Plage" in other sources.

221 **The designation was used:** Ibid., p. 97.

221 **In all, the defense at Port Lyautey:** Annexes to final report to commander Western Task Force, Sub-taskforce Goalpost plans and reports, p. 3; Records of the War Department Special and General Staffs, Record Group RG 165, Entry 418, Box 1292, National Archives Building, College Park, MD.

222 **He was hoping for little opposition:** Truscott, *Command Mission,* p. 93.

222 **The assignments given to the three:** Ibid., p. 95.

223 **"I should like to call your attention":** Martin Blumenson, ed., *The Patton Papers* (New York: Da Capo Press, 1996–1998), p. 100.

224 **Patton's own central attack group:** Samuel Eliot Morison, *History of United States Naval Operations in World War II,* vol. 2, *Operations in North African Waters October 1942–June 1943* (Boston: Atlantic Little, Brown, 1954), pp. 50–51.

224 **"Soldiers: We are to be congratulated":** Blumenson, ed., *Patton Papers,* p. 102.

226 **When the guns opened fire:** René Malevergne, *The Exfiltration of René Malevergne* (unpublished diary), p. 184.

CHAPTER 30

"Viva la France eternelle"

227 **With zigzagging and evasive maneuvers:** Samuel Eliot Morison, *History of United States Naval Operations in World War II,* vol. 2, *Operations in North African Waters October 1942–June 1943* (Boston: Atlantic Little, Brown, 1954), p. 51. The actual distance, as the crow flies, was substantially less.

227 **Megaphones from the craft:** Brigadier General Arthur R. Wilson to Chief of Staff, memorandum, December 12, 1942, p. 4, available at http://www.60thinfantry.com/North%20Africa%20Report%20of%20Operations.swf.

228 **"I believe that navy personnel":** Annexes to final report to commander Western Task Force, Sub-taskforce Goalpost plans and reports; 60th Combat team report, p. 1. Records of the War Department Special and General Staffs, Record Group RG 165, Entry 418, Box 1292, National Archives Building, College Park, MD.

228 **"We found ships everywhere":** Lucian Truscott, *Command Mission, a Personal Story* (New York: Dutton, 1954), p. 96.

229 **"My heart sank":** Ibid., p. 96. According to Morison (*History of United States Naval Operations,* vol. 2, p. 71), the decision to broadcast at 0200 Algiers time (an hour ahead of the time in Casablanca) had been made a couple of weeks earlier. George Patton knew about it but apparently hadn't informed Truscott. It was the contention of Eisenhower and the president that this foreknowledge would have no impact on the invasion in Morocco.

229 **"I am Viktor Prechak":** René Malevergne, *The Exfiltration of René Malevergne* (unpublished diary), p. 185.

229 **"Be forewarned":** Truscott, *Command Mission,* p. 96.

230 **"dry clacking of machine guns":** Ibid., p. 186.

230 **"sad and without brilliance":** Malevergne, *Exfiltration of René Malevergne,* p. 186.

230 **"You're a writer, Mr. Cronkite":** Walter Cronkite, *A Reporter's Life* (New York: Ballantine Books, 1996), pp. 84–85.

231 **"The great belch of yellow flame":** Ibid., p. 84.

231 **"If they had asked":** Ibid., p. 84.

231 **"Great chains of red balls":** Truscott, *Command Mission,* p. 97.

232 **"At mouth of river":** Ibid., p. 97.

233 They were told either: "Craw grave no. 1 at Port Lyautey," *New York Times,* March 25, 1943.

233 "exhaust all the French profanity": Lewis Wood, "Hamilton tells of African Exploit," *New York Times,* April 29, 1942.

234 Afterward, as the French paused: Harry Semmes, *Portrait of Patton* (New York: Appleton-Century-Crofts, 1955), p. 122.

235 Here they stayed: Sub–task force Goalpost plans and reports, p. 8.

236 "large numbers of French troops": Sub-taskforce Goalpost plans and report, 3rd battalion report, p. 2.

237 "I answered that it was possible": Malevergne, *Exfiltration of René Malevergne,* p. 189.

237 "before indicating our intention": Ibid., p. 189.

238 "tinkered ineffectively": Truscott, *Command Mission,* p. 110.

239 Truscott headed back to headquarters: Ibid., p. 113.

240 *God is with us:* Martin Blumenson, ed., *The Patton Papers* (New York: Da Capo Press, 1996–1998), p. 103.

240 a searchlight appeared in the skies: Morison, *History of United States Naval Operations,* vol. 2, p. 73.

241 The only items saved: Blumenson, ed., *Patton Papers,* p. 105.

241 A destroyer in the American group: Morison, *History of United States Naval Operations,* vol. 2, pp. 74–76. On board the *Brooklyn* was Lieutenant Commander Samuel Eliot Morison, a Harvard historian, who was already beginning to collect notes for his monumental history of U.S. naval operations in World War II.

241 "naval war is nice": Blumenson, ed., *Patton Papers,* p. 106.

242 "God was very good": Ibid., p. 106.

CHAPTER 31

"Crack it open quickly"

243 booted him "with all [his] might": Martin Blumenson, ed., *The Patton Papers* (New York: Da Capo Press, 1996–1998), p. 108.

243 "The men were poor": Ibid., p. 108

243 Of the nearly twenty thousand troops: David H. Lippman, "World War II Plus 55," http://worldwar2plus55.com/, November 9, 1942.

244 "the ground near this pestilential lagoon": Harry Semmes, *Portrait of Patton* (New York: Appleton-Century-Crofts, 1955), p. 121.

245 Semmes had other concerns: Ibid., p. 118.

246 "We will always have a warm spot": Ibid., p. 125.

246 At the same time: Annexes to final report to commander Western Task
     Force: Sub-taskforce Goalpost plans and reports; 60th Combat team re-
     port, p. 1. Records of the War Department Special and General Staffs,
     Record Group 165, Entry 418, Box 1292, National Archives Building,
     College Park, MD.

248 As K Company came within 1,200 yards: Ibid., p. 3.

249 "Algiers has been ours": Blumenson, ed., Patton Papers, p. 109.

CHAPTER 32

The Dallas *Goes First*

250 "It's okay," Malevergne said: René Malevergne, *The Exfiltration of René
     Malevergne* (unpublished diary), p. 190.

252 "a familiar growl": Ibid., p. 191.

253 eyeing the progress: Lucian Truscott, *Command Mission, a Personal Story*
     (New York: Dutton, 1954), p. 119.

253 "A glance over the side": U.S.S. *Dallas* war diary, p. 2. Records of the
     Office of the Chief of Naval Transportation, 1875–1989, Record Group
     38:765 war diaries, U.S.S. *Dallas*. National Archives building, College
     Park, MD.

254 "Captain, there is no depth there": Malevergne, *Exfiltration of René Malev-
     ergne,* p. 192.

254 the *Dallas* opened her own: Samuel Eliot Morison, *History of United
     States Naval Operations in World War II,* vol. 2, *Operations in North
     African Waters October 1942–June 1943* (Boston: Atlantic Little, Brown,
     1954), p. 130.

255 They waved at one another: Malevergne, *Exfiltration of René Malevergne,*
     p. 194.

255 "like a Dutch canal boat": Morison, *History of United States Naval Op-
     erations,* vol. 2, p. 131.

256 Reconnoitering on the ridge: George F. Howe, *United States Army in World
     War II: The Mediterranean Theater of Operations; Northwest Africa: Seiz-
     ing the Initiative in the West* (Washington, D.C.: U.S. Army Center of Mili-
     tary History, 1991), p. 167.

256 From the ancient crenellated walls: Truscott, *Command Mission,* p. 115.

257 "great clouds of smoke": Ibid., p. 120.

257 Late in the morning: Daniel Rathbun, http://www.portlyautey.com/Rathbun
.htm.

CHAPTER 33

Twelve Desperate Miles

260 "You are going to be released": René Malevergne, *The Exfiltration of René
Malevergne* (unpublished diary), p. 195.

261 Exactly when Captain John: "The Voyage of the Steamship 'Contessa'
from American to African Shores," p. 9; Historical Records, 1942–1944,
Folder 2, November 1–December 31, 1942. Records of the Office of the
Chief of Transportation, 1917–1966, Record Group 336 51-1.5, National
Archives Building, Philadelphia, PA.

261 "Leṣlay": Malevergne, *Exfiltration of René Malevergne,* p. 196.

261 "that the impossible be done": Ibid., p. 196.

262 Malevergne thought it was Panamanian: Ibid., p. 196.

262 a load essential to the commandos: Ibid., p. 196.

263 "a sitting duck": Betty McLaughlin, widow of Hazelton McLaughlin, interview with the author, August 10, 2010.

264 "churning up mud and sand": Bertram Fowler, "Twelve Desperate Miles,"
Saturday Evening Post, August 28, 1943.

266 Soon gaping holes: George F. Howe, *United States Army in World War II: The
Mediterranean Theater of Operations, Northwest Africa* (Washington,
D.C.: U.S. Army Center of Military History, 1991), p. 168.

267 Occasional sniper fire continued: Ibid., p. 169.

267 Semmes relayed Hamilton's message: Annexes to final report to commander Western Task Force, Sub-taskforce Goalpost plans and reports,
p. 13. Records of the War Department Special and General Staffs, Record
Group RG 165, Entry 418, Box 1292, National Archives Building, College
Park, MD.

267 Rumors of enemy troops: Howe, *United States Army in World War II,*
p. 179.

268 For René Malevergne, still lingering: Malevergne, *Exfiltration of René
Malevergne,* p. 198.

CHAPTER 34

Armistice Day

270 **a self-lubricating bearing:** Bill Kimbel, interview with the author, March 3, 2010.

270 **Ernest Shackleton, for instance:** Deirdre O'Regan, "Lignum Vitae—The Bosun's Favorite Wood," http://www.lignum-vitae.com/customer-stories.html.

271 **"Working twenty-four hours a day":** "The Voyage of the Steamship 'Contessa' from American to African Shores," p. 10; Historical Records, 1942–1944, Folder 2, November 1–December 31, 1942. Records of the Office of the Chief of Transportation, 1917–1966, Record Group 336 51-1.5, National Archives Building, Philadelphia, PA.

271 **"It should not be omitted":** Ibid., p. 10.

272 **Despite numerous requests:** Ibid.

272 **"to lend something of a military display":** Lucian Truscott, *Command Mission, a Personal Story* (New York: Dutton, 1954), p. 122.

272 **"a brightly colored pageant":** George F. Howe, *United States Army in World War II: The Mediterranean Theater of Operations, Northwest Africa* (Washington, D.C.: U.S. Army Center of Military History, 1991), p. 170.

273 **"only the Sherman tanks":** Samuel Eliot Morison, *History of United States Naval Operations in World War II,* vol. 2, *Operations in North African Waters October 1942–June 1943* (Boston: Atlantic Little, Brown, 1954), p. 164.

274 **received word from Admiral Darlan:** This is the same Darlan who had refused to see Malevergne when he returned from France after his trial. Eisenhower's deal with Darlan, a notorious Fascist sympathizer despised by de Gaulle, would be the subject of much criticism in the days, weeks, and months to come. Darlan himself was assassinated in December 1942.

274 **"General Noguès and Admiral Michelier":** Blumenson, ed., *The Patton Papers* (New York: Da Capo Press, 1996–1998), p. 110.

275 **"I had my orders":** Morison, *History of United States Naval Operations,* vol. 2, p. 164.

275 **Like Truscott's regional proposal:** Howe, *United States Army in World War II,* p. 174. It should be noted that the draft terms failed to account for the subjects of the sultan of Morocco.

275 **"To the liberation of France":** Ibid., p. 174.

EPILOGUE

"The little Contessa *did the trick"*

276 **"It's impossible to change":** Aljean Harmetz, *Round Up the Usual Suspects* (New York: Hyperion, 1992), p. 280.

277 **"Casablanca had sold":** Ibid., p. 282.

277 **"We've got an old rule":** Walter Cronkite, *A Reporter's Life* (New York: Ballantine Books, 1996), p. 86.

278 **"You cut every road":** Ibid., p. 86.

278 **"I later learned":** Ibid., p. 90.

279 **"Please tell [General] Gross":** George Patton to Brehon Somervell, November 22, 1942. Records of the War Department Special and General Staffs, Record Group 165:418:1291: Doc109 National Archive Building, College Park, MD.

279 **"By his outstanding professional":** The Captain John commendation is attached to "The Voyage of the Steamship 'Contessa' from American to African Shores," p. 11; Historical Records, 1942–1944, Folder 2, November 1–December 31, 1942. Records of the Office of the Chief of Transportation, 1917–1966, Record Group 336 51-1.5, National Archives Building, Philadelphia, PA.

281 **"M. Malevergne volunteered his services":** The family of René Malevergne maintains a Web site honoring his memory and accomplishments: http://www.malevergne.free.fr/. His commendations and citations can be found there.

282 **Correspondence between the two:** The postwar correspondence between William Eddy and René Malevergne can be found among the William Alfred Eddy Papers at the Seeley G. Mudd Manuscript Library, Princeton University, Princeton, New Jersey. A few years after René's death, Germaine contacted Eddy looking for the diary, which had, for obscure reasons, been passed among American foreign service offices in North Africa and disappeared. By the end of the 1960s, it had been rediscovered and was back in Germaine's hands. Germaine was now living in Grenoble, France, near her sons, René and Claude. A professor of history at the University of Texas–Arlington, Leon Borden Blair, became interested in the manuscript and translated it into English. René and Claude Malevergne still live in Grenoble, where René works as a neurosurgeon and Claude is in public relations.

283 In August 1969: Details of the passing of Captain John and Bess come from interviews with family members, including grandsons Louis and Tim Koerner, and family friend Bill Kimbel.

284 The *Contessa* came back to the Gulf: Mark H. Goldberg, *Going Bananas* (Kings Point, NY: American Merchant Marine Museum Foundation, 1993), p. 216.

INDEX

About the Author

TIM BRADY is the author of two books, including *The Great Dan Patch and the Remarkable Mr. Savage* (Nodin Press, 2006), winner of a 2006 Midwest Book Award. He is a frequent contributor to the *History Channel* magazine and PBS history documentaries. A graduate of the Iowa Writers' Workshop, he lives with his family in Saint Paul, Minnesota.